WAR MEMORIALS

By the same author

ARCHITECTURAL SCULPTURE IN ROMANESQUE PROVENCE
EUROPEAN SWORDS AND DAGGERS IN THE TOWER OF LONDON
HEADS AND HORSES
ARMS AND ARMOUR IN BRITAIN
THE VANISHING PAST

WAR MEMORIALS
FROM ANTIQUITY TO THE PRESENT

ALAN BORG

LEO COOPER · LONDON

First published in Great Britain in 1991 by
LEO COOPER
190 Shaftesbury Avenue, London WC2H 8JL an imprint of Pen & Sword Books Ltd.,
47 Church Street, Barnsley, S. Yorks. S70 2AS.

A CIP catalogue record for this book is available
from the British Library

ISBN: 0-85052-363-X

Printed in Great Britain
by Redwood Press at Melksham

164 7 104566 12016

CONTENTS

ACKNOWLEDGMENTS

I am grateful to many friends and colleagues for help and advice in preparing this book, although needless to say faults and omissions are entirely my own. Particular thanks go to my colleagues at the Imperial War Museum, especially the Department of Photographs in whose dark rooms my photographs were printed. My family have been especially long-suffering, putting up with long detours in the car to see a particular memorial and surviving emergency stops when one is sighted unexpectedly out of the corner of an eye. This in itself is sufficient reason (but there are countless others) to dedicate these pages to Caroline, Leonora and Helen Borg.

PREFACE

'And some there be, which have no memorial; who are perished,
as though they had never been; and are become as though they
had never been born; and their children after them. But these
were merciful men, whose righteousness hath not been forgotten. With their seed shall continually remain a good inheritance,
and their children are within the covenant.'

(*Ecclesiasticus,* Chapter 44, verses 9-11)

War memorials are the most numerous and widespread of all public
monuments. Every town and most villages in Britain has one, often
more than one, and the same is true of every country which took part in
either or both of the two World Wars. Other memorials stand on the
battlefields themselves or adorn the war cemeteries which are to be found
across the world. It is probably because they are so common that these
memorials seldom attract much attention, although they represent the
biggest communal arts project ever attempted. Taken individually, they
range from important and impressive public works to curious and even
sometimes frankly bizarre monuments, but as a group they blur into the
urban background.

The greatest period of memorial construction followed in the wake of
the shattering tragedy of the First World War. The more limited wars of
the 19th century produced their crop of memorials, and there was a great
outburst of memorial construction following the Boer War (which resulted in more than 900 memorials), but it was the unprecedented scope
of the First World War and its appalling statistics of death which caused
the greatest upsurge in memorial building. Throughout the western world
committees were set up to supervise the design and construction of memorials and a wide variety of solutions were adopted. In many cases these
memorials were barely complete when the world began to slide towards
the Second World War, and this is partly the reason why comparatively
few memorials were erected in the post-1945 era; for the most part existing memorials were adapted to include the more recent conflict. There
were exceptions, such as the creation of the RAF memorial at Runny-

mede, as well as a whole series of new battlefield memorials. Occasionally a town or community would decide to make a new and separate memorial for the later war, as at Great Yarmouth and at Weston-super-Mare, where Second War memorials stand alongside those to the First War, the two forming a single memorial complex. There were also exceptions in those countries for which the Second World War was the first or the major war of the century, notably the Soviet Union where many hundreds of memorials were built to commemorate the 'Great Patriotic War'. More recent conflicts have also produced their crop of memorials, from Vietnam to the Falklands, but it remains the First World War that has given rise to the greatest number of memorials and the decade between 1920-1930 is the classic era of memorial construction. For this reason this book concentrates, in its second part, on the First World War memorials and only makes reference to later examples when they illustrate a particular point.

There is as yet no complete count or inventory of modern war memorials but the total certainly runs into hundreds of thousands worldwide. They fall, however, into a limited number of categories and types. Inevitably these types did not spring from a void; quite the reverse, for most of the committees that commissioned them and the artists who designed them were consciously drawing upon existing traditions. To understand the present it is necessary to look back into the past and one purpose of this book is to examine the memorial tradition and to trace some of the various elements which have contributed to 20th century memorial concepts.

Ever since wars first began the victorious dead have been buried with pomp and ceremony and their achievement has been celebrated in monumental form. A characteristic of ancient war memorials is that they commemorate war itself, and specifically victory, rather than recording the loss and suffering of individuals. Modern memorials on the other hand are much more concerned with the sacrifices of war, with the loss of young life in the defence of freedom. *For your tomorrow we gave our today* is a recurrent theme. Yet it would be a mistake to assume that the elements of state glorification are entirely absent from 20th century memorials, and one of the continuing strands that can be defined is a traditional assertion of the justice of the cause for which the war has been fought.

One reason for this is that the great majority of memorial art is officially inspired and promoted. In the present century there has been a general reaction against the idea of art sponsored by the state or by a particular community, yet in the past such official patronage was the norm. The arts of Egypt, Greece, Rome and medieval Europe were largely the product of royal, state, or communal patronage and, we must assume, in most cases the artist had to produce what the client wanted. The official commemorative art of the ancient world required the approval of authority, just as the war memorials and other public works of art erected in the present century have needed official sanction. We have no difficulty in seeing Assyrian palace friezes, Greek temples, or Roman triumphal arches as works of art, but many still find it difficult to treat the official art of our own century with an equally open mind.

There have of course always been artists with a private rather than a public vision, but it was only with the Romantic movement that individual expression of internal feeling came to be the dominant qualification of artistic integrity. When Goya painted the *Night of 3rd May, 1808* and etched the *Disasters of War* he unleashed a stream of artistic expression about conflict that had been largely dormant before this. It was a reaction against the traditional and official view, in which suffering had been rarely depicted with reality and was nearly always reserved only for the enemy. Suddenly the horror and terror of war became a legitimate subject for the artist and as the momentum of modern technological war increased the revulsion felt by all was mirrored in the reactions of the artists, from the poetry of Wilfrid Owen to the painting of Picasso. Public art no longer seemed in tune with the spirit of the modern world, almost as if people could no longer believe that states which were responsible for producing such carnage could also produce genuine public reactions to war. However, most of the new war memorials did respect the traditional values, showing the nobility of the soldier even in death and reinforcing the righteousness of the cause for which he had fought. All this came to be unfashionable in the decades which followed the wars, with the result that the war memorial movement has been fiercely criticized, but now perhaps we can see things in a clearer perspective. There is much genuine feeling and much genuine artistic integrity in our war memorials, and many can well stand comparison with the official art of the past. In the following pages I trace the memorial tradition from antiquity to the present day with the intention of demonstrating that modern memorials deserve as much attention, and certainly derive from many of the same precepts as those of the past.

One thing has changed, however, and that is the scale of what is commemorated. The Great Mound at Marathon carried the names of the 192 Greek soldiers who died in that epic battle against the Persians in 490BC; the Menin Gate at Ypres records the names of 54,896 men who died there and who have no known grave. Still they ran out of space and had to fit another 35,000 names on the wall of the cemetery at Tyne Cot. Statistics such as these will always appal and it is is obvious why those responsible for the programmes of memorial building in the years after the First World War took their task very seriously. To produce fitting memorials to such a tragedy was a daunting project and one that called for artists who could draw upon a deep knowledge of the highest artistic traditions of their culture. It is not surprising that society as a whole did not regard this as a suitable field for artistic experiment, but rather as an opportunity to bring together all that seemed best and most noble in the artistic tradition of the civilisation they had fought to preserve. This was the aim and in large measure the results justify the high ambition.

This book is divided into two parts. The first examines the depiction and memorialization of war from ancient times to the 20th century. The evidence here is fragmentary, as for all historical studies, but even so the size of the canvas is so large that my selection is necessarily partial. The second part illustrates how the various memorial types defined in the first were taken up and adapted by the memorial builders of this century. I have restricted myself to the western civilizations, and the study of 20th century memorials is based mainly but not exclusively on British examples. Numerous gaps remain, some of which are intentional; for example, I have confined myself very largely to external public monuments, despite the fact that many war memorials are in churches and in media such as stained glass. However, some limitation of the field seemed inevitable.

Within my chosen sphere the coverage remains uneven. There is a treasure trove of virtually unexplored documentary material in local libraries and County Record Offices, describing the ways in which memorial committees were established and how they set about their work. Even the national archival sources, held by bodies such as the Public Record Office and the Commonwealth War Graves Commission, are far from being fully exploited. There is little existing secondary literature, although there are many contemporary pamphlets describing particular local memorials and giving details of unveiling ceremonies as well as catalogues of exhibitions of memorial sculpture. There is an excellent book by James Glidea on Boer War memorials[1] and one describing British Public Schools Memorials.[2] Most recently there has been a valuable survey of First World War memorials by Derek Boorman[3] and a study of the different forms of information that may be gleaned from memorials by Colin McIntyre.[4] However, virtually the only attempt at an art historical analysis was made shortly after the Second World War by Arnold Whittick.[5] His is an interest-

ing and good book but it is now difficult to obtain and its value is somewhat marred by the fact that one of its main purposes was to influence
the new types of memorial that were then being planned. A recent historical study of American memorials is concerned less with their artistic
development than with their social and political meaning[6] and there is a
similarly wide focus in an excellent book on New Zealand's war memorials.[7] There are also good and thought-provoking studies of memorials
in Canada[8] and France.[9] A pioneering exhibition was devoted to war
memorials at the RIBA in 1977[10] and there have been studies of some
of the more important memorial artists and valuable exhibitions of their
work, notably Lutyens in 1981,[11] Charles Sargeant Jagger in 1985[12] and
Gilbert Ledward[13] and Charles Holden[14] in 1988. The memorials on the
Western Front are reasonably well known from the publications of the
Commonwealth War Graves Commission[15] and various battlefield gui-
des.[16] There is also now a major project to produce a National Inventory
of War Memorials, under the auspices of the Imperial War Museum and
the Royal Commission on Historical Monuments. When complete, this
will provide for the first time an overview of the subject and so will
become the standard reference point for matters of conservation and preservation. The database will also be an essential research tool for art historians and genealogists.

This book should be seen against the background of current knowledge. My intention has been to construct a framework, for both past and
present, which allows us to place the memorials round us in their context. Some of my assertions and conclusions will be modified in the light
of future work but I hope the framework itself will stand. There are many
memorials that really do deserve our attention. In towns and villages
across the land there are excellent, sometimes outstanding works of art,
which most of us currently ignore. If we begin to appreciate war memorials as part of an ancient and continuing artistic tradition, it becomes
easier to assess how well they fulfill their primary purpose. The wars of
the 20th century must not be forgotten and the memorials are there to
remind us. On the whole they do an outstanding job and it is we who
fail by failing to notice them. If this book makes more people aware of
our rich heritage of memorials to war and thereby also brings a reminder
of the cost of war itself, then it will have served its purpose. To adapt
Christopher Wren's epitaph *Si monumentum requiris, circumspice.*

NOTES

1 Gildea, J., *For Remembrance and in Honour of those who lost their lives in the South African War*, London, 1911
2 Kernot, C., *British Public School War Memorials*, London, 1927
3 Boorman, D., *At the going down of the sun*, York, 1988
4 McIntyre, C., *Monuments of War; How to read a war memorial*, London, 1990
5 Whittick, A., *War Memorials*, London, 1946
6 Mayo, J., *War Memorials as Political Landscape: The American Experience and Beyond*, New York, 1988.
7 Maclean, C., and Phillips, J., *The Sorrow and the Pride; New Zealand War Memorials*, Wellington, 1990
8 Shipley, R., *To Mark Our Place: A History of Canadian War Memorials*, Toronto, 1987
9 Becker, A., *Les Monuments aux Morts, Memoire de la Grande Guerre*, Paris, 1988
10 See the exhibition catalogue by Stamp, G., *Silent Cities*, London, 1977
11 At the Hayward Gallery, London, organised by the Arts Council and with an excellent catalogue
12 At the Imperial War Museum and with an important catalogue by Compton, A., (ed), *Charles Sargeant Jagger: War and Peace Sculpture*, London, 1985
13 At the Fine Arts Society, London
14 At the RIBA, with an excellent catalogue by Karol, E., and Allibone, F., *Charles Holden, Architect 1875-1960*, London, 1988
15 See Longworth, P., *The Unending Vigil: A History of the Commonwealth War Graves Commission*, London, 1968, and Gibson, E., and Kingsley Ward, G., *Courage Remembered*, London, 1989.
16 For the Western Front the best of these remains Coombs, R., *Before Endeavours Fade*, London 1976 (and subsequent editions).

CHAPTER 1

SYMBOL AND MYTH

'And in those times there was no peace to him that went out, nor
to him that went in, but great vexations were upon all inhabitants of the countries. And nation was destroyed of nation, and
city of city: for God did vex them with all adversity.'

(*Chronicles*, Book II, Chapter 15, verses 5-6).

Any reader of the Old Testament knows that warfare was an almost
constant preoccupation in the ancient Near East, that area which
formed the cradle of our own western civilization. Great empires grew
up on conquest, especially in Egypt and Mesopotamia, while smaller city
states often had to be prepared to fight for their very existence. It is
hardly surprising, therefore, that two closely linked themes dominate
ancient art and particularly ancient memorials: power, both human and
divine, and war. He who is victorious in war achieves power, but the
reverse of this — he who is in power achieves victory in war — is neither self-evident nor historically accurate. Perhaps this is why most ancient
military art is devoted to asserting that the second statement *is* true, for
its main theme is the inevitable and unremitting victory of the ruler in
war, and the humiliation and death of his enemies. Sometimes the ruler
has divine aid in his victories, and it is always clear that the gods desert
the losers. Such sentiments dominate the earliest memorials to war and
were to influence all that followed them.

This ancient art is not so much an instrument of propaganda as of reassu-
rance, intended to remind the ruler of his invincibility and incidentally
to terrify potential enemies into submission. Almost certainly the attitudes to war which we see represented in art were not developed by the
artists themselves, but reflect the political and religious views of the state.
In such circumstances it would have been unthinkable to portray anything but the continuous, unremitting and inevitable victory of the ruler.

The ancient portrayal of war is about power, but there are two main
and distinct ways of illustrating the power of a ruler over his enemies.
These may be termed symbolic on the one hand and narrative on the

1

other. The symbolic type, presenting simple, timeless forms and images, first clearly emerges in Egypt and spread from there to the rest of the ancient world. Narrative, which will be considered in the next chapter, was first developed in Mesopotamia.

The power of symbolic images rests in their simplicity and recognizability and this makes them especially suitable for expressing the linked concepts of power and military supremacy. The simplest form of monumental symbol is probably the block of stone, which the Egyptians (and others) created as the embodiment of a god. Initially such god symbols were plain rectangular blocks of stone, such as the examples which survive in number at the Nabatean city of Petra.[1] The most famous of all such god-blocks is the Kaaba at Mecca, although it was later purged and purified by the prophet Mohammed.[2] The Egyptians, however, developed a more sophisticated god-block, elongated and pointed at the top, which we know as the obelisk. Originally associated with the sun god, obelisks came to be used as symbols of power by the divine rulers of Egypt, the pharaohs, who believed themselves to be the children of the sun god.[3] From here it was but a short step to use an obelisk to proclaim the king's military prowess and to record his victories. According to Herodotus, the pharaoh Sesostris erected many such pillars on battlefields, inscribed with his name and the nature of his victory.[4] In fact comparatively few surviving obelisks were inscribed in this way, but Tuthmosis III (1479-1425BC) erected two at Karnak to proclaim his victory over his enemies in Asia, and the upper part of one of these survives in Istanbul (1).* The hieroglyphic inscription describes how the king crossed the Euphrates with his army and slaughtered his foes, and it was probably the exceptional nature of this military enterprise which gave cause for the erection of the obelisks. By contrast, the obelisks of Ramesses II, make only generalized and probably excessively boastful references to his military victories, describing him as 'the bull who tramples the foreign lands and kills the rebels'.

If the memorialization of victory was only one of many meanings which the ancient Egyptians attributed to their obelisks, it was to be the key reason why so many of their powerful successors removed these stones from Egypt and set them up in their own cities as symbols of victory. The Romans more than any others did this, with the result that there are still today more standing ancient obelisks in Rome than in any city in the world. The first such obelisk to be removed from Egypt stands now in the Piazza del Popolo, and so great was the achievement in bringing it to Rome that the ship which transported it was long preserved as an adjoin-

*Numerals in brackets refer to the illustrations following page 146.

ing exhibit in the capital. When one considers that the stone is almost 100 feet tall and weighs 235 tons this pride in achievement is understandable. The obelisk was originally set up in 10BC in the Circus Maximus to commemorate the conquest of Egypt by Augustus. It was followed by many more, thirteen of which survive today, although none is in its original location. Equally, not all the obelisks of Rome were so clearly intended to commemorate victories, since it became an imperial fashion to erect an obelisk from Egypt. Nonetheless, it is from the Romans rather than from the Egyptians themselves that the obelisk as a specifically military memorial derives, and it was from Rome that the form entered the vocabulary of western memorial motifs. The practice of obelisk removal was continued by the later Roman emperors in their new capital of Constantinople, and the last to be taken in antiquity, that of Tuthmosis III mentioned above, is also the only one to remain in its original Roman setting, in the centre of the Hippodrome and mounted on the sculpted base made for it by the Emperor Theodosius I in the year 390AD. Most of the sculpted scenes refer to the events and prizes awarded in the Hippodrome games, with only one showing the embassy and homage of some barbarians, so perhaps the obelisk was not brought to Constantinople to mark a military triumph. However, the Hippodrome also provides the earliest example of a western-built obelisk (1) (that is to say it was not brought from Egypt and it is not monolithic but constructed of separate stones). It stands almost 100 feet high and an inscription on its base records that it was sheathed in bronze by the Emperor Constantine Porphyrogenitus (912-59), because it was decayed at that time. It probably dates from the earliest period of the Christian city, and although its original purpose is unknown it may well have been some form of victory symbol.[5]

From these classical sources obelisks were taken up by artists and designers of the Christian world and used as decorative motifs associated particularly with death and with victory. They were also used in what might be termed a miscellaneous monumental role, as in the case of the Martyrs' Monument in Edinburgh which was raised in 1793 to commemorate those who were banished for advocating parliamentary reform, or that built by Nash in Bath, to mark the city's gratitude for the benefits bestowed on them by the Prince of Wales. Another somewhat unusual example is the obelisk erected by Brass Crosby, Lord Mayor of London, in 1771 at the centre of St George's Circus in London (and moved to the park outside the Imperial War Museum in 1905), which recorded the distances from Westminster, Fleet Street, and London Bridge (3). However, the 19th century revival of the ancient practice of obelisk removal was to re-emphasize the memorial role of such stones. Egyptian obelisks went to Paris, London, and New York, and one, now known as Cleopatra's Needle and standing on the Embankment in London (2), was acquired specifically as a victory symbol.[6] Ironically, however, the victory commemorated was over the French, not the Egyptians. British victories over the French fleet at Aboukir in 1798 and over the French army at Alexandria in 1801 drove the Napoleonic forces from Egypt and to record this triumph an obelisk was awarded to London by the Egyptians for driving out the French. It was not actually removed and re-erected on its present site until 1878, after an extraordinary journey which reveals how skilful the ancients must have been to move these massive stones. The obelisk also took on a secondary memorial role when the pedestal and one of the two bronze sphinxes which flank it was damaged by a bomb dropped during the first German air raid on London, on 4 September, 1917, and the resulting scarring was left unrepaired as a testimony to this event.[7]

This was just part of the revival of the use of obelisks as victory and memorial symbols and well before Cleopatra's Needle had appeared in London Sir Robert Smirke had designed and built the Wellington Testimonial as a massive obelisk in Dublin (1861), while the Washington Monument of 1877-84 in Washington DC can claim to be the world's largest obelisk, at around 500 feet.[8] A number of obelisks were built specifically as war memorials before the present century. There is a battlefield example at Drumclog near Strathaven, the site of the Covenanters' only victory over the English, in June, 1679. Several more were erected to commemorate the Duke of Marlborough's victories over Louis XIV, while an obelisk at Concord, Massachusetts, marks the spot on which the first shot in the American Revolution was fired. A granite obelisk in the main court at Chelsea Hospital in London commemorates the battle of Chillianwallah, the decisive engagement of the Second Sikh War in 1849, and others were used to commemorate the Crimean War, as at Portsmouth. Another striking example is in the British cemetery outside Florence Nightingale's hospital at Scutari, on the Asian shore of the Bosphorus. This consists of an obelisk made of granite from Aberdeen, set on a base sculpted with four large angels.[9] Perhaps it was this memorial which started a trend for 20th century memorial obelisks in the Black Sea region, for the British memorial at Cape Helles to the men who fell during the Gallipoli campaign is of this form, as is the Soviet war memorial in the Crimean city of Odessa. In fact, however, obelisks were to become one of the commonest of all 20th century war memorial forms, found both in isolation and in combination with other elements. They were also to prove especially

4

popular on coastal sites, where they could be used as a landmark for shipping.

Like the obelisk, the memorial column dates from antiquity. However, although they are related visually, columns differ from obelisks in their manufacture and in their meaning. Antique obelisks are monolithic, single pieces of stone carved out of the bedrock as telling symbols of the divine creation of the earth and closely related to the god-blocks mentioned above. Columns, on the other hand, are (for the most part) built up of separate pieces and are more clearly an expression of man's mastery over his environment. In other words a column does not have the divine associations which were essential to ancient obelisks and which, in a sense, they have always retained, despite the fact that many post-classical obelisks are not monolithic but are built up of separate pieces. This is also perhaps why the memorial column was not widely used by the earliest civilizations of the Near East, although both columns and obelisks were used in isolation or in pairs to mark the entrance to a holy place, an example being Phar'oun's Pillar at Petra.[10] Columns and pillars were also used as tombstones, particularly in the Lycian kingdom of southern Anatolia, a well-known example being the so-called Harpy tomb from the city of Xanthos (4). This monolithic pillar, some 18 feet tall, supported a series of sculpted reliefs, dating from around 480BC, while the tomb chamber was inserted in the top of the column itself.[11] Honorific columns and tower tombs can be seen together at Palmyra,(5) while Herodotus mentions that a memorial column was erected by the government of Samos in memory of the Samian sailors who fought in the Battle of Lade. He also describes the memorial columns which were erected on the battlefield of Thermopylae, where Leonidas and his Three Hundred perished.[12] But commemorative columns were first developed on any scale by the Romans, who also popularized the idea of a column as a victory memorial, often crowned by a statue of the victorious commander and decorated with reliefs recording his achievement. The most famous example is Trajan's column in Rome (6), which will be considered in more detail in the next chapter. Here it is only necessary to note that the idea of a column as a memorial was to become a standard element in western iconography, particularly as a celebration of imperial victory. The Emperor Constantine placed a great column, surmounted by a figure of himself in the form of Apollo, at the centre of the forum in Constantinople, to mark the foundation of the city as the new capital on 11 May, 330, and this survives today as a battered fragment (8). Another emperor, Napoleon, erected a memorial column in 1806 for his victory at Austerlitz, which stands in the Place Vendôme in

Paris and which was based on Trajan's memorial (7).[13] Another pair of Trajanic columns, decorated with relief spirals, flank the facade of Fischer von Erlach's Karlskirche in Vienna (dating from 1716), although here they record another sort of victory, over the plague. Indeed, columns became a common way of commemorating plagues in eastern Europe and Fischer von Erlach can again be cited for his splendid *Pestsäule* in the Graben in Vienna.[14] London provides a plain example of a memorial column in the Monument, designed by Sir Christopher Wren to commemorate the Great Fire of 1666. There is also a 19th century war memorial column outside the west front of Westminster Abbey (12). It was erected in 1861 to commemorate the old boys of Westminster School who died in the Crimean War and was designed by Sir George Gilbert Scott.[15] In Paris the Colonne de Juillet in the Place de la Bastille rises to a height of 170 feet and commemorates the Parisians killed in the revolutions of 1830 and 1848. Their names are engraved on the base of the column, while, at the top, the statue represents the Spirit of Liberty. Berlin has a Victory Column, erected in 1869-73, to commemorate the defeat of Denmark, Austria and France (11). The shaft of the column is adorned with the barrels of captured cannon, while a gilded figure of Victory crowns the monument. Finally, in the United States the West Point military academy has a column memorial to its Civil War dead.

The commonest use of memorial columns has been as pedestals for hero statues, and a series of such honorific columns can be seen in the eastern Roman cities of Palmyra and Apamea, where they were erected in memory of notable citizens.[16] This was also the original function of Trajan's column, although the bronze statue of the Emperor that initially crowned it disappeared in the 7th century. A mediaeval example of this practice, which stressed its classical origins, is provided by the two famous columns that flank the entrance to the Piazzetta in Venice, facing the Grand Canal. These are antique monoliths which were brought to Venice from the east by Doge Vitale Michiel II at the end of the 12th century. One is surmounted by an oriental lion, representing St Mark, the other by a figure of St Theodore, the torso of which is made from a Roman imperial figure.[17] A similar idea lies behind the two classical columns which were erected in the Crusader castle of Edessa (the modern city of Sanli-Urfa in eastern Turkey). In more recent times the Duke of Marlborough received both a column and a triumphal arch at Blenheim, while Nelson, the archetypal British hero, was posthumously awarded several monuments, with memorial columns in Dublin (1808), Great Yarmouth (1817), and London (1838). The Yarmouth column, designed by William Wilkins, is 144 feet

high, a mere 12 inches less than that in Trafalgar Square, and was originally intended to be crowned by a sculpture of a Roman galley, to emphasize the antique link. In the event a statue of Britannia was substituted
(10).[18] The combination of column and statue was similarly fortuitous in
London. A competition was held to design a Nelson memorial and the
winner, William Railton, proposed a Corinthian column. Second prize
went to E. H. Bailey for a figure of the Admiral, but there was no great
enthusiasm for either scheme, so they were combined to produce a
column surmounted by a figure. Shortage of money meant that the series
of bronze reliefs had to be added later, and the flanking lions were contributed by Landseer.[19] The nearby column to the Duke of York, designed
by Benjamin Wyatt, was intended from the first to support the bronze
statue of the Duke by Sir Richard Westmacott and was erected in 1834.[20]
In France, Napoleon was the recipient of a number of columns; a good
example is the Colonne de la Grande Armée outside Boulogne, on the site
of the base camp for the proposed invasion of England in 1804-5 (9).
Napoleon's column in the Place Vendôme in Paris has had a variety of
crowning figures; the emperor dressed as Caesar came first, but was
replaced in succession by Henri IV, Napoleon again, a huge fleur-de-lys,
and two further figures of the emperor. Even (or perhaps especially) on
top of a column one is subject to the whims of political and social fashion.
Rulers less significant and powerful than Napoleon might also seek columnar immortality, such as Ludwig I of Darmstadt, for whom a Victory
Column was erected in 1841, crowned with a figure of the locally famous
Duke. Elsewhere, politicians might be deemed worthy of a column, such
as Cobden in Newcastle, and even a writer, Walter Scott, received a
column in Glasgow.

A third, equally fundamental memorial form is the cross, which not
unnaturally in the Christian world, is the commonest symbol of all. In fact,
monumental crosses formed no part of the memorial vocabulary in the
ancient world but as the instrument of Christ's Passion and Resurrection
the cross immediately provided the combination of sacrifice and triumph
which is fundamental to the concept of the modern war memorial. The
cross was of course used as a Christian symbol from the time of the Crucifixion onwards, but its specifically military associations derive from the
Emperor Constantine's victory at the Battle of the Milvian Bridge (312),
when a vision of the cross inspired the soldiers to victory: *In hoc signo
vinces.*[21]

Monumental crosses were also erected by the early church, notably the
great jewelled cross on the site of Golgotha in the Church of the Holy

Sepulchre, Jerusalem, and some idea of how this must have appeared is preserved in the apse mosaic of the Church of Santa Pudenziana in Rome. But the cross did not have specifically military or memorial connotations until some 900 years later when it was adopted as the sign of the Crusaders. Then the martial link was strengthened by the cruciform shape of the mediaeval sword, which was interpreted as a direct analogue of the cross of Christ.[22] However, there is one group of early mediaeval crosses which was especially important in the development of the 20th century war memorials. These are the standing Celtic crosses, erected in Northumbria and the Celtic lands during the 7th and 8th centuries.[23] They have always been something of a puzzle to historians, for they were created at a time when virtually no other large-scale standing monuments were being built in Europe, and some of them, notably the Ruthwell and Bewcastle crosses, are decorated with sculpture which can only have been inspired by late antique work from the Mediterranean area. Indeed, the whole form of these monumental crosses suggests a link with the classical obelisk and column tradition, but exactly how these ideas were transmitted to Britain is unclear. Certainly the most southerly of the crosses, at Reculver in Kent, of which only fragments survive, had a round shaft, decorated with figures, which derives ultimately from Trajan's Column or some related monument.[24] Whatever their origin, standing crosses have been used as a central motif in war memorial design, although the crosses themselves do not seem to have had any clear memorial purpose. They appear to have been erected out of simple piety and perhaps marked places of prayer in remote areas sparsely supplied with churches. Equally, it was not the figure sculpture on the crosses, which so intrigues art historians today, that enthused the memorial designers, but the forms of the crosses themselves. This is typically a long free-standing shaft surmounted by the cross itself, often enclosed by or enclosing a circle. A second aspect to be taken up was the non-figurative decoration, which consists of interlace patterns derived from Celtic and Scandinavian art.

The reason for the popularity of these cross forms as war memorials lies in their Christian symbolism, the striking nature of the original monuments, and the fact that they were rightly perceived as a distinctively British type. Indeed, despite their Mediterranean associations, it may well be that they link up with the Celtic tradition of standing stones. In this context it is interesting to note that a series of large free-standing cross monuments were produced in the 16th and 17th centuries in Brittany, an area which shares the Celtic tradition of standing stones.[25] One of these Breton crosses was to be transported to Flanders, together with a dolmen, to form the First World War memorial to the French 87th and 45th Divisions at the Carrefour de la Rose, near Ypres.

England also produced specifically memorial crosses in the Middle Ages, most famously in the twelve Eleanor Crosses. Eleanor of Castile was the wife of Edward I, who died at Harby in Lincolnshire in 1290. Her body was brought to Westminster Abbey for burial, and a cross was erected at each place the cortège stopped on its journey to London. These have been largely destroyed or rebuilt, but they were canopied structures related to contemporary metalwork shrines, as can be seen from the fine surviving example at Geddington in Northamptonshire. The tradition continued when they were rebuilt and at the last stopping place, Charing Cross in London, there is an elegant Victorian gothic version designed by E. M. Barry in 1863.[26] The form was also to inspire a number of First World War memorials.

It is therefore surprising that crosses were not widely used as war memorials before the 20th century, but this reflects the fact that individual or communal war memorials were not themselves common in mediaeval or early modern Europe. One of the few exceptions is a cross on the site of the battle between Charlemagne and Marsilio in 778, near Roncesvalles in the Pyrenees. The present cross is a fourteenth century example, erected here in 1880 to replace the original one destroyed by the French in 1794. Another cross on the battlefield of Crécy (**18**) marks the spot where King John the Blind of Bohemia, ally of King Philippe VI of France, was killed. The monument is set on a modern base, but the plain cross itself appears to be old and there is no reason to doubt the tradition that it was erected shortly after the battle in 1346. These remain unusual memorials, and the majority of monuments found on mediaeval battlefields are later commemorations, although the cross marking the site of the Battle of Towton (1461) appears to be old. The present era has made up for this, and the cross is now the most familiar of all memorial symbols, especially in the form of the Cross of Sacrifice, designed by Sir Reginald Blomfield, which has a cruciform sword applied to the face of the cross (see chapter 5).

Obelisks, columns, and crosses are three of the most common symbolic forms in the memorial vocabulary. There are many others, notably cenotaphs and arches, which have come to be closely associated with public monuments, but these will appear in other contexts later in these pages. At this point it is appropriate to turn from symbolic forms to the closely related field of symbolic representations.

A symbolic representation is a figure or figures which are immediately recognizable as standing for a general concept, such as victory, death or peace. Such representations were first developed in the ancient world but have achieved a currency that spans the centuries. Once again it was the Egyptians who originated some of these forms. In the early Dynastic age Egyptian kings set up a series of shield-shaped stones to mark the site of important victories. The shield-shaped stone is one memorial symbol that did not survive antiquity, but the form of their decoration was to prove more influential and provide some of the earliest and longest-lasting examples of the symbolic representation of victory. One of the first extant survivals is found on the best-known of these early Egyptian sculpted stones, the Narmer palette (13), which dates from c3200BC and is today preserved in the Cairo museum.[27] It is a victory monument, Narmer being the first king of the First Dynasty, who united for the first time Upper and Lower Egypt under one rule. The stone is carved on both sides, and the surface is divided into registers by means of a flat baseline on which all the figures are placed. There is no attempt to convey any illusion of space or depth. On one side we see the king standing before a kneeling enemy, whose hair he grasps in one hand. In his other hand he holds a raised mace, with which he is clearly about to deliver a death blow to his helpless opponent. In the lower register are the bodies of two enemies who have been previously despatched.

This form of symbolic victory recurs many times in ancient art and is obviously no more than a generalized statement about the military might of the ruler concerned, even when it relates to a specific battlefield memorial. The reverse of the Narmer palette shows another generalized scene in the topmost register, with the king, depicted as usual on a larger scale that anyone else, preceded by his standard bearers, inspecting the dead bodies of his enemies. The bodies are naked, manacled, and headless, neatly arranged in two rows and with each head carefully placed between the feet of its former owner. The symbolic nature of the scene is self-evident, and like the victory scene on the other side does not show the actual process of war, but only the results of war to those who oppose the king.

If symbolic representations of victory were established through such monuments, the ferocious imagery of Narmer's palette was to be toned down by later, more civilized societies. The Greeks in particular developed the symbolic representation of war through the use of myth. In this they differed very clearly from the Romans who, as we shall see, delighted in realistic representations of battle, and this fundamental difference in approach in fact provides one of the basic distinctions between the two great classical cultures.

10

The Greeks were not, of course, the first people to have or to illustrate myths, but they were the first to develop in a conscious and rigorous manner their symbolic and allegorical meaning. All mythologies are rich in stories of battles and these provide ready metaphors for actual military affairs. A favourite Greek example was the battle between the Centaurs and the Lapiths. The wild Centaurs, part human part horse, were invited by the king of the Lapiths to attend his wedding, but in a remarkable abuse of his hospitality they tried to carry off all the Lapith women. They were defeated in the ensuing battle and it is clear that the struggle represented for the Greeks the victory of civilization over barbarism, and more specifically the victory of Greeks over Persians. For this reason the subject was commonly used on memorial temples, such as the Parthenon, built in the time of Pericles in celebration of Greece's victory over the Persians,[28] as well as on the internal frieze from the temple at Bassae. Equally common and even more directly related to the Persian wars were the frequent depictions of battles between Greeks and Amazons. The Amazons were believed to dwell in Asia Minor and their identification with the Persians is often stressed by showing them in Persian dress and with Persian weapons.[29] Once again the Parthenon provides an example which is repeated in numerous other temples of the 5th century BC. But undoubtedly the most spectacular use of myth on a war memorial in ancient times was the Great Altar at Pergamon (14), built in the reign of Eumenes II (197-159BC) to commemorate his victory over the Gauls.[30] This large structure, decorated on all sides with reliefs showing the victory of the Gods over the Giants, is today preserved and re-erected in the Pergamon Museum in Berlin. The carving is of immense virtuosity, representing the peak of the realistic and dynamic Hellenistic style. Pergamon will feature again in the story, both as an early example of a complex of memorial structures and for the famous and dramatic sculptures of dying Gauls, which were in the precinct of the temple of Athena and represent one of the earliest artistic expressions of compassionate death. The Great Altar alone assures the city of a key place in the history of memorial development.

By using symbolic representations in this way the Greeks divorced their memorials of war from particular events and allowed them to stand as essentially timeless statements about victory. No doubt some believed that the stories portrayed had their origins in real events, but by the time they became the subject for sculptors and painters they had assumed an entirely mythical role, bearing the same sort of relation to reality as the legend of King Arthur does for us. This allowed Greek myth portrayal to escape the confines of pure narrative, in which the artist attempts to retell

11

a series of events as they occurred. There was no need to represent all the episodes of a well-known myth, since the story would be entirely familiar to the viewer. Instead, each part of the story could be represented by a single picture, so that we have a series of highlights rather than a continuous narrative. The method may be compared with the technique of illustrating a book, when, if the story being told is well-known, a few well-chosen pictures will remind the reader of the whole narrative. A further advantage of this highlight technique is that, as well as recalling the whole story, the individual scenes can symbolize particular qualities such as courage, treachery, or suffering. Thus it is clear that for the Greeks the portrayal of myth and legend had a direct bearing on life, and this was an attitude which was handed down to modern times. The victory of the Gods over the Giants was the victory of Greek civilization over Barbarism, and the deeds of the heroes of the *Iliad* and the *Odyssey* stood for the deeds (or potential deeds) of every Greek soldier. In this generalized presentation of warfare Greek artists provided a strand of the memorial tradition which has survived to the present day.

Besides creating generalized metaphors for conflicts, the Greeks also developed a number of individual symbolic images which have survived the centuries as part of the memorial vocabulary. The most striking and long-lasting of these was undoubtedly the figure of Nike, or Victory, which had emerged by the end of the 6th century BC as a winged female figure, clothed in a long robe. She was shown with various attributes, such as a palm, a wreath, or a crown of victory, and for the Greeks she was most commonly associated with achievement in the athletic or poetic fields. However, she was also to accompany military victors and this was to be her lasting duty. The Winged Victory of Samothrace (15), today in the Louvre, is only the best known version of a subject which has appeared in various guises ever since. This figure was set in the prow of a sculpted ship and placed so that it could be seen on the skyline from the theatre of Samothrace. Clearly intended as a memorial, it was a votive offering from Demetrius Poliorcetes after the naval victory of Salamina.[31] The image was taken up by the Romans, for whom the Victory figure was an essential element in any depiction of military triumph. New versions of the type were popularized, such as Victory writing on a shield to record her triumphs, or Victory as a charioteer, and these images were later to be revived by artists in the Renaissance.[32] Such revivals were facilitated by the fact that the pagan Victory was transformed into the Christian angel. Without undergoing any change in pictorial form, and indeed little change in meaning, the pagan deity became the Christian messenger of God,

12

conferring divine blessing upon those whom He favoured. Thus, on early Christian sarcophagi we find winged angels bearing the monogram of Christ which are indistinguishable from pagan Victories bearing wreaths.[33] Indeed, we can see the change taking place on early Byzantine coins, where figures of Victory are gradually replaced by angels. In many Byzantine works of art angels are depicted as winged soldiers in armour, while the archangels Michael and Gabriel frequently appear in an undisguised military role.[34]

The Greeks contributed other symbolic figures, notably the weeping or mourning woman, represented as a draped figure with head bowed, and sometimes a reversed torch, symbolizing death through the extinction of light. There is a famous relief of Mourning Athena in the Acropolis Museum in Athens, which was formerly interpreted as the goddess reading the names of Athenian war dead listed on a stele in front of her. This view is no longer accepted, and indeed the 'mourning' aspect of the figure has been questioned, but it is worth noting that she leans on a reversed spear, just as many later soldiers reverse their arms in mourning.[35] Penelope pining for her husband Odysseus is often shown in mourning, while the family of Meleager are seen mourning at his death bed and tomb. One of the most striking of classical examples is the great sarcophagus of the Mourning Women from the royal necropolis at Sidon, dated to around 350BC and preserved in the Archaeological Museum in Istanbul. This depicts a series of female figures in various attitudes of lamentation set in niches around the sarcophagus. From here it was but a short step to showing the actual family of the deceased as mourners and this practice was adopted by the Romans on their tombstones.[36] However, it was in the middle ages that the representation of family and friends as mourners became common, and such weepers stand in niches around countless mediaeval sepulchres. Indeed, by the 14th century such weeping figures were a key element in every grandiose tomb and are carved to demonstrate all possible aspects of mourning. Some of the most famous examples were created by Claus Sluter for the Burgundian royal family in their mausoleum at the Chartreuse de Champmol.[37] The tradition reached an extraordinary climax in the tomb of the Emperor Maximilian I who died in 1519 and was buried in the Hofkirche at Innsbruck. Here the weepers, his ancestors and relatives, have stepped away from the sarcophagus and are represented as over-lifesize sculptures in bronze surrounding the tomb.[38] In this monument we see the immediate ancestors of the full-size mourning soldiers who stand around the base of many a modern war memorial.

The Christian world has also provided its own symbolic figures, in the form of saints, some of whom have acquired universal significance of a sort which relates them to Greek images. Among the best known military saints are George and James, and although the imagery used to depict them drew upon the traditional vocabulary of hero presentation (which will be discussed in chapter 3) they both evolved specific and readily recognizable forms. St George, in full armour and often mounted on a charger in his role as dragon slayer, provided a splendid and timeless image of virtue and power triumphant over the forces of evil. Since he was also patron saint of England, this image came to be seen as a national symbol and in this form it entered the memorial repertoire. Another particularly influential version was the sculpture of the Saint which Donatello made in 1416 for Or San Michele in Florence, and this standing image of a handsome youth, fully armoured and ready to fight for God and King, was to be widely revived in the 19th and 20th centuries.[39]

Both St George and St James occasionally took part in actual battles, appearing before Christian troops in the form of a vision and leading them to victory over the infidel. St James first did this at the Battle of Clavijo in the 9th century, at the start of the reconquest of Spain. On this and other occasions he was credited not only with the overall victory but was believed to have despatched personally thousands of the enemy, and this led to his distinctive Spanish presentation as Santiago Matamoros, St James the Moor Slayer.[40] In this guise he is seen, mounted on a white horse, enthusiastically lopping off the heads of surrounding infidels. Not only does this image appear in many Spanish churches, but pilgrims to Santiago de Compostela can to this day buy tokens and trinkets depicting the warlike Apostle killing his enemies. Such heavenly intervention has continued to be a theme for artists in the present century, and one of the odder paintings from the First World War is John Hassall's 1915 Vision of St George over the Battlefield (19). This shows the trenches of the western front suffused by a magical pink glow, with the mounted saint dressed as a mediaeval crusader appearing in the clouds above.[41]

There are other figures that appear in a Christian context, but which are also essentially pagan in conception, disguised by a thin veil of faith to become angels of Peace, or representations of Fame or Immortality. Other female personifications emerged, notably Liberty, who was to become closely associated with the French Revolution and Republic. Here the image, which is normally classically based, combines several different attributes; as Marianne she symbolizes the spirit of the Republic, sometimes warlike, as in Rude's famous relief of La Marseillaise on the Arc de Triomphe, elsewhere the embodiment of serenity and good order. She was also exported and New York's Statue of Liberty remains one of the best known versions of the theme.[42] Her British equivalent, Britannia, inspired one of the most extraordinary but unbuilt monumental concepts; in 1799 John Flaxman designed a 200-feet-high statue of Britannia, to be placed on Greenwich Hill, next to the Observatory, as a memorial to British naval victories over the French.[43] Drawings and models for this project survive and inevitably bring to mind the 20th century memorial at Volgograd in the Soviet Union, with its giant female figure (see below, chapter 6).

The only figure to survive more or less unchanged over the centuries was Victory, who appeared on monuments at all periods. Among influential modern versions were the 26-feet-high gilded figure by Friedrich Drake on top of the Victory Column in Berlin (16) and the striking figure created by Thomas Brock for the Victoria Memorial, outside Buckingham Palace. This was unveiled in 1911 but only finally completed in 1924, and the splendid monument provided a sort of touchstone for many memorial artists in the 1920s. Victory had also figured prominently on a number of Boer War memorials and another powerful image was that made in 1903 by the American sculptor Augustus Saint-Gaudens for his memorial to General Sherman in New York. Here the General is mounted on a charger which is being led by Victory. In England a similar iconography had been proposed by Alfred Gilbert for a Boer War memorial, but only a maquette was made. It is, however, interesting that the imagery of Victory leading a mounted figure can be traced back directly to Byzantine sources and is found, for example, on coins of the Emperor Justinian.[44]

These various symbols, both animate and inanimate, were taken up by the memorial artists of the 20th century but, with the exception of Victory, they seldom reproduced classical themes directly. Like Roman artists borrowing from Greek traditions, they have combined elements and expanded themes to produce an iconography that is recognizably of our own time. It is one of the central themes of the following pages that the official memorial art of the 20th century can stand comparison, indeed demands to be compared, with that of the past. It will also be argued that, for the most part, the memorials of modern war represent the successful re-interpretation of a living tradition, not the sterile reproduction of outmoded forms.

1 At Petra these are commonly known as the Djin blocks and some of them are hollow, suggesting that they were tombs. Others are solid and therefore qualify as god-blocks. See Khouri, R, *Petra*, London, 1986, pp 31-2.

2 Although the Kaaba has the form and appearance of a god-block it is in fact a built structure, with the sacred stone, a black rock possibly of meteoric origin, built into one corner. See Creswell, K, *Early Muslim Architecture*, London, 1958, pp 1-2.

3 For a general discussion of ancient obelisks see Habachi, L, *The Obelisks of Egypt*, London, 1978.

4 Book II, p 167, in the Penguin Classics translation by Aubrey de Selincourt, London, 1985.

5 The third extant monument on the *spina* of the Hippodrome is the Serpent column from Delphi. Thus it would seem that the Hippodrome was the site for trophies of various sorts and this makes the original meaning and intention of the built obelisk still more puzzling.

6 For a detailed description of the removal and transportation of Cleopatra's Needle see Noakes, A, *Cleopatra's Needles*, London, 1962.

7 Quite a large number of First World War memorials have preserved subsequent war damage, to redouble the memorial message, an example being the Guards Memorial in London, which was damaged by a bomb in 1944. Some of the scars were retained at the request of the sculptor, Gilbert Ledward. See Skipwith, P, 'Gilbert Ledward RA and the Guards' Division Memorial' *Apollo*, January, 1988, pp 22-26.

8 Later obelisks, and the memorial tradition generally, are discussed by Curl, J, *A Celebration of Death*, London, 1980.

9 The Crimean obelisk is located in the cemetery used by the British community in Istanbul, to which the military cemetery for the two World Wars has been added. The whole is now under the care of the Commonwealth War Graves Commission and is a beautifully maintained oasis in the middle of a modern Turkish maritime and military complex.

10 The High Place at Petra also provides a good example of paired obelisks marking the entrance to a sacred area. See Browning, I, *Petra*, London, 1973, pp 207-8.

11 The sculpture from the Harpy Tomb is in the British Museum. See Cook, B, *Greek and Roman Art in the British Museum*, London, 1976.

12 Herodotus, Book VI, 15, and Book VII, 220.

13 The column was designed by the architect J Godoin, and the bronze reliefs are fashioned from the 1200 cannon captured at the battle. A figure of Napoleon in Roman costume originally surmounted the column. See Saint Simon, F de, *La Place Vendôme*, Paris, 1983.

14 See Coudenhove, G, *Die Wiener Pestsäule*, Vienna, 1958. The idea of building memorials to plagues is an ancient one. If Pausanias, who wrote in the 2nd century AD, is to be believed this was one of the reasons why a splendid temple was constructed at Bassae in the 5th century BC.

15 See Byron, A, *London Statues*, London, 1981, p 355, although one may question his view that the monument is a monstrosity.

16 Browning, I, *Palmyra*, London, 1979, pp 169. 207-8.

17 MacAdam, A, *Blue Guide to Venice*, London, 1986, p 90.

18 The figure of Britannia does not face the sea but looks towards Nelson's birthplace of Burnham Thorpe. See Mee, A, *Norfolk*, London, 1972, p 360. On the subject of the commemoration of Nelson generally see Yarrington, A, 'Nelson, the citizen hero: state and public patronage in monumental sculpture, 1805-18,' in *Art History*, Vol 6 no 3 (1983) pp 315-329.

19 Physick, J, *The Wellington Monument*, London, 1970, pp 19-21.

20 It was said that the Duke was placed so high to keep him out of the reach of his creditors. See Byron, *op cit*, pp 218-9.

21 The Battle of the Milvian Bridge is described by Eusebius, *The History of the Church* (trans G. Williamson), London, 1965, 368-70.

22 This symbolism was described in detail by a Catalan writer, Ramon Llull, whose work was translated into English and published by Caxton as *The Book of the Ordre of Chyvalry*.

23 There is a large literature on the Celtic crosses, but see Clapham, A, *English Romanesque Architecture before the Conquest,* Oxford, 1930.

24 The Reculver cross has been discussed in detail by Kozodoy, R, 'The Reculver Cross', *Archaeologia,* Vol CVIII, 1986, pp 67-94.

25 Good examples may be seen at Guimilau, Lampaul-Guimilau, and St Thegonnec.

26 The Eleanor Crosses were both unusual and influential. See the discussion and bibliography in Alexander, J, and Binski, P, (eds), *Age of Chivalry; Art in Plantagenet England 1200-1400,* London, 1987, pp 361-66.

27 For a basic introduction to these Egyptian sculpted stones see Aldred, C, *Egyptian Art,* London, 1980.

28 The original intention was to leave the war-damaged temples on the Acropolis as a memorial to the Greek struggle, but Pericles persuaded the Athenians to rebuild them. However, the idea of preserving war-damaged buildings as memorials is one that has survived, a modern example being the incorporation of the remains of the bomb-damaged structure in the rebuilt cathedral at Coventry.

29 Redlich, R, *Die Amazonensarkophage des 2 und 3 Jahrhunderts nach Christus,* Berlin, 1942.

30 Pollitt, J, *Art in the Hellenistic Age,* Cambridge, 1986, pp 97-110.

31 That the winged Nike goes back at least to the 6th century BC is witnessed by a figure from Delos preserved in the National Museum in Athens. See Richter, G, *The Severe Style in Greek Sculpture,* Princeton, 1970. On female personifications generally see Warner, M, *Monuments and Maidens: The Allegory of the Female Form,* London, 1985.

32 For examples see Bober, P. and Rubinstein, R, *Renaissance Artists and Antique Sculpture,* London, 1986.

33 There are many examples, including what is perhaps the earliest Christian sculpture to have survived in Constantinople, the 4th century Sariguzel sarcophagus in the Archaeological Museum, Istanbul. See Beckwith, J, *The Art of Constantinople,* London, 1961, pp 20-21.

34 Again many examples, but the mosaics of San Apollinare in Classe, Ravenna, may be cited, where Michael and Gabriel both carry the *labarum,* a Roman military standard bearing the Christian monogram.

35 For this and much related material see Panofsky, E, *Tomb Sculpture, London,* 1964. On the Mourning Athena see specifically Ridgway, B, *The Severe Style in Greek Sculpture,* Princeton, 1970, pp 47-8. In Britain the practice of reversing firearms at funerals dates at least to the 16th century. See the description of the funeral of Sir Peter Carewe in 1575 in Field, C, *Old Times Under Arms,* London, 1935, p 255. I am grateful to Mrs Sarah Barter-Bailey, Librarian of the Royal Armouries, for this reference.

36 See Walker, S, *Memorials to the Roman Dead,* London, 1985.

37 The tomb of Philip the Bold, Duke of Burgundy (d 1404) is the only one of Sluter's royal tombs to survive complete, and here the weepers include a famous series of cowled monks. This tradition of mourning figures can be traced equally in England and in France.

38 The Innsbruck figures may ultimately be derived from the life-size sculptures in the west choir at Naumburg, which was built in the middle of the 13th century as a memorial chapel to the benefactors of the cathedral.

39 Some 20th century memorials include actual reproductions of Donatello's figure, for example on the Boer War memorial at Huntingdon.

40 For a thorough and entertaining investigation of this tradition see Kendrick, T, *St James in Spain,* London, 1960.

41 Imperial War Museum, Department of Art.

42 A detailed study of this exists by Agulhon, M, *Marianne into Battle: Republican Imagery and Symbolism in France, 1789-1880.* On the Statue of Liberty see Warner, *op cit.*

43 Physick, J, *Designs for English Sculpture 1680-1860,* London, 1969, pp 165-8. This giant figure may itself have been inspired by an unrealized French plan, dating from 1793, to erect in Paris a colossal monument representing the People, to be cast from captured canon; the apparently male statue was to hold the figures of Liberty and Equality in one hand, while leaning on a great club with the other. See Agulhon, *op cit.* pp 18-19.

44 Warner, *op cit,* and Greenthal, K, *Augustus Saint-Gaudens, Master Sculptor,* New York, 1985.

CHAPTER 2

THE NARRATIVE OF WAR

'One picture is worth more than ten thousand words.'
Chinese proverb

Despite the symbols developed by the Egyptians and by the Greeks, the most common form of memorial to war in the ancient world was the narrative depiction of its campaign. The desire to tell a story is universal and war has always provided some of the best and most dramatic material. Naturally the king always triumphed and the whole purpose of such memorials was to record the achievements of the ruler. This narrative tradition has a long and almost unbroken history from the dawn of representation to the present day and it is no accident that the stylized reliefs of some modern war memorials conjure up memories of Assyrian palaces.

The idea of using narrative scenes to depict the events of war seems to have started in Mesopotamia, where the Sumerian kingdoms were emerging as powerful city-states in the third millenium BC, at much the same time as the First Dynasty was establishing itself in Egypt. The Mesopotamians did not eschew symbolic forms, adopting a characteristic type of obelisk, with a stepped rather than a pointed top, and using symbolic representations of victory that are similar to the Egyptian. Many of these can be seen on the earliest cylinder seals, often in the form of contests between a king-hero and wild beasts.[1] However, among the extraordinary treasures found by Sir Leonard Woolley in the Royal Cemetery at Ur is what may well be the earliest extant narrative depiction of war.[2] This occurs on a magnificent but mysterious object usually known as the Standard, which is today preserved in the British Museum (20). Dating from c2450 BC, it is a curious wedge-shaped hollow box of unknown purpose (perhaps part of a musical instrument) which is decorated on its two long sides with figures cut from shell and set in a ground of lapis luzuli. A straight baseline divides the picture surface into registers, three on each side, which are to be read from bottom to top, the action moving from left to right.

The lowest tier of what may be termed the front of the Standard shows a battle in progress, represented by four chariots. Each chariot contains two people, a driver and a soldier. However, it is not clear whether these four chariots are to be understood individually or collectively; in other words, are we looking at a single moment in the battle involving four chariots, or are we looking at the progress of the battle, represented by the same chariot at four different moments? Certain details suggest that the latter is the case. Firstly, the chariot appears to gain speed, from a gentle walk on the left to a full gallop on the right. Secondly, the soldier is shown weaponless in the first chariot, in the second he takes a spear from the spear-box at the front, in the third he wields an axe, while in the fourth he again holds a spear. This could mean that we are seeing the actions of one man (no doubt the king) throughout the battle, rather than a single moment in time. Such an interpretation might seem to attribute to the Standard a sophistication which, splendid though it is, it does not otherwise possess; yet, with the hindsight of knowing that it is in Mesopotamia that the war narrative evolves, I think we are justified in seeing this as a battle story.

The scene above shows a group of prisoners being led off after the battle, while the top register depicts the victorious king (placed centrally and slightly larger than anyone else) with his empty chariot and attendants behind him, inspecting a group of prisoners.

If the front of the Standard may be said to show the fate of the enemy, the back clearly depicts the fruits of victory. In the lowest tier we see the spoil, including chariot teams; in the middle register we have a procession of men and animals, which may represent either further booty or the preparations for the topmost scene, the victory feast, where the king is seated with his generals, drinking and listening to music.

While the Ur Standard may be read as narrative, it still has a lot in common with the symbolic type of victory seen on Narmer's palette (see Chapter 1). Again the two sides may be taken to represent defeat of the enemy and the rewards of victory. We do not know if a specific victory is commemorated; there is nothing to make it specific and it may be no more than a generalized statement about war. Equally, it is clearly the king's triumph, since on both sides the topmost scene shows the all-powerful monarch, on the one hand dealing with the defeated, on the other celebrating the spoils of victory. The glorification of the king is all the more apparent if we identify him as the warrior in the battle scene — an identification which is strengthened by the presence of the empty chariot in the topmost scene.

It is also worth noting that here, as in most pre-Greek art, there is an absence of emotional content. We identify the scenes in a hieroglyphic manner, recognizing a chariot as a warlike machine, and a prostrate figure as a dead body. There is nothing to suggest the horror of war, and little to indicate, except symbolically, its triumph.

This mixture of symbolic and narrative presentation is even clearer in another important early monument, the stele of Eannatum or, as it is often known, the stele of the Vultures which dates from around 2450 BC and is now in the Louvre (21).[3] Only fragments survive, but they are enough to reconstruct the main themes of the whole stone and to show that one of the two faces was entirely narrative, the other symbolic, although both referred to the same event. Another departure was the addition of a long inscription, giving precise details of the event portrayed. From this we learn that the monument commemorated a boundary dispute between the cities of Lagash and Umma, which was only resolved when Umma was defeated. The stele was erected on the re-established boundary line and decorated with scenes of the victory of the Lagash forces under the command of King Eannatum. Like the Ur Standard, the narrative scenes are divided into registers by straight lines, but in this case the story is read from the top downwards. First we see Eannatum, at the head of a phalanx of shield-bearing troops; the battle is presumably in progress, since the troops march over the bodies of fallen enemies. To the right is a great pile of bodies, with vultures feasting on them — hence the nickname of the stone. In the second register we see Eannatum in his chariot, with foot-soldiers behind, and in the lowest register we see again the king, now after the battle making a thank-offering, and a great pile of corpses. The living carry baskets of earth on their heads to pile over these bodies to make a burial mound. This form of proper burial contrasts with the vulture feast above and has led to the suggestion that this is the men of Lagash burying their own dead, while the enemy are left to the scavengers. Thus we are witnessing the creation of one of the first known burial mounds — a form of memorial that will be considered in chapter 4. Here we should simply note that the introduction of such features as the basket-carriers and the vultures brings a dramatic realism to the scene of battle which has been absent before.

By contrast, the reverse of the stele is entirely symbolic, although the image is both powerful and poetic. A large seated figure clasps a net, which is full not of fish but of men. This is the great net which Eannatum cast over the men of Umma, and having caught them in it, despatched them with ease. The seated figure is probably that of the King himself, although it has also been interpreted as that of the god Ningirsu, acting as a reminder that human actions are subject to divine regulation.

The stele of Eannatum, like all the monuments mentioned so far, preserves the horizontal baseline and the consequent division of the pictorial space into registers. The first surviving monument to break with this tradition, and indeed one of the most remarkable of all these early stone reliefs, is the stele of the Akkadian King Naramsin (22), who ruled in Mesopotamia towards the end of the 3rd millenium BC.[4] This is a monument to a victory, not a depiction of a battle, but it is important for presenting us with a single unified composition. We see the victorious king leading his troops up a hillside, at the crest of which are the emblems of the gods. The troops are arranged in three parallel files, but there is no baseline and they are marching upwards, giving the whole composition a surging movement. There is also a minimal attempt to present landscape, in the form of trees, which separate the victorious troops from the defeated enemy. It is true that the figure of the king still dominates, and is larger than the rest, but the picture as a whole does seem to represent a move towards a more expressive form. This is not just another symbolic and eternal vision of royal supremacy, but a particular statement about Naramsin's own achievement.

It is also significant that, in common with a number of other such victory monuments, the stele of Naramsin survived because it in turn became a trophy of battle and was carried off by the Persians to their city of Susa. There in due course it was discovered by French archaeologists and today it is preserved in the Louvre.

The next large step in the development of the battle narrative seems to have been taken, somewhat surprisingly, in Egypt. We have already seen that symbolic forms of victory were the norm in Early and Middle Kingdom Egypt. There are a few exceptions, such as a scene of the siege of a town, portrayed with remarkable vividness, in the Old Kingdom tomb of Inti at Deshasheh in Upper Egypt, or in a similar scene in a 6th Dynasty tomb at Saqqarah, but these are unusual. Certainly, they do not lead us to expect the dramatic artistic and cultural changes which came with the 18th Dynasty of the New Kingdom.

The turning point was what would now be called a cultural revolution, led by the heretical pharaoh Akhenaton around 1370 BC, who set up a monotheistic religion and moved his capital from Thebes to a new site known as Tel-el-Amarna.[5] The new religion and the new capital gave birth to a new artistic style, which began to break away from the rigidity of existing Egyptian conventions. As on the Mesopotamian stele of Naramsin, the Amarna artists moved to abandon the horizontal groundline and large areas were treated as a single compositional unit. There is a consciousness of space and a new freedom of choice in subject matter. Politically, the Amarna experiment was a disaster; artistically, it was to have lasting results and to bear fruit in a series of royal reliefs created for the 19th Dynasty pharaohs Seti I and Ramesses II.

Seti's reliefs at Karnak are remarkable examples of the new compositional unity and in a series of battle scenes we see the king actively involved in the fray, often apparently in personal danger, portrayed with a sense of drama never before seen. Artistically and compositionally, Seti's reliefs are among the most striking results of the Amarna revolution. Still more interesting from the point of view of war narrative are the reliefs made for Seti's successor, Ramesses II, to commemorate the Battle of Qadesh.[6]

Qadesh was a small town in Syria where Ramesses fought the Hittites. Although he did not win a great victory, it seems likely that the Pharaoh's own role was, as it is depicted, considerable and this was why he wanted all the details of the action commemorated. This is probably also why the battle is represented on four different monuments: on Ramesses' temple at Abydos, at Luxor, on the Ramesseum at Thebes, and at Abu Simbel (23). The battle is also recorded in lengthy literary texts and the reliefs have inscriptions. The chronological order in which the four representations of the battle were made is uncertain, but they all contain the same basic elements, with the Abu Simbel version being the fullest — and therefore perhaps the last to be done.

The main events of the story are simple. Ramesses had gone to Qadesh with a body of troops and pitched camp. Captured spies revealed that this camp had been surrounded by the Hittite forces, so allowing the Egyptians to send out a call for reinforcements. The camp was then overrun by the Hittites, but instead of pushing home their attack they spent time in looting, allowing the reinforcements to arrive and the Egyptians to regroup. The counter-attack was led by Ramesses himself, breaking out towards the city of Qadesh and driving the enemy into the River Orontes. When further Egyptian support arrived the Hittites were routed, although the city itself did not fall.

This series of events is shown at Abu Simbel in two sections, one placed above the other and separated by a stylised band of opposed chariots. Yet this is a long way from the traditional register composition, and the upper and lower scenes are treated as a consistent narrative. This begins at the lower right-hand side, where the Pharaoh is seen interrogating the spies.

The scene to the left of this takes a different viewpoint, showing the whole camp overrun by the Hittites, with the relieving forces arriving on the extreme left. The upper scene is still more remarkable, for on the left we see Ramesses battling in his chariot, almost entirely surrounded by the enemy. The city of Qadesh is depicted as a moated stronghold, while the River Orontes winds across the pictorial space, with the second relieving force arriving on the opposite bank. On the extreme right is a formalized victory parade, but Ramesses in his chariot looks back on the scene of the action rather than towards his own troops.

Here, perhaps for the first time, is a true episodic battle narrative and, despite the clumsiness of the transition from scene to scene and despite the lack of a unified viewpoint, the story comes across vividly and dramatically. There are also a number of specific details to enliven the narration: the messenger setting off to seek reinforcements and (only in the Ramesseum version) the Prince of Aleppo, having been driven across the river by Ramesses, is held upside down to drain. A laconic inscription explains "The wretched chief of Aleppo is turned upside down by his soldiers after His Majesty hurled him into the water."

The Battle of Qadesh reliefs, remarkable as they are, had no successors in Egypt. It is to Assyria that we must turn to find the full development of narrative art, although it has indeed been suggested that the Assyrian artists were directly influenced by the Egyptian royal reliefs of Seti and Ramesses. This is not, however, the only possible origin of the Assyrian palace reliefs and they may be more directly related to internal Mesopotamian tradition which goes back to Ur. It is also of interest that the earliest Assyrian narratives are found on symbolic obelisks, which in Mesopotamia had stepped rather than pointed tops. The so-called White Obelisk from the Temple of Ishtar at Nineveh, now in the British Museum, is dated between the 11th and 9th centuries BC and shows the victorious campaigns of an unnamed king. These scenes are perhaps the true forerunners of the famous palace reliefs.

The reliefs were found in a series of palaces, dating from the 9th to the 7th centuries BC, notably at Nimrud and Nineveh (in what is today Iraq). A great deal of material has been recovered, mostly in the course of excavations carried out in the 19th century, and much of it was transported to western museums.[7] This means that the reliefs are both well known and well studied, although it still requires something of an effort to imagine them as part of a great royal palace rather than in the antiseptic atmosphere of a museum gallery.

One of the most immediately striking things about the Assyrian reliefs is the apparent reduction in the symbolic, hieratic elements and their replacement by something much closer to factual reporting. The change is more apparent than real, but we are presented with an entirely narrative depiction and, for the first time, the king is shown as an ordinary mortal, often appearing the same size as his subjects and his enemies. There is also an absence of religious content or reference; there are no gods in evidence and the Assyrians are left to win their battles without divine aid. The outcome of events is never exactly in doubt, since we know the Assyrians are going to win, but it remains a subject for dramatic speculation. Incidents are related in a fresh and vivid manner, while there is a variety of pose, movement, and even expression which makes the Egyptian reliefs look stilted and dull by comparison. The attention to detail is such that we can reconstruct every item of apparel and every weapon with confidence. Above all, we see a series of master carvers at work. Obviously not everything is of the same standard, but the best is very good indeed. The portrayal of musculature and movement make it certain that the artists had studied nature acutely. This is especially true of the depiction of animals, mainly horses in the battle scenes, but including a variety of wild beasts in the hunting scenes, which were virtually the only other subject to decorate the palaces. The realism is such that one suspects that at least some of the carvers must have seen war at first hand and were not merely using long-established conventions. Of course, the conventions remain — notably the eternal profile of ancient art — but there is a new freedom in the handling of spatial concepts. The horizontal baseline and the tier arrangement is used in some cases and not in others. There is even a suggestion of perspective, although this may be accidental.

The best way to appreciate the Assyrian narrative achievment is to look at particular examples in some detail. Two are selected here, both of which are in the British Museum. One, the Siege of Lachish by Sennacherib in 700 BC, is an event recorded in the Bible, while the other, the Battle of Ulai fought by Ashurbanipal in 653 BC against the Elamites and the Babylonians, is arguably the finest ancient narrative to have survived.[8]

The Siege of Lachish is of particular interest because the reliefs are not the only record we have of it (24). Sennacherib's campaigns are described in the Assyrian Annals and the siege of the town is specifically mentioned twice in the Bible (2 *Kings* 18, v.13-17 and 2 *Chronicles* 32, v.9). In addition, the site has been excavated, revealing weapons, armour and signs of destruction which correspond to the period of the siege.[9] It seems that this was an important victory and it was commemorated in a key site in the royal palace at Nineveh. The reliefs were found in Room 36 of the palace, which was the third in a series of reception halls opening off a great courtyard. The scene of the siege itself was placed centrally in the room, so that it could be seen from both the preceding halls and from the courtyard itself. The episode of the siege was prefaced by reliefs of the army gathering and on the march and followed by the processions of booty and prisoners. Finally, Sennacherib himself, seated upon his throne, received the surrender of the city.

The central episode of the siege is depicted against a patterned background, resembling fish-scales and perhaps intended to represent rocky terrain. This makes it rather difficult to 'read', while the problem of depicting a single mass of action within the register composition was not satisfactorily solved. However, we must remember that originally all the reliefs would have been painted and this would have made the storyline clearer. The registers do in fact help to give some impression of the formality of a siege, but they also make it hard to show direct action. Yet the detail and variety of the action is vivid. The Assyrians built a ramp to attack the walls with battering rams and this ramp is shown using diagonal registers. The rams are carefully depicted as small tank-like structures, no doubt covered in thatch since the defenders hurl lighted torches at them. An occupant of one ram carriage pours water over the roof to protect it from fire, while archers shower the defenders with arrows. This sort of detail gives remarkable vitality to the scene, even if it still lacks overall cohesion. There is also a continuity to the narrative. While the siege continues we already see a column of prisoners or exiles issuing from a postern gate. This line develops into the full-scale booty and prisoner procession, with the various items of loot clearly shown, as well as the gruesome fate of some of the prisoners, who are flayed alive. At last we come to Sennacherib himself, a truly majestic figure on a splendid throne: a symbol at the end of the narrative.

The Lachish reliefs are a fascinating historical document, especially when taken together with the other evidence of the event, but as narrative art the central episode remains confused. To find the supreme achievement of Assyrian narrative art we must move to another room in the palace at Nineveh and go forward fifty years in time. In 653 BC King Ashurbanipal defeated the Elamites, who lived in what is now southern Iran, at the Battle of the River Ulai. Like the Lachish reliefs, the Ulai story was uncovered in the 19th century and brought to the British Museum.

The Ulai reliefs (25) follow the same general formula as those of Lachish. The army assembles, the battle takes place, the aftermath is depicted. The great central scene is the battle itself, and here there are two distinct improvements on the Lachish scheme. Firstly, the whole composition is easier to read and, secondly, the action progresses steadily from left to right. The opening of the battle on a hillside is shown as a curving line which breaks the horizontal registers; its end is seen when the remaining enemy are driven into the River Ulai, which similarly flows across the normal registers. Within these two framing lines the action unfolds dramatically. The most remarkable element is the inclusion of a particular and detailed episode, the flight and death of the Elamite King Teumann. This takes place in the midst of the action and the events are explained by cuneiform inscriptions. Teumann has been wounded by an arrow and he flees to the forest for safety. His chariot collapses, perhaps with a broken axle, and the King is thrown out. The depiction of the crash and the panic of the horses is masterly. Tammaritu, Teumann's son, has also escaped and he takes his father's hand to lead him to safety. In vain, for they are caught by a band of Assyrian soldiers and, although Tammaritu tries valiantly to protect his father, they are both slain. Teumann's head is cut off and sent by chariot to Ashurbanipal.

This dramatic episode, one that surely occurred, gives an immediacy to the battle scene that is entirely new. Despite the fact that the story is told in an entirely unemotional way, it introduces a personal element which is only to be found previously in the Qadesh reliefs of Ramesses II.

The subsequent phases of the narrative revert to the usual triumphal themes. In this case we see a puppet king installed in Teumann's palace, while Ashurbanipal receives ambassadors. Above an inscription records his victories, opening with the traditional but ever-impressive Assyrian formula: *I am Ashurbanipal, King of the Universe, King of Assyria, Conqueror of my enemies.*

Nineveh, and with it the Assyrian empire, fell in 612 BC. The heritage of Egypt and Mesopotamia moved both east and west — to Persia on the one hand and Greece on the other. However, as discussed in the previous chapter, the Greeks favoured the symbolic and mythical presentation of war, largely to the exclusion of narrative. There were some exceptions to this rule. Appropriately enough, the temple of Athena Nike on the Acropolis of Athens, built in the years following 427 BC, had a frieze depicting unspecified battles betweeen the Greeks and Persians.[10] The accidental nature of our surviving evidence undoubtedly also gives an unbalanced picture; for example, a fragment of a votive relief preserved in the Eleusis Museum shows a dramatic moment from a battle between the Anthenians and the Spartans during the Peloponnesian War. This monument was in honour of Pythodorus, a general who witnessed the peace with Sparta in 421 BC, and it indicates that Greek war narratives may have been rather more common than now appears.[11] Pausanias and others describe a number of large battle paintings, including the Battle of Marathon in the Painted Colonnade at Athens, but unfortunately none of these survive. It is also clear that some of the Greek-influenced city states in Asia Minor preferred the narrative tradition and employed Greek artists to depict battle scenes, notably on the tomb of the Nereids at Xanthos[12] and the Heroon at Gjolbaschi-Trysa,[13] both of the late 5th century BC. However, it was the Romans who really inherited the Assyrian love of realistic war narrative and developed the form with a new zeal.

Battle epics proliferate in Roman art, decorating civic monuments the length and breadth of the Empire — an Empire which owed its very existence to the efficiency of the imperial army. Roman battle scenes, like those of the Assyrians, are filled with detail and precise observation, providing a prime source of information about life in Roman times. Yet they also took from the Greeks the idea of using myth as symbol and extended the highlight technique of representation. They also derived the idea of symbolic ruler images from the Egyptians, and, because Roman art has always been the most accessible form of classical culture for later western artists, it is the Roman memorial vocabulary that has most directly influenced Europe. Within this vocabulary, narrative played an especially important role.

The Roman revival of narrative may be traced back to Etruscan beginnings. A number of early tomb paintings include scenes of battle, some derived from myth, others apparently representing actual events.[14] The Romans took over this kind of historical painting and in an early example found near the church of S Eusebio (and now in the Museo Nuovo Capitolino in Rome) we see a battle scene and a parley between two commanders before a city. It includes what seems to be one of the first 'triumphal' scenes in Roman art — a theme that was to have a long history.

A number of depictions of victories survived from the Republican period, but it was under the Empire that the art of war reached its highest level. The best-known example is Trajan's Column (6), created in 113 AD to commemorate the Emperor's campaigns against the Dacians on the Danube frontier.[15] Much has been written about its decoration and the origins of the spiral reliefs which depict the campaigns. It has been compared to the illustrations of a book-roll, and may even be a stone version of an actual roll which is now lost. Equally, it may be linked with the sort of triumphal painting mentioned above.

The traditional nature of the narrative on the column becomes clear as soon as the scenes are examined. In the first place they preserve but re-interpret the ancient concept of a composition in registers, for one register winds up the column in a spiral, forming a continuous picture strip some 150 feet long. This depicts the two main campaigns of the Dacian wars, with a figure of Victory separating the two expeditions. The scenes are set against landscape and architectural backgrounds and at first sight it is difficult to distinguish between individual events, but it soon becomes apparent that scenes showing the Emperor himself recur in a regular fashion, punctuating the action. These scenes are formal and stately: the Emperor receives ambassadors, performs a sacrifice, or addresses his troops. Passages of vivid action separate these formal scenes, but the method of storytelling is basically the same as that found on the Assyrian reliefs. What makes the column different (and the heir to Greek invention) is the detailed and personal way in which the action is shown; no longer are there merely monotonous lines of troops, chariots, or captives, but each scene is individually observed and often clearly derived from actual events. The one strikingly traditional feature is that scenes of action are shown almost exclusively in profile, continuing the ancient tradition of action portrayal. Nonetheless, the actuality of the combat comes across with startling realism, and here it seems we have a sort of newsreel in stone. This impression is of course misleading, because the formal presentation, with the recurrent Emperor theme, means that the account is only partially historical. Individual scenes may well be reasonably accurate reflections of particular events, based on written accounts or even veterans' memories, but overall the column is not so much a depiction of history as a monument of individual triumph. In this, Trajan's memorial differs little from those of Ramesses II or Ashurbanipal.

Trajan's Column set a fashion for narrative columns that lasted into the early Byzantine period, although the two examples in Istanbul, that of Theodosius erected in 386 and of Arcadius in 453, are lost.[16] Had they all survived they would have formed a splendid source for the development of Roman narrative, but as it is, only the column of Marcus Aurelius in Rome, erected at the end of the 2nd century AD, bears direct comparison with that of Trajan.[17] Interestingly enough, there is already a decline in narrative incident on the Aurelian column. The scenes are less crowded, less full of realistic detail, and the compositions are simpler, with less feeling of depth. Looked at in terms of the history of narrative, this seems to be a throwback to a much earlier tradition. Looked at in terms of the future the column of Marcus Aurelius marks the beginning of a tendency towards simplification of forms which was to characterize Late Antique art and to become the legacy of the Byzantine and mediaeval world.

This development is most easily seen on the Arch of Constantine in Rome (26), erected after the Emperor's victorious rise to power in 312 AD.[18] For reasons which have never been entirely understood, it was decided to incorporate several old pieces of sculpture in the new work, notably parts of a great frieze commemorating Trajan's victories over the Dacians, which may have come from a temple. Like the scenes on the column, the frieze panels are illusionistic and the action of battle is depicted in vivid emotional detail. The contrast with the new panels made for Constantine's arch could hardly be greater. For example, the depiction of the Siege of Verona presents a series of identical attackers and identical defenders, arranged in ranks on a two-dimensional picture surface. Dramatic action is confined to a figure falling stiffly from the city walls. Apart from a greater depth of relief, this scene could almost come from an Assyrian siege picture; the concept is the same, with key scenes showing Constantine distributing largesse to the people after his victories.

It was once believed that the contrast between the sculpture of Trajan and of Constantine could be explained in terms of the gradual decline of Roman art. This is no longer accepted as the root cause, although it has to be admitted that Constantine's reliefs are far from top quality. Fundamentally, however, we are seeing the Romans returning to symbolic representation. Narrative gradually became less popular and artists dealt more and more in symbols. Narrative art tends to blur any simple message and, as the Empire crumbled around them, the later Roman Emperors were increasingly concerned with a straightforward statement of their power. A general conclusion may be drawn: narrative art is only used for political purposes by rulers who feel secure in their possession of power.

It was partly for this reason, and partly because of the requirements of the new Christian religion, that narrative, especially war narrative, did not flourish in the first centuries of mediaeval Europe. Christians differed from pagans in having a single holy book, the Bible, and the illustration of the well-known stories in it naturally tended to be in abbreviated narrative form. Biblical illustration was close in spirit to Greek myth portrayal, with highlights usually replacing continuous narrative. There were some conscious revivals of classical forms, especially in Byzantium. The Joshua Roll, an illustrated version of an antique *rotulus* made in the 10th century AD, is a notable example and some other extended biblical cycles do have a narrative form.[19] However, there is only one outstanding war narrative to have survived from the early middle ages — the Bayeux Tapestry.

It is probably not coincidental that the Bayeux Tapestry (27)(technically an embroidery) is one of the very few secular works of art to have survived from this period. It is clear that the art made for the castle or the palace was very different from that made for the church and it is probably only because the Tapestry was later preserved in Bayeux Cathedral that it has survived. If it represents a survival rather than an isolated revival of narrative art, the lost intermediary links were almost certainly to have been found in royal halls rather than in churches. There are descriptions of battle paintings adorning the council chamber at Ingelheim in the time of the Carolingian emperor Louis the Pious, while Henry I of Germany commanded that his defeat of the Hungarians in 933 be painted on the walls of his palace at Merseburg. There is in addition the allegorical poem by Abbot Baudri of Bourgueil, addressed to William the Conqueror's daughter Adela, which describes the secular decorations, including wall hangings, in 'the Countess's bedroom'. These are all lost and the nearest extant precursors of the Bayeux Tapestry are the tapestry fragments which were found in the Viking ship at Osberg.[20] These appear to have formed long strips of wall hangings decorated with scenes from Norse mythology and their form is similar to that of the later Tapestry.

The Bayeux Tapestry is so familiar that it need not be described in any detail.[21] It was probably made in England for Odo of Bayeux within living memory of the battle. The story is told in three sections: firstly, there is Harold's visit to Normandy, which leads him to become Duke William's vassal; secondly, there are preparations for war, and finally the battle itself. The very last section of the Tapestry is lost, but it almost certainly showed King William seated in victory on his throne, just as the beginning shows Edward the Confessor seated on his. It has long been recognized that the telling of the story is very much a propaganda exercise, giving the specifically Norman version of the truth and attributing an especially important role to Bishop Odo. It has also been convincingly suggested that it in part follows the form of a *chanson de geste* with the wronged master eventually overcoming the treacherous vassal. Equally, it can be viewed as one of a line of war narratives which stretches back to Nineveh, if not to Ur. This does not mean that the designers of the Tapestry had seen any of the previous examples discussed here, particularly Trajan's Column (although they could well have been familiar with an Early Christian or Byzantine version of a classical narrative) but it does seem that we are dealing with a continuous tradition. The formula of preparation, battle and aftermath is perhaps no more than the obvious sequence, but the way in which the story unfolds, preserving a register composition which is firmly held between the decorative borders, is comparable with the Assyrian reliefs. Once again, the tradition of showing battle scenes exclusively in profile persists, while in the rest of the Tapestry, frontal and three-quarter views are frequently found. Again, like the Assyrian carvers, the designers of the Tapestry delight in showing horses: at the start of the battle the Norman cavalry are seen moving from the walk, to the trot, to the gallop. A splendidly vigorous illustration of two horses falling conveys equine panic in a way that recalls Teumann's crashing chariot at the Battle of the River Ulai. However, the real link between Bayeux and its ancient past is that it is an attempt to show in a coherent way the whole history of a campaign from beginning to end. It therefore acts both as a record and as a memorial.

The loss of the great majority of mediaeval secular decoration gives the Bayeux Tapestry a singularity and importance which it may not wholly deserve. There are fragmentary survivals to suggest otherwise. In the Tour Ferrande at Pernes in southern France a series of rather crudely executed wall paintings, dated to around the year 1300, show episodes from the conquest of the Kingdom of Sicily by Charles of Anjou in 1266-68.[22]

It seems probable that these paintings at Pernes are a provincial version of a larger, now lost work, and they do suggest a continuing tradition. This tradition flourished most notably in the tapestry workshops of the late middle ages and it is well recorded in documents and inventories. For example, the Battle of Rosebecque in 1382 was the subject of a tapestry listed in the 1404 inventory of Philip of Burgundy, who had himself taken part in the battle.[23]

The most striking survivor of this tradition is a curious and much neglected Renaissance painting. This is an enormous fresco covering the whole length of one wall in Philip II's royal palace of El Escorial in Spain (28).[24] The room, which is consequently known as the Hall of Battles, is some 175 feet long and the gigantic fresco is a *trompe l'oeil* tapestry, shown hanging from imaginary fixings and folded back over the doorways. This gives credence to the story that in 1587 a huge damaged picture was found in some old chests in the Alcazar at Segovia and Philip II was so impressed by it that he ordered it to be copied for his new palace. Clearly the Segovia find was a tapestry, or rather series of tapestries. The battle represented is that of La Higueruela, which was fought by King John II of Castile against the Moors on 1st July, 1431. The task of recreating the tapestries as fresco was entrusted to four Italians called Granello, Tavarone, Castello and Cambiasso, and their achievement is the most impressive evidence for the survival of the battle narrative tradition. It is one of the largest battle narratives ever undertaken, full of fascinating details and executed in a curious mixture of mediaeval and Renaissance style. The Italian painters clearly made an effort to copy the costume and armour of the original and indeed most of the details seem to have been accurately observed, suggesting by their form that the lost Segovia tapestries dated from the middle years of the 15th century, only a few years after the battle.

The painting of the Battle of Higueruela, given its vast expanse, is inevitably a little confusing and one's eye is easily diverted by amusing or alarming detail. Yet the traditional structure remains intact: the army assembles, marches out, encounters the enemy, and is victorious. Some details suggest that the original Segovia version may have been incomplete, since the narrative sequence occasionally breaks down; thus, we see the Christian army marching against the ranks of the Moors, whose lines stretch diagonally across the surface. Immediately behind this the main battle is taking place and this lack of continuity is best explained by imagining that scenes which were originally depicted on separate tapestries have been conflated. The need to produce a series also explains the proliferation of fighting scenes in the fresco. In addition to the main battle there is an attack on a fort and a variety of 'mopping up' operations.

The Escorial fresco can be seen as a grandiose revival of the ancient tradition of battle narrative. Some elements go right back to ancient forms, notably the predominance of profiles in the action scenes as well as the traditional form and structure of the picture. There is little doubt that Ashurbanipal would have felt quite at home with King Philip's decorations. However, this ancient tradition was drawing to a close and it is symptomatic that the Escorial fresco is a copy rather than an entirely original work. There is a similar quality of pastiche about the rare post-Renaissance war narratives, such as Napoleon's column in the Place Vendôme in Paris (29) which is directly based on Trajan's Column. Nonetheless, the bronze reliefs, designed by Etienne Bergeret, give a splendid picture of the campaign, with a wealth of detail and precise observation. The story is taken from August to December, 1805, with a series of traditional depictions of the army making ready, on the march, laying siege and fighting pitched battles. The ancient usage of profile predominates but the number of appearances of the Emperor is greater than in the equivalent ancient works. This may be a pastiche, but it still has considerable style and vivacity.[23]

The reason for the general decline in war narratives is probably that war itself was becoming a broader and more complex subject. No longer was it a question of a single army assembling, going forth to battle, and returning victorious. Several armies might be engaged on several fronts over a long period, making it difficult to reduce the events to a single storyline. Consequently the depiction of battles began to concentrate on single moments in the action, which might perhaps be taken as representative of the campaign as a whole. There have been some attempts in the 20th century to revive pure narrative representation but these are mostly defeated by the complexity of their topic. For this reason the majority of modern war narrative is episodic, deriving from the highlight tradition of Greek art. The problem is that the episodes shown are not always immediately recognizable, as scenes from classical mythology would have been. Nonetheless, the narrative presentation has contributed much to the memorial tradition and provided some of the finest examples of the artist's response to war.

NOTES

1 The theme of a man fighting beasts, normally lions, is extremely common in ancient Mesopotamian art and may well derive from an episode in the story of Gilgamesh, King of Uruk, who killed some lions in the course of his wanderings. The texts of the story, normally known in English as *The Epic of Gilgamesh*, represent the earliest work of literature known, dating from the 3rd millenium BC.

2 For detailed discussions of all aspects of the evolution of ancient narrative see the publication of the 57th meeting of the Archaeological Institute of America, held in Chicago in 1955, *Narration in Ancient Art: A Symposium* published as volume 61 of the *American Journal of Archaeology* 1957. To this should be added Brilliant, R, *Visual Narratives: Storytelling in Etruscan and Roman Art*, Cornell, 1986.

3 Preserved in the Louvre Museum.

4 The stele of Naramsin was taken to Susa in Persia by Shutruk-Nahhunte of Elam about 1000 years after its manufacture. Like Egyptian obelisks, many Mesopotamian victory stones themselves became trophies of victory, especially for the Persians.

5 The revolutionary nature of the period is discussed by Schafer, H, *Amarna in Religion und Kunst*, Leipzig, 1931.

6 The Qadesh reliefs are discussed at length by Kantor, H, in *Narration in Ancient Art*, cited in note 2.

7 The full story of the early discoveries in Mesopotamia is told by Lloyd, S, *Foundations in the Dust*, London, 1947.

8 See Guterbock, H, *Narration in Ancient Art*, for a full discussion of these reliefs.

9 Some of the material excavated at Lachish is exhibited in the British Museum alongside the reliefs.

10 The temple of Athena Nike has been largely reconstructed, following its partial demolition by the Turks. Four blocks from the frieze were acquired by Lord Elgin and are in the British Museum.

11 This fragment is discussed by Kanta, K, *Eleusis*, Athens, 1979.

12 The complete tomb was dismantled and removed to the British Museum by Charles Fellowes in 1842.

13 These reliefs are in the Kunsthistorisches Museum, Vienna.

14 See Stenico, A, *Roman and Etruscan Painting*, London, 1965.

15 The best general study is Rossi, L, *Trajan's Column and the Dacian Wars*, London, 1971, but see also Richmond, I, *Trajan's Army on Trajan's Column*, London, 1982.

16 On historiated columns generally see Becatti, G, *La Colonna coclide istoriata*, Rome, 1960, and Brilliant, R, *Visual Narratives*.

17 Strong, D, *Roman Sculpture*, London.

18 L'Orange, H, & von Gerkan, A, *Der spatantike Bildschmuck des Konstantinsbogens*, Berlin 1939.

19 The manuscript is Vatican gr. 431. See Beckwith, J, *The Art of Constantinople*, London 1961.

20 Sjovold, T, *The Osberg Find and the other Viking Ship Finds*, Oslo, 1976.

21 There are many publications of the tapestry, most recently Wilson, D, *The Bayeux Tapestry*, London, 1986, and Bernstein, D, *The Mystery of the Bayeux Tapestry*, London, 1986, especially Chapter VI, Continuous Narrative; Distinctive Format and the Idea of Triumph.

22 Giraud, H, & Igolen, J, *Pernes, ancienne capitale di Comtat Venaissin*, Paris, 1927 and specifically on the paintings Deschamps, P, & Thibout, M, *La Peinture Murale en France au debut de l 'epoque gothique de Philippe-Auguste à la fin du regne de Charles V*, Paris, 1963, pp 229-34.

23 Martindale, A, 'Painting for Pleasure', in *The Vanishing Past* (ed. Borg, A, & Martindale, A), Oxford (BAR International) 1981, pp 109-131.

24 Fortunately, a detailed set of engravings of the reliefs on the column were published by Ambrose Tardieu, *La Colonne de la grande armée d'Austerlitz*, Paris, 1822-3. These are reproduced by Saint-Simon, F de, *La Place Vendôme*, Paris, 1983.

CHAPTER 3

THE CONQUERING HERO

'See, the conquering hero comes!
Sound the trumpets, beat the drums!'

Thomas Morrell, *Joshua*, pt.III

Heroes have been conspicuously absent from the war narrative considered so far. Of course, in one sense the king is always the hero, but he is seldom seen performing heroic deeds. Ashurbanipal or even William the Conqueror are shown as the winners of victories which have an inevitability that does not call for individual heroism. The king's role is to direct and guide affairs, and to receive the praise and the prisoners after the battle. There is comparatively little depiction of personal bravery in the arts of Egypt and Mesopotamia. Once again, it was the Greeks who first firmly established the image of the hero.

Heroes had existed long before Greek times in myth and literature and they were sometimes given visual expression in symbolic terms. Thus, on Sumerian cylinder seals we find Gilgamesh, the earliest of all heroes, killing a lion with each hand.[1] Yet the heroic idea did not really find a satisfactory pictorial expression until the Greeks took it up. Even then it came about through the portrayal of myth rather than fact. Not only did this accord with the Greek temperament but is partly explained by the fact that the deeds of real-life heroes aspire to and indeed often become in time the deeds of myth; the hero is, almost by definition, a super-human figure, whose actions raise him to the level of a Hector or a Lysander. Thus the portrayal of the hero begins with the depiction of myth and only gradually comes to show the real-life personality. Even when this happens history and myth are frequently confused, since the deeds of human heroes can acquire mythical status rapidly. Still today, in an age of almost instantaneous communication, it is possible for news to become distorted and confused and for actions of individual bravery to be (intentionally or unintentionally) inflated. In the past, when information travelled slowly, often by word of mouth, news of victories and defeats, of individual courage and achievement, were frequently wildly

35

distorted and this sometimes allowed the actions of one man (especially if he were the king) to be transformed into the fabulous deeds of a hero.

In archaic Greek art heroes are only distinguished by identifying labels or symbols; a soldier armed with a spear and a sword is, we are told, Priam. A little later the adoption of the highlight technique of narration allowed the viewer not only to identify the hero but to recall the whole story of his exploits. Thus, representations of the deeds of Heracles, as depicted on Greek vases, allow the informed viewer to recall often quite complex episodes through a series of single scenes. This method proved popular and successful, allowing as it did the deeds of actual heroes in Greek history to be compared or identified with the deeds of legend.

It was only a matter of time before the direct association between real and mythical heroes was made, although the democratic city states of central Greece tended to have rules forbidding the public depiction of prominent men. Such restrictions did not apply on the fringes of the Greek world, and when Philip of Macedon became effective ruler of all Greece the portrayal of the leader as hero became common. Philip had statues of himself and other members of the ruling family made by the Greek sculptor Leochares and set up in the sanctuary at Olympia. These do not survive, but a number of heroic depictions of Philip's son and successor, the myth-making figure of Alexander the Great, are known.[2] The splendid mosaic from Pompeii showing the Battle of the Issus is a Roman version of a lost Greek painting by Philoxenus. The battle itself, fought in 333 BC, was that in which Alexander defeated the Persian king Darius and the painter has selected a highly dramatic moment in the action when, in the midst of a mass of armed and fighting men, the two leaders come face to face. The incident is probably fictitious, but that is not the point. At the centre of the clashing armies are the two generals, Alexander on horseback and Darius in his chariot. The Persian is raising his hand in horror as one of his officers throws himself in the path of a spearthrust which was meant for Darius himself. There is an expression of terror on the Great King's face which contrasts strongly with the god-like confidence of the young Alexander. Here is the supreme hero of Greek myth translated into actuality: Apollo come to life.[3]

The hero is seen here in action, the fulcrum around which all activity turns. Alexander may also serve as a prototype for a second hero figure, in which the image is given specifically god-like characteristics.[4] This seems to have been created for him by the court sculptor Lysippos and in several early heads he wears a lion skin, which associates him directly with his mythical ancestor Heracles. In a further series of both contemporary and commemorative busts we see the ever-handsome, ever-youthful hero, with rugged face and wind-blown hair (30). This image was to form part, but not the whole part, of the commonest Roman hero type, the free-standing imperial statue. The concept was developed in the Hellenistic world and at first such statues were reserved for the gods, but gradually the victorious commander adopted the style. Thus Aemilius Paulus erected a monument to himself at Delphi, in memory of his victory at Pydna in 167 BC[5]. The monument seems to have consisted of a tall rectangular column, capped by a frieze, and with a statue of the victorious general on horseback on the top. The frieze survives and shows a lively combat between Romans and Macedonians.

The Romans took over the idea of the free-standing civic statue and developed it into an instrument of state propaganda. The image of the benevolent conqueror is related to that of the victorious king receiving homage at the end of a war narrative, but, extracted from a narrative context, it receives a generalized meaning which in turn recalls the symbolic rulers of Egyptian art. Trajan, on his column, carried connotations of both types of hero; we do not actually see him in action, but his ritual appearances are closely associated with the action scenes. The imperial statues, on the other hand, are totally divorced from action and radiate a calm and peaceful dominance. Augustus set the pattern. A young-middle-aged commander, dressed in rich armour, with one hand raised in a gesture which at once conveys victory, lordship, and protection (31). The best-known example is the statue of the Emperor from the Villa of Livia at Prima Porta, which is probably a contemporary marble copy of a bronze original. It is of particular interest to note that the richly decorated cuirass he wears is embossed with a representation of the return to Rome of the imperial standards lost in 53 BC at the Battle of Carrhae. The recovery of the standards itself confirmed that the Emperor was supreme and godlike and the statue reveals him as the embodiment of the *Pax Romana*, bringing peace and good government to the people of the empire.[6] Later these imperial statues were often over life-size, so perpetuating the tradition that made the ruler larger than life, literally head and shoulders above his subjects and his enemies. A fine example is the bronze figure of the Emperor Marcian set up in Barletta in southern Italy,[7] but virtually every Roman provincial city was furnished with its emperor images, all conveying the same basic meaning.

Important though free standing emperor images were in the propagation of the heroic image, a still more influential form was that of the equestrian figure. The hero on horseback has an added authority and command, and is raised above the surrounding crowd with no increase in size. Moreover, the horse itself can play a key part in the image, appearing as a noble yet arrogant beast that has been mastered by the hero on its back. In fact, the first record of an equestrian portrait that I have come across is one in which the horse itself was the hero. Herodotus records how King Darius I of Persia came to the throne in 521 BC with the aid of a neighing horse and a clever groom and that consequently his first royal act was to erect a stone monument of a man on horseback, with the inscription: "Darius, son of Hystaspes, by the virtue of his horse and of his groom Oebares, won the throne of Persia."[8] However, the most famous and most influential of all antique equestrian memorials was the Granikos Monument by Lysippos, set up at Dion in Macedonia to commemorate Alexander's first victory over the Persians.[9] This consisted of at least twenty-five bronze equestrian figures, perhaps accompanied by some infantry, and including a portrait of Alexander himself. It was transported to Rome in 146 BC and no trace of it survives, although it is thought that a small bronze statuette of Alexander on horseback, found at Herculaneum, might be based on his figure in the group. Even so, a single figure can give no impression of what this amazing and important monument must have been like and there can be little doubt that it set the trend for heroic equestrian figures in the future.

The most famous and most influential of surviving antique equestrian figures is the bronze statue of Marcus Aurelius from the Capitoline Hill in Rome (32).[10] The Emperor is suitably noble, though more benign than arrogant, in the *Pax Romana* tradition, and he rides a splendidly imperious beast, which originally crushed a fallen enemy beneath its raised front leg (the figure is long since lost). The motif of a horseman trampling on a defeated enemy was already ancient. The Greek soldier Dexileos, who fell in the Corinthian War, was commemorated on a stele which showed him as the mounted warrior crushing the enemy underfoot,[11] and similar scenes can easily be found in battle friezes before this. However, it was the free-standing Roman version of the theme which made it part of the standard heroic vocabulary. This was due, at least in part, to a misunderstanding, for the Christians of the Middle Ages thought that the statue of Marcus Aurelius in fact represented the first Christian Emperor, Constantine, and the fallen figure beneath the horse's hoof was that of Paganism, defeated by the new religion. Such "Constantine" images can be found in many medieval churches, particularly in western and southern France.[12] Yet this misinterpretation does not explain the continuing popularity of the image, which lies in the fact that actual heroes and heroic rulers, whether Roman emperors or medieval knights, were likely to be equestrians. The image of a man on horseback matched both the real and imagined perception of a conquering hero.

The two main types — the hero in action and the hero in triumph — therefore became recurrent themes in western art. However, knowledge of hero representation in the middle ages is scanty, largely because of the wholesale destruction of secular art in castles and palaces. Certainly the secular literature of the time is full of the stories of battles and the doings of heroes, but the art that has survived is primarily that of the church. In churches Christ was the hero, in action breaking down the Gates of Hell or in triumph as Judge of the World. This Christian iconography was largely derived from Roman imperial forms and provides the best-known example of the survival of the classical tradition. Yet Christian iconography certainly had its secular counterpart, which derived from the same roots, but all too little of this has survived.

One clue as to the strength of the secular tradition is that two of the most famous heroes, albeit largely mythical ones, invaded the Christian sphere of church decoration. Roland and Oliver, the companions of Charlemagne who were celebrated in the greatest of medieval epics, *The Song of Roland,* are to be found looking slightly uncomfortable in a number of ecclesiastical settings.[13] At Verona, for example, they stand sentinel on either side of the cathedral doorway, while their story is shown in the stained glass at Chartres. Roland also appears in a genuinely secular and heroic context, sculpted free-standing and over life-size, in the market squares of a number of German towns. Such gigantic Rolands, mostly dating from the 14th and 15th centuries, are the medieval counterparts of Roman imperial statues and they appear to symbolize civic pride, liberty and independence. Dressed as a contemporary knight and carrying a huge unsheathed sword, the Roland figure was often raised further above the crowd by a tall pedestal. At Magdeburg the Roland statue, now lost, was placed on top of a column, like Trajan.

An impressive group of medieval hero figures are the life-size sculptures of the founders in the choir of Naumburg cathedral, dating from the middle of the 13th century.[14] These are startlingly lifelike portraits and must be based upon contemporary figures, although they represent long-dead benefactors. Dressed as solid, respectable knights and accompanied by their ladies, they embody all the virtues of medieval German urban society, bringing the Roman image of Augustus once again to mind. The Naumburg figures, like the civic Rolands, give just a hint of the sort of secular iconography that has been lost and which would allow us to follow the full story of medieval hero portrayal.

There is a similar lack of evidence for equestrian figures in the Middle Ages, although there are indications that they existed. The Byzantine emperor Justinian had a large bronze equestrian portrait of himself erected in Constantinople. There is a small bronze of the Emperor Charlemagne mounted on a charger, in the Roman manner, which was probably inspired by the full-size mounted bronze sculpture of the Emperor Theodoric, which was brought from Ravenna to Aachen in 801 and set up in Charlemagne's palace.[15] Although long since lost, it is probable that this and other antique survivals inspired large-scale copies. The figure of Justinian in Constantinople certainly survived until the mid-16th century and was frequently commented upon by visitors to the city, so what appears to us as a revival of the equestrian hero in the Renaissance may in fact be merely a survival of a continuing type.

Medieval heroes are best known to us in death; the knight's tomb is where his earthly triumph is linked with the heavenly triumph of Christ. There is a seemingly endless series of armoured knights adorning churches in Britain and elsewhere, all of whom are depicted in death as heroes, dead but armed for the Resurrection and ready to fight for Christ as they had fought for the true religion on earth. The association between earthly combat and heavenly purpose, and the role of the tomb as a heroic memorial, was stressed by the very common practice of placing the dead warrior's arms above his tomb, as symbols of his valour on earth and an indication of his readiness to continue the fight. There is more than an echo here of the ancient custom of providing the dead with grave goods for use in the afterlife, although in Christian terms the arms were returned to God, from whom they were received in the first place.

The custom of making weapons part of the memorial was an ancient one, and the evolution of the trophy of arms will be considered in the next Chapter. However, in so far as the practice continues in the 20th century, its immediate origins are medieval. Significantly, such funerary arms often were, or were reputed to be, those with which the deceased had won famous victories, such as the shield and helm of Henry V which hang above his tomb in Westminster Abbey and which are by tradition those used by the King at the Battle of Agincourt. Perhaps the finest medieval combination of tomb and arms to survive is the monument to the Black Prince in Canterbury Cathedral. The Prince had given detailed instructions about this in his will, dated 7th June, 1376: "our image in relieved work of latten gilt shall be placed in memory of us, all armed in steel for battle . . . and (at the funeral) our helmets shall go before out the said body."[16] Today both the image and the arms survive, and although we see the hero in death and repose the tomb serves to recall most vividly the hero in action on the battlefield.

From here it was a short step to the preservation of famous weapons specifically as memorials to heroes. Great swords such as the legendary Excalibur and Durendal were physical extensions of their first heroic owners, and would give the current user something of the hero's power. Swords or banners captured on the Crusades became memorials to Christian victory and this use of captured arms became still more common with the invention of cannon. As has been mentioned, the Austerlitz Column in Paris was decorated with reliefs made from cannon captured in the battle and similarly the figures on the Guards Crimean memorial in London were made from captured Russian guns (17). Actual weapons were also preserved as memorials, such as the mortar from the 1812 Siege of Cadiz which, mounted on a fantastic carriage, forms a little-known memorial on Horse Guards Parade. The apotheosis of this idea was marked by the institution of the highest British award for bravery, the Victoria Cross, for the medals were made from the metal of captured guns.[17]

The topic of trophies and captured weapons as memorials may seem to be separate from the subject of the hero, but the two are linked in the tombs of medieval knights. However, as we have seen, the medieval picture is incomplete and this leaves some of the best heroic images as the military saints, such as George and James, whose role was discussed in Chapter 1. It is only with the advent of the Renaissance in Italy that a clear picture of the secular hero emerges once again.

It is not surprising that the hero image should regain its traditional form in Italy, the home of Roman heroes, nor that this revival should be closely linked with that of the *condottiere*. Put bluntly, for these hard-bitten professional soldiers to be seen as heroes was good for business. The need for a leader or a commander to establish for himself an heroic image is a continuing thread of history, and it sometimes seems that the need increases in inverse proportion to the candidate's merit. Certainly, many of the *condottiere* were far from admirable characters, but they left behind them among the most striking hero images in western art.

The process begins as an extension of the heroic tombs of medieval knights, in which the recumbent figure was gradually replaced by that of a mounted and victorious commander, either in the form of a free standing statue or, as with Uccello's famous fresco of the English mercenary Sir John Hawkwood, in paint (33). [18] This is a splendid image, even in its much restored state, which clearly reveals its Roman ancestry and which in turn inspired a series of similar memorials, such as that to Niccolo da Tolentino painted by Andrea del Castagno (also in Florence Cathedral). Very rapidly these mounted figures, while remaining commemorative, escaped the confines of the tomb and began to appear in the squares and public places of the towns for which they had fought. There are a number of fine 14th century examples, such as the monument to Cangrande della Scala, who died in 1329, in Verona, but the two outstanding figures are of the 15th century. Firstly, there is Donatello's noble vision of Erasmo da Narni, better known as Gattamelata, or the Honeyed Cat, in the Piazza del Santo at Padua (34). Gattamelata was renowned for courage and for keeping his word and certainly Donatello portrays him as the epitome of the just and honest commander. This is traditionally said to be the first cast equestrian statue to survive since that of Marcus Aurelius, with which it shares the same air of calm yet powerful assurance.[19] Very different is the famous dramatic image of Bartolomeo Colleoni by Andrea del Verrocchio which stands in the Campo SS Giovanni e Paulo in Venice (35).[20] This is the definitive expression of mounted might, managing to combine nobility, power, arrogance and unstoppable force. The sculpture is placed on a tall pedestal, dominating the surrounding square. Colleoni is mounted on a splendid, controlled horse, while the fully armed figure of the *condottiere* adopts an aggressive yet commanding pose. Even today every visitor to Venice who stands many feet below him in the square is immediately mesmerised by his face, with its piercing stare; here is not only the triumphant hero but also the avenging angel.

There are few other equestrian figures to match the power of this, but the basic formula was firmly re-established. Within a few years there was to be hardly a city in Europe without its sculpture of some local or national hero, mounted on his stallion. An example of the type is the statue of the Great Elector, Frederick William of Brandenburg (1703), in Berlin.[36] It is the work of Andreas Schluter, who depicted the Elector in part Roman and part contemporary dress, with figures of slaves at the base, representing his enemies. Another is the figure of Peter the Great in Leningrad, by Falconet and dating from 1782. In London there is a good equestrian series, which starts off with Le Notre's Charles I in Trafalgar Square(10) and ends less successfully with Alfred Hardiman's figure of Lord Haig in Whitehall, dating from 1937. London's most grandiose essay in the genre was a huge bronze statue of the Duke of Wellington by M. Cotes Wyatt which was erected on top of Decimus Burton's Constitution Arch at Hyde Park Corner in 1846. After a great deal of controversy and unseemly squabbling, this was

42

removed and the figure now stands forgotten at Aldershot.[21] The official memorial to Wellington is in St Paul's Cathedral, consisting of a tall canopied tomb by Alfred Stephens and crowned incongruously with an equestrian figure by John Tweed.

At the end of the 19th century a particularly accomplished sculptor of equestrian heroes was the American Augustus Saint-Gaudens. His monument to General John Logan in Chicago, dating from 1897, presents an impressive mounted figure, with one hand raised and bearing a standard. The form relates to the monument to Joan of Arc in the Place des Pyramides in Paris, cast from a figure made by Emmanuel Fremiet in 1874, which Saint-Gaundens would have known from his soujourns in France. Still more impressive is the Sherman monument in New York, mentioned above as an example of Victory leading a mounted figure. The sculpture is imbued with confidence and gives an impression of power and triumph, making it one of the few modern equestrian sculptures that can compare with those of Antiquity and the Renaissance.[22]

Since horses are no longer a normal form of transport, equestrian images have become less common and the most recent hero statues stand on their own feet. However, there is one other form of equestrian portrayal which should be mentioned, for from the time of Uccello such images have been commonly created in paint. Titian's *Charles V on horseback,* Van Dyck's *Charles I,* and Velasquez' *Count Duke Olivares* are among many memorable state equestrian portraits and these painted versions were as inflential in establishing the type as the sculpted ones. However, there is perhaps only one which can compete with Verrocchio's *Colleoni* in its power and force. This is David's wildly romantic portrait of Napoleon, windswept but triumphant on a mettlesome rearing stallion, crossing the Great St Bernard pass on his way to victory at Marengo. On the rocks below are carved the names of those other great heroes who had trodden the same path, Hannibal and Charlemagne, while in the background the army labours to cross the mountains. Nothing could better epitomize the hero aspiring to the condition of myth.[23]

David's Napoleon is a triumphant hero and at the same time a hero in action. The modern development of this second type of hero representation can also be traced from Uccello, whose Sir John Hawkwood has already been cited as the Renaissance statement of the triumphant mode. In the three panels which make up the *Rout of San Romano* (37) Uccello produced one of the first great battle pictures of modern times.[24] The panels, which are today distributed between the National Gallery in London, the Louvre in Paris, and the Uffizi in Florence, were originally designed to go at one end of Lorenzo de Medici's bedchamber. The other walls were apparently decorated with scenes of hunting and animal combat, producing a subject mix which recalls that of the Assyrian palaces. The event which was so prominently commemorated was in fact a comparatively minor affair which took place on 1st June, 1432, and although the paintings themselves are undated they clearly belong to the middle of the 15th century. It is also of some interest to note that many of the finest battle pictures record what history would regard as minor engagements, reflecting more on the vanity of commanders than on their historical objectivity. At San Romano the Florentine commander, Niccolo da Tolentino, was attacked by Siennese forces under the command of Bernardino della Carda. After resisting for several hours, the Florentines were relieved by a force commanded by Micheletto da Cotignola. Uccello's interpretation of these events is famous in the annals of art history for its experimentation with perspective and movement, but here we may concentrate on the manner in which the story is told. In many ways it follows the battle narrative tradition and (reading from left to right) the first panel (National Gallery) shows Tolentino, on a rearing white stallion, leading the charge against the enemy; the second panel (Uffizi) depicts a moment in the fray, with the unhorsing of a knight who is presumably the Siennese commander della Carda; the third panel (Louvre) shows the relieving forces, with Cotignola in the middle, sword raised, horse rearing. The triptych is not, therefore, a true narrative and the two outer wings concentrate on the hero in action. The figure of Tolentino on the first panel recalls that of Alexander on the Battle of the Issus mosaic, while both Florentine commanders are in traditional triumphal poses, almost as if they were public equestrian monuments set down in the midst of a battle scene. Equally interesting is the fact that the central panel shows the defeat of the enemy, for this is what the whole picture is really about. It is a demonstration of Florentine power and invincibility, rather than the celebration of two particular commanders.

Since Uccello's time the hero in action has developed in a number of ways, gradually taking on more complex strands of meaning. A different approach was used in one of the most famous of war paintings, Leonardo da Vinci's *Battle of Anghiari* which survives only in descriptions and in a number of copies. However, one of these is by Rubens, an artist fully capable of capturing the spirt of the original.[25] Leonardo's work was commissioned in 1503, as one of two paintings to be set up in the town hall by the city of Florence, in order to commemorate the great victories of the state. The best artists of the day were to be employed, and the second painting was by Michelangelo, entitled *Bathing Soldiers,* which is now also lost.

Leonardo chose to illustrate a highly dramatic moment in the battle, the struggle for the standard. The composition is a whirling mass of men and horses, the latter playing a vital role in both the form·and expression of the picture, recalling the horses on the Bayeux Tapestry or those in Ashurbanipal's palace. Here they convey the maelstrom, the ferocity, and the terror as clearly as the human participants. Yet the composition focuses on the fully armed figure with raised sword who is defending the standard from attack. Here is the Renaissance hero in action, a Gattamelata or a Colleoni in battle — a man who might justly expect to be rewarded with a victory statue in his home town. This figure holds the centre of the composition, much as Alexander forms the key in the Issus mosaic. The picture itself shows the horror of war but contains no pity. War, for Leonardo, is terrifying and terrible and he knew this at first hand, having started his career as a military engineer. Yet the victor is, through his victory, the inevitable hero; the *Battle of Anghiari* was in no sense an anti-war picture (its period, commission and setting preclude the possibility) but it is a relentless one and its hero is a totally unromantic figure.

Another type of conquering hero appears in the equally famous war painting by Velasquez, the *Surrender of Breda,* dating from 1635. This presents the triumphant hero, receiving and forgiving his enemies after struggling with Leonardo-like fury.[26] The result is a memorable interpretation of the beneficent hero type, first promulgated by Augustus in his *Pax Romana* statues. The Siege of Breda in the Netherlands was a *cause célèbre* of the Thirty Years War, taking place in 1624-5. It was particularly notable for the sufferings both of the Dutch defendants and the Spanish attackers, and for the generous terms of the eventual surrender. Moreover, this surrender was not accompanied by the usual frenzy of butchery and looting by the victors. Ten years after the event Velasquez (who was not of course present at Breda) turned the surrender into a major propaganda statement, reviving the theme of the merciful hero, in contrast to the avenger. We see the victor, Spinola, the only fully armed figure in the picture, reaching out with a gesture of benevolence to the defeated Prince of Nassau, who proffers the keys of the city in a suitably deferential manner. The contrast is further emphasized by the two retinues, with the Dutch ragged, dirty and bewildered, while the Spaniards are neat, confident and well drilled (their vertical lances being one of the famous compositional characteristics of the painting). Despite its mastery and despite its fame it is clear that the *Surrender of Breda* conveys a traditional concept. Action, power, and compassion are the hallmarks of the conquering hero and Velasquez provides Spinola with all three.

Post-Renaissance artists added, or rather popularized, one further important concept to the traditional forms of hero portrayal. This is the death of the hero, a subject which breaks dramatically with the scheme outlined above. In the pre-Classical world it was axiomatic that the hero did not die, it was only his enemies that perished. Yet in reality kings and heroes did die, and sometimes the manner of their deaths was final proof of their heroic qualities. "Whom the gods love die young" and heroes are traditionally divine favourites. They often died facing insuperable odds, at the moment of triumph, saving friends, or at the will of an unkind fate. However, while the living hero, defying death or triumphant in victory, is a reassuring and valuable image, the dying hero was potentially unsettling and dangerous.

The Greeks were very conscious of the poignancy of heroic death, but restricted it almost entirely to mythology, whereby it makes its appearance in art. However, as we have seen, the portrayal of myth is relatively safe and the Greeks seldom allowed the depiction of the death of real or recently dead heroes. The break with this tradition came not in Greece itself but at the Hellenistic court of Pergamon, where a school of virtuoso sculptors had emerged in the second century BC. In the courtyard of the temple of Athena, the goddess of victory, the Pergamene kings set up tableaux recalling their victories over the Gauls (38). These famous figures of dead and dying Gauls, known exclusively from later Roman copies, are perhaps the first examples of the serious treatment of heroic death in the visual arts. It was permissible to depict death in this way because the figures concerned were the enemy, but nonetheless these sculptures have a nobility and a power that is unsurpassed. It has been suggested that at Pergamon (and at a similar Pergamene monument erected in Athens) only the defeated Gauls were shown, without the triumphant victors, and certainly the surviving Roman copies show only the enemy. Such an unusual approach would be in tune with the theatrical nature of the Pergamon court and would again emphasize the heroic nature of the Gauls' sacrifice.[27]

Despite the bold and dramatic achievements at Pergamon, Roman sculptors tended to follow the traditional Greek lead and to treat death with circumspection. It would have been unthinkable to show the death of an Emperor in battle (not that this happened very often) or that of a great general, no matter how mighty his deeds. This convention survived the Pergamene experiment, but was ripped assunder by the Christians. The death of Christ, the Christian hero, was at the very centre of the new religion. Yet of course Christ triumphed over death and it was this that

46

made the representation of His death acceptable. Nonetheless, early Christian versions of the Crucifixion do not show suffering or even death, but present a living, triumphant Christ on the cross, with eyes open and fully clothed. Thus the figure of Christ is merely a symbol of victory over death, presenting an iconography which could easily be accepted by the early church. The dead Christ, with eyes closed and naked body slumped on the cross, is a later form which only developed once the Church was firmly established and could afford to show what every Christian knew to be only a temporary defeat.

It remained impossible to show the death of human heroes, although the literature of the middle ages abounds in the deaths of legendary ones. Sometimes, as in manuscript illustrations of the Roland story, the death of an heroic knight is seen, but these are sufficiently removed from reality. In this particular case the fact of death itself produced one final heroic act, for with his last remaining strength the dying Roland struck down an infidel with his horn to prevent him taking the famous sword Durendal, and this incident is often illustrated.

Even the Renaissance, with its self-confidence and increasing freedom of artistic expression, was unable to cope with the visual concept of the dying hero except in religious or mythological terms. Only in the 18th century were the barriers finally broken down, allowing the glorious death of the hero on the battlefield to be celebrated as well as mourned. It was of course essential, if the hero was to remain (or become) a hero, that he should die in triumph, the battle won. The moral of history must remain and the hero's life could not be seen to have been pointless or wasted. Thus, in those cases where the hero does stand alone, the battle lost, the viewer knows from subsequent history that defeat was to turn into victory.

One of the first examples of this new mode was Benjamin West's picture of the Death of General Wolfe on the Heights of Abraham on 13th September, 1759 (39). [28] Wolfe's exploit had all the elements of heroic enterprise and his death at the very moment of triumph was the ideal heroic tragedy. West's famous picture is a marvellous romantic concoction and the eye can easily miss the fact that the composition is taken directly from the traditional Christian formula for the Deposition from the Cross. Here Wolfe's slumped body replaces that of Christ, the standard replaces the cross, the groups of anxious soldiers are arranged as the mourners at the Deposition, and one can see the musket and bayonet at Wolfe's feet as the Instruments of the Passion.

Once introduced, the powerful image of the dying hero was widely

taken up. Within a few years John Singleton Copley was producing another of the great works of the age, the *Death of Major Pierson* on 6th January, 1781, which took place during the courageous defence of St Helier,
following the French invasion of Jersey.[29] It is a picture of splendid dash
and action, but the Deposition grouping remains, with once more the standard in place of the cross. Another small but probably intentional detail
is the presence in the background of a free-standing hero statue, around
which the battle rages. Indeed, this picture contains almost all the elements
of war depiction, for in addition to heroism, death and violent action,
there is also pity in the form of terrified women and children running
from the fray.

Both West and Copley were Americans working in London, and it was
a third American, this time working in his homeland, who produced a
whole series of dying heroes from the War of Independence. John Trumbull, himself the son of a famous soldier, created the heroes of the Revolution in paintings which contributed directly to the American national
myth. *The Death of General Warren at Bunker Hill, The Death of General
Montgomery at Quebec*, and *The Death of General Mercer at Princeton*
are all versions of the same theme.[30] Trumbull balanced these with a
series of noble surrender pictures, in the tradition of *The Surrender at
Breda*, of which *The Surrender of General Burgoyne at Saratoga* is typical.

In less than fifty years the theme of the dying hero had become standard. The tradition continued in the 19th century, with dying heroes from
Nelson to Gordon immortalized with artistic brush and poetic licence. It
is often instructive to check the dates of such pictures, for in many cases
they were painted a decade or more after the event they commemorate.
A good example is *The Last Stand at Gandamak*, (40) an event which took
place on 13 January 1842, during the First Afghan War. The sole survivor
of the battle, Dr Brydon, rode to Jalalabad with news of the disaster, which
inspired W. B. Wollen to depict the last moments of the action, when the
wounded remnants of the defensive square faced the final onslaught of
the enemy. Yet not only was the artist not personally involved, but his
picture was painted in 1898, 56 years after the event.[31] In this case we
are looking at a piece of romantic history painting, far from the realm of
historical reporting and this was typical of 19th century military art. It
achieved its finest expression in the work of Lady Butler.[32] *Scotland for
Ever*, depicting the charge of the Scots Greys at Waterloo, was actually
painted in 1881, but it remains one of the most dramatic battle pieces
ever produced. It also introduces yet a further development of the heroic
idea, the representation of a corporate heroic act. Increasingly, in the

works of Lady Butler and her contemporaries, we find instead of or along-side the individual hero the heroic company, usually fighting until the last man drops. In fact the corporate heroic act often results in death, making this a form of the dying hero concept. The classic example is Robert Gibb's picture of the Highlanders at Balaclava, *The Thin Red Line*, and Lady Butler produced another statement of the idea in her *Defence of Rorke's Drift*. A final variation on the theme is provided by one of her best known and most influential pictures, *The Roll Call*, which depicts the Grenadier Guards after an engagement in the Crimean War. We deduce that the Guards have been victorious, for the fleeing enemy are visible in the distance and a single Russian helmet lies in the blood-stained snow, but the price of victory has been high. The men are exhausted, wounded, in some cases dying, but they are clearly all heroes. When this picture was exhibited at the Royal Academy in 1874 it created an enormous sensation, and the recent reassessment of Lady Butler's much neglected art confirms that she was a painter of exceptional emotional power whose hero images influenced a whole generation.

The dead or dying hero did not of course replace entirely the more conventional types. However popular and emotive such scenes might be, the enemy could not be relied upon to kill the hero every time. Equally, it was coming to be realized that however valuable individual heroics might be, the job of a commander was to direct strategy and tactics and this could only be done successfully if he stayed alive. From the 17th century a growing number of battle pictures show the action taking place in the background, with the foreground taken up with the suitably martial and heroic commander, who is nonetheless out of the way of the actual fighting. A good example of the type is John Wootton's picture of George II at the Battle of Dettingen in 1743 (41).[33] Significantly, this was the last occasion on which a British monarch led his troops in battle. Wootton shows the action taking place on the horizon; the King, on a splendid grey horse, is not even looking at the soldiers but stares out of the picture with an air of confidence. Close by are his officers, also mounted and similarly exuding supreme disinterest in the outcome of affairs. The portrait of the King is essentially that of the traditional equestrian hero, as he had been portrayed across the centuries, transposed as if by accident to the proximity of the battle.

As war became increasingly organized and scientific it was not only the king who retreated from the battlefield. More and more the generals and the politicians directed war from behind the front lines and this shift of emphasis helps to explain the popularity of the dying hero imagery, since generals who died in battle were themselves becoming a rare breed. Equally, the battlefield hero was increasingly seen to be the ordinary soldier, who fought and died without questioning the reason why.[34]

It is clear that the depiction of heroes has much in common with the personification of myth and mythical qualities such as Victory. In visual terms the most enduring quality of the hero is nobility of spirit, and this applies whether the heroic figure is seen in splendid isolation, like Colleoni, in violent action, like Alexander, or in death, like General Wolfe. Whatever his activity or condition, the hero is by definition heroic and he is portrayed accordingly. The greatest change in heroic portrayal in the 19th and 20th centuries has been the introduction of the anonymous hero, the ordinary soldier. Kings and generals have been in large part replaced by generalized and unnamed figures, depicted with all the panoply of the ancient heroic tradition. These are the heroes who people the war memorials of the twentieth century and it is interesting to reflect that they share their anonymity with some very distant predecessors, the Dying Gauls of Pergamon.

NOTES

1 The subject is widely known as the Gilgamesh motif. See Lloyd, S, *Art in the Ancient Near East*, London, 1961.
2 Pollitt, J, *Art in the Hellenistic Age*, Cambridge, 1986. This is the most recent comprehensive study in English of the period.
3 Pollitt, *op.cit.*, argues that Darius is the focus of the composition and is evidence of an anti-heroic strain in Hellenistic art. I am unable to accept this view, although the figure of Darius should be seen as a foil and balance to that of Alexander.
4 Pollitt, *op.cit.*, pp 20-37.
5 This was the largest of three such monuments at Delphi, the others being dedicated to Eumenes II of Pergamon and Prousias of Bithynia. The frieze is in the Delphi museum.
6 On the iconography of Augustus see Walker, S, and Burnett, A, *The Image of Augustus*, London, 1981, (British Museum exhibition catalogue).
7 The identification of the figure has been disputed. See Weitzmann, K, (ed) *Age of Spiri-*

tuality, New York, 1979, no 23. However, Beckwith, J, *The Art of Constantinople*, London, 1961, argued in favour of Heraclius (610-619).
8 Herodotus, Book III, 86.
9 Pollitt, *op.cit.*, pp 41-43.
10 Knauer, E, *Das Reiterstandbild des Kaisers Marc Aurel*, Stuttgart, 1968.
11 In the Kerameikos Cemetery, Athens.
12 For example on the west front of Parthenay-le-Vieux, c 1120. Such Constantine figures are studied by Adhemar, J, *Influences antiques dans l'art du Moyen-Age francais*, London, 1939.
13 Lejeune, R, & Stiennon, R, *The Legend of Roland in the Middle Ages*, London, 2 vols, 1971.
14 Kidson, P, *The Medieval World*, New York, 1967, pp 140-142.
15 Lasko, P, *Ars Sacra*, London 1972, pp 18-19.
16 Mann, J, *The Funeral Achievements of Edward, the Black Prince*, London, 1951.

17 The original guns are preserved at Woolwich and turn out to be of Chinese origin, rather than Russian from the Crimea, as was intended. See Blackmore, H, *The Armouries of the Tower of London*, I Ordnance, London, 1976.

18 Borsook, E, *The Mural Painters of Tuscany*, London, 1960.

19 Janson, H, *The Sculpture of Donatello*, Princeton, 1957, II, pp 162-187.

20 Panofsky, E, *Tomb Sculpture*, London, 1964.

21 Physick, J, *The Wellington Monument*, London, 1970.

22 See Greenthal, K, *Augustus Saint-Gaudens, Master Sculptor, New York, 1985.*

23 Elsen, A, *The Purposes of Art*, New York, 1967, pp 242-3.

24 Berenson, B, *The Italian Painters of the Renaissance*, Oxford, 1930.

25 Clark, K, *Leonardo da Vinci*, Cambridge, 1939. The Rubens copy, which is in the Louvre, appears to be based on an engraving. A few of Leonardo's sketches for the mural survive.

26 It has been suggested that Velasquez also used as models Roman homage scenes, of the sort found on the columns of Trajan and Marcus Aurelius. Lafuente Ferrari, E, *Velasquez*, London, 1943.

27 Pollitt, J, *op.cit.*, pp 83-97.

28 In the National Gallery of Canada, Ottawa. This and the following pictures are discussed in Keegan, J, and Darracott, J, *The Nature of War*, London, 1981.

29 In the Tate Gallery, London.

30 In the Yale University Art Gallery.

31 In the National Army Museum, London.

32 Underwood, P, and Spencer-Smith, J, *Lady Butler, Battle Artist*, Gloucester, 1987. This is an extensive exhibition catalogue which includes a major reassessment of the artist.

33 In the National Army Museum, London.

34 For a general study of paintings of the army in the 19th century see Hichberger, J, *Images of the Army: The Military in British Art 1815-1914*, Manchester, 1988.

CHAPTER 4

MEMORIAL FORMS

'Let fame, that all hunt after in their lives
Live register'd upon our brazen tombs,
And then grace us in the disgrace of death;'
Shakespeare, *Love's Labour's Lost*, Act 1:1

The previous chapters have been concerned with the types, symbols, and traditions which go to make up the memorial vocabulary. However, from ancient times there has been an accepted formal repertoire associated with memorials of war and much of this has been influential in modern times, even though the commemorative aim has partly changed. Ancient memorials concentrate on the triumph of war, whereas their modern counterparts tend to emphasize the sacrifice of those who have died. Yet it remains true to say that many 20th century memorials retain a significant aspect of triumph and this is one of the reasons why contemporary critics have either condemned or ignored them. However, to interpret the cultural climate of the first quarter of this century in the light of that prevailing in the last quarter is not especially helpful. The great majority of people alive in the decade after the First World War regarded the outcome as a victory for the civilized values they believed Britain stood for, and this is a judgment which we can still agree with, even if the methods by which victory was achieved leave more room for doubt. Some of those who had fought in the trenches thought differently, but even among soldiers they were a minority. The element of triumphalism that remains in the memorials was intended and it serves no purpose to condemn it. Rather we should try to understand and to seek its origins in the models which the memorial makers chose for themselves.

One of the most ancient memorial forms is a mound over a burial place. This is a prehistoric tradition and was certainly very ancient by the 3rd millenium BC when the Egyptians were already creating stylised mounds in the form of pyramids. The earliest of these was the Step Pyramid at Saqqara, dating from c2680 BC, and although its form is normally interpreted as a series of *mastabas* (rectangular brick burial monuments) of

52

diminishing size and superimposed one on the other, the effect was to produce a stylised mound. This in turn led to the Great Pyramids of the Fourth Dynasty, whose timeless form and massive bulk has impressed successive generations.[1] Actual mounds were the most visible features of Mycenaean tholos tombs, mostly dating from 1600-1200 BC. The so-called Treasury of Atreus at Mycenae is the most famous example and its great conical tomb chamber lends support to the suggestion that one origin of the mound form was the ritual burial of a house.[2] The discovery in 1977 of the tomb of Philip of Macedon (who was killed in 336 BC) within a great mound at Vergina was one of the most exciting archaeological events of the century, showing for the first time the royal contents of such a monument in the Hellenistic period. The rich armour, weapons and treasure it contained reveal a splendour that must have been common to all royal burial mounds in antiquity.

Mounds were also among the earliest forms of memorial to battle and to victory, deriving in the first instance from the need to bury the dead where they had fallen. The Stele of the Vultures, discussed in Chapter 1, shows the creation of an early battlefield burial mound, but the best ancient example is the Great Mound at Marathon, raised over the ashes of the Athenian soldiers who fell defending their land from the Persians in 490 BC. On this mound stele were erected recording the names of the 192 Greeks who died, although the Persian casualties were put at 6,400.[3] A separate mound was raised to the Plataeans, the allies of the Athenians, and this has been excavated to reveal the graves where they were buried (unlike the Athenians, who were cremated). Yet although these are burial mounds they are primarily monuments to victory and those who died are to be praised but not pitied; no one mourns at Marathon.

These mounds are also exceptional in the Greek era, reflecting the supreme importance attached to the battle. A special cult of the fallen was established at Marathon, but normally Athenians killed in war were returned to the city for state funerals. Each year also the names of the war dead were inscribed on ten stele, one for each tribe, and set up in the form of a monument. Unfortunately none of these Athenian memorials has survived, but it seems likely that some of the individual military monuments, such as the stele of Dexileos in the Kerameikos cemetery, reflect in some sense these annual state memorials.[4]

Many of the great tomb structures of antiquity can be seen to derive from the idea of a burial mound, notably the famous tomb of King Mausolos, who died c353 BC at Halicarnassus. The tomb, built by his sister and wife Artemesia, became one of the Seven Wonders of the World and gave us the word mausoleum. It was clearly conceived as both a funerary and a victory monument and, although it finally collapsed around a thousand years later, it has been possible to reconstruct its form.[5] On a huge rectangular base was a colonnade, supporting a pyramidical roof, surmounted by a colossal sculpture of Mausolos riding in a four-horse chariot. There were a series of friezes depicting battles of Greeks against Amazons and Lapiths against Centaurs. The remnants of these sculptures, revealing Greek workmanship of the highest quality, are preserved in the British Museum.

The great circular mausolea of the Roman world also derive from tumulus tombs, which in Etruscan and early Roman times were provided with a circular retaining wall. The first of these imperial mausolea was the tomb of Augustus, built in 28 BC in the Campus Martius in Rome, and with a large figure of the emperor placed on a column at the centre. Hadrian's mausoleum, now known as Castel Sant' Angelo, is equally impressive and these great monuments established the Roman fashion for circular tombs. Pyramids also continued in a limited and more modest way, a striking example being the tomb of Gaius Cestius, built in the time of the Emperor Augustus in Rome. Rising to over 100 feet, it remains a familiar landmark in the city.[6]

In addition to stylised architectural mounds there was a continuation of actual mound building. By far the most impressive example from antiquity is Nemrud Dag in eastern Turkey, the burial place of Antiochus I, King of Commagene.[7] Like Mausolos, Antiochus was a man of little importance outside his small realm, but despite or perhaps because of this he determined to build himself a funerary monument without equal in the world. He therefore chose the highest mountain in his kingdom, Nemrud Dag, which rises to almost 6,500 feet, and built on top of it a great mound, rising a further 230 feet in the air. On the east and west sides of the mound he created great terraces and a sacrificial altar, and decorated these places with colossal statues representing his divine ancestors. The giant heads of these sculptures today litter the terraces, adding a surreal element to the already strange atmosphere of the monument. On a series of relief panels Antiochus himself is depicted shaking hands with the various gods, clearly on an equal footing.

Nemrud Dag was not Antiochus' first essay in mound building. At the foot of the mountain he constructed a large and unusual mound as the burial place of the royal ladies. On one side of the valley of the River Kahta lies the King's summer capital of Arsemia, and on the other, dramatically sited and visible from the capital, is the mound. Placed around the mound at the cardinal points are Doric columns surmounted by sculptures, including another hand-shaking scene, an eagle and a lion. This combination of memorial columns and mound seems to be unique to the kingdom of Commagene, although remains of a further example survive in Antiochus' domain (42).

Mounds were also a very common form of memorial in the northern European cultures. Many, like Silbury Hill in Wiltshire (43), the biggest man-made prehistoric mound in Europe, are difficult to date but plant remains in the core have given a radio carbon dating of 2145 BC.[8] The custom continues well into historic times, with the Vikings being notable mound builders. In some instances, as at Gamla Uppsala in Sweden, there is a group of huge mounds suggesting some form of royal necropolis.[9] There is a similar though smaller group at Sutton Hoo, where the largest mound revealed the amazing ship burial and its treasures. Interestingly, Sutton Hoo appears to have been a true memorial rather than a burial place, since no trace of a body has been found. It would seem to be a cenotaph or memorial to an important ruler whose body lies elsewhere, perhaps lost at sea or on the battlefield.[10]

The building of mounds on battlefields also continued. It is recorded that Drusus, brother of the Emperor Tiberius, built a large mound on the site of his defeat of the Marcomanni in 9 BC. Germanicus in 16 AD produced an apparently more wasteful memorial when he constructed a vast pile of enemy arms to commemorate the victory of the Campus Idistavisius and in this case the resulting mound clearly stood in triumph rather than mourning. The custom died out in the Middle Ages, but was revived when a recent battlefield mound was constructed on the field of Waterloo, erected as a memorial in the 1820s and crowned with a colossal cast-iron lion. Lion Hill remains the dominant feature of the site today.[11]

The pile of enemy arms made by Germanicus leads to a common association between mounds and trophies. In its original form a trophy was a lopped tree on which captured arms were hung and to which prisoners were chained. Such real trophy trees were soon replaced by more durable versions in stone. One such appears to have been placed by Drusus on top of his mound, while another is depicted on the Roman triumphal arch at Carpentras in southern France. This link between mound and trophy was to be stressed by the Romans in a series of vast battlefield memorials, two of which survive in more or less reconstructed form. One is in southern France at La Turbie, a name which derives from the Latin *tropaeum*.[12] This was built in 6 BC under the Emperor Augustus to record his victories over 44 Gallic tribes, whose names were inscribed on the huge square base of the monument, along with sculpted trophies of arms.

Above the base was a great circular colonnade, with statues of the commanding generals, and the whole was surmounted by a gigantic hero statue of Augustus himself.

The monument at La Turbie, even in its fragmentary and restored state, is a vast and impressive statement. Still more interesting is the trophy at Adamklissi in Romania, which forms part of what may properly be termed a complex of war memorials.[13] The trophy is the work of the monumentally inclined Emperor Trajan, and is on the site of (or at least in the area of) his victories over the Dacians — the same victories which are so fully recorded on his column in Rome. In addition to the trophy there are two other monuments in the immediate area, one a mausoleum, the other an altar which are contemporary with each other and a little earlier than the trophy.

The date of these two monuments is uncertain, but there is a clue in the name of the senior officer who died in the action and who was commemorated on the altar. The inscription gives his town of origin as Pompeii and subsequently as Naples, which suggests that his death occurred after the destruction of Pompeii in 79 AD. In this case the two monuments probably commemorate a defeat, that of Oppius Sabinus at the hands of the Dacians in the reign of the Emperor Domitian. The first of the two monuments is a circular mausoleum, presumably a memorial to the battlefield commander, and clearly derived from the burial mound tradition. Some 200 yards from this and directly aligned with it is the altar, 40 feet square and carved on its sides with the names of the 3,800 Roman soldiers who fell in the battle. The inscription states that these were *fortissimi viri qui pro republica morte occubuerunt*, and this wording, with its reference to sacrifice, separates the Adamklissi altar from the Mound at Marathon and makes it one of the earliest war memorials, in the sense that we understand the term today. Its commemorative and ceremonial purpose is emphasized by the open space between the altar and the mausoleum, which forms a parade ground suitable for anniversary marches and sacrifices.

The defeat commemorated here was to be avenged by Trajan, and the other great monument at Adamklissi(44) is an unashamed victory trophy, reminding the now defeated Dacians of the omnipotence of Rome and the price of Roman retribution. It is not without significance that the Trophy was by far the most prominent, most elaborate, and most spectacular of the three monuments, and there can be no doubt that the important thing to commemorate was the Emperor's victory, rather than to dwell on the price of that victory in human lives. Trajan clearly had a liking for trium-

56

phal monuments, as is witnessed by his great narrative column in Rome and it is instructive to compare the column and the trophy, monuments to the same wars. The column is a victory statement, on the one hand symbolic and deriving from Egyptian obelisks which were symbolic statements of the ruler's power, and on the other narrative and related to the ancient battle narratives considered in Chapter 2. Since the Emperor's ashes were subsequently buried in a casket beneath the column it is also a mausoleum, making it a monument of considerable complexity and sophistication. By comparison, the trophy is relatively simple in conception, being a monumental recreation of a victory mound combined with a gigantic trophy. Like the column, the circular base was decorated with scenes from the wars, but no attempt was made to produce a narrative — perhaps because there were not artists of sufficient skill available. Instead, the highlight technique was used, with fifty-four separate panels showing aspects of the conflict, carved in a rather naive style. On the battlemented cornice above were carved the figures of prisoners, each tied to a trophy tree and each dressed differently, to represent the various tribes defeated by Trajan. At the top of this mound-base was the trophy itself, consisting of a huge stylised lopped trunk adorned with arms.

The trophy at Adamklissi is today drastically restored. Its clean, new lines inevitably bring to mind some contemporary memorials, especially those built by totalitarian regimes. The comparison is not all that inappropriate, for there is a grandiose similarity about such monuments whatever their date, and the present state of the Adamklissi trophy does at least convey something of its original power and purpose. Roman public monuments, and especially their memorials to victory, were statements about imperial power, intended to impress the subject peoples. Many of these monuments are now destroyed, although the site of one further Roman trophy has been excavated at St Bertrand-de-Comminges in the Pyrenees and this appears to have incorporated a series of monumental sculptures of captured barbarians; but in the Roman empire the captured enemy were not allowed heroic nobility in death, such as is given to the Gauls at Pergamon.

Great monuments on battlefields were always comparatively rare, and the standard type of Roman victory monument was a form of urban decoration, the triumphal arch. This type, like the equestrian hero, was to live on in the western artistic tradition up to the present century. Originally such arches were erected in Rome and in provincial cities to mark important entrances or crossing points. The idea of using arches in this way was not new, for it can be seen in the Ishtar Gate in Babylon, dating from the time of Nebuchadnezzar, but the specifically memorial character of such arches was first fully exploited by the Romans.

A triumphal arch could be either particular or general; sometimes, as on the Arch of Titus in Rome (45), a particular victory was commemorated. In this case it was the capture of Jerusalem in 70 AD and the sculpted decoration records these events in detail, including the sacking of the Temple and the removal of the Menorah or seven-branched candlestick. This arch also presents the simplest form of such monuments, consisting of a rectangular block of masonry pierced by a single opening, with the decoration applied as a series of frieze-like panels.

The triumphal arch at Orange in southern France presents a contrasting and apparently more developed type. In the first place it appears to commemorate Roman victories in general, rather than one specific action. Secondly, in place of the simple architectural form of the arch of Titus, Orange is a sophisticated architectural composition, consisting of a triple opening, with a tall centre arch flanked by two smaller ones. Above there is a double attic cornice and the whole surface is covered in elaborate sculptural decoration. It is in fact a rather surprising monument to find in what was a relatively unimportant provincial town, founded as a colony for old soldiers, and so its date and purpose have been much discussed. A puzzling element is the appearance of a whole range of naval trophies, which appear to be a reference to the Battle of Actium in 31 BC, since this was the last naval action of any consequence in which the Romans were involved. Yet it seems the occasion for building the arch was the defeat of a rebellion led by a certain Sacrovir in 21 AD, since his name occurs on the structure. The inscription giving the date of construction is lost, but a study of the position of the holes which held the pegs of the brass letters has allowed it to be read as giving the date of 26 AD, in the reign of the Emperor Tiberius.[14] Also lost is the bronze group which crowned the arch, showing the heroic emperor riding in his chariot.

It was no doubt the popularity and widespread usage of triumphal arches by the Romans which led to their continued use in post-Roman times. In the medieval period the form was adapted to provide the standard lay-out for church facades. Not only does the three-portal form common to most cathedrals derive from the triumphal arch, but also the form and arrangement of the Christian decoration reflects the same sources. Roman imperial imagery was translated into Christian terms, with Christ replacing the hero-emperor. The scenes of campaign and battle found on arches such as those of Titus and Constantine become the scenes of the birth, life and passion of Christ, which could be regarded as the campaign and victory of Jesus. Looked at in these terms the facades of the great gothic cathedrals, of Chartres or of Amiens (46), are closer to the Roman past than is first apparent.[15]

The most Roman of medieval emperors, Charlemagne, made frequent use of the triumphal arch form and the gatehouse of his abbey at Lorsch has been interpreted as a version of the arch of Constantine.[16] A silver reliquary presented by Charlemagne's biographer Einhard to the church of St Servatius, Maastricht, was in the form of a miniature triumphal arch, with the Arch of Titus as the apparent model. Destroyed in the French Revolution, this remarkable object is known from a 17th century drawing.[17] A full-size triumphal arch was built by the Emperor Frederick II at Capua in 1247 and decorated with sculptures in the classical manner.[18] This arch was destroyed in the 16th century, but it probably provided the inspiration for the existing triumphal arch gate into the Castel Nuovo in Naples, erected in the middle of the 15th century to commemorate the entry of Alphonso I to the city. The sculptural reliefs depict the King's triumphal procession, while a free-standing image of St Michael replaces the traditional emperor figure on the top. A similar idea lies behind the triumphal arch erected by the Emperor Charles V in Palermo (47) in the mid-16th century or that put up in the 17th century in honour of the Venetian general Leonardo Foscolo in the island city of Korcula.[19]

What may well be a specific example of the use of an arch as a war memorial in the middle ages is provided by the Erpingham Gate of Norwich Cathedral. This is a splendid gateway in the Perpendicular style erected by Sir Thomas Erpingham, a valiant and noble soldier who had fought at Agincourt in 1415. The gate was apparently intended as a memorial and thank-offering, for on it we see Sir Thomas portrayed in full armour in the gable, surrounded by the apostles, saints, and heraldic devices. However, it was only in the Renaissance and after that the classical Roman form of triumphal arch was widely revived.

By the 19th century there was hardly a city of any importance in Europe which could not boast at least one triumphal arch. The most famous is of course Napoleon's victory monument in Paris, the Arc de Triomphe, (48) which can claim to be the largest of all such structures, ancient or modern.[20] Placed superbly at one end of the Champs-Elysées, it was begun in 1806 but not completed until 1836. It is decorated with a series of friezes, representing the Emperor's campaigns and including the Battle of Austerlitz. Larger compositions decorate the piers themselves, including Rude's famous sculpture of departing volunteers, 'La Marseillaise', which won the Prix de Rome for sculpture in 1812. Within

59

the arches are inscribed the names of the hundreds of Napoleonic generals, with those who died in battle underlined. Thus the status of the arch as a war memorial was established and this was emphasized by the burial of France's Unknown Soldier here in 1920. Yet the triumphal aspect predominates and was stressed by General de Gaulle's symbolic passage through the arch after the Liberation of Paris by the Allies in 1944. The final episode in this heroic saga was the renaming of the Place de l'Etoile, which surrounds the arch, as the Place Charles de Gaulle after the modern hero's death.

The Arc de Triomphe was in fact only the culmination of a series of Parisian victory arches, inaugurated by the Porte St Denis in 1672, to commemorate Louis XIV's victories over the Dutch. Based on the Arch of Titus, its sculptural decoration includes a splendid depiction of King Louis crossing the Rhine. Two years later the Porte St Martin was built nearby, also of single arch form and decorated with allegorical sculptures, in celebration of more of Louis XIV's campaigns. The Arc du Carrousel (49) was another monument to the Battle of Austerlitz (1805) and was modelled on the arch of Septimus Severus in Rome. It was intended as the base for a particular trophy, the captured bronze horses from San Marco in Venice, but these were returned to Italy in 1815 and replaced in 1828 by a bronze group representing the Restoration driving a four-horse chariot.

The modern Parisian story of triumphal arches can be paralleled (but not surpassed) in a number of European cities. Thus in Germany the fashion for such arches was introduced from France with the Brandenburg Gate in Potsdam of 1770 and continued to the impressive Victory Gate in Munich of 1843-54. Yet from earliest times there has also been a tradition of giving memorial buildings a more practical meaning. The idea was to make the memorial part of the daily life of the people, and the commonest way of doing this was through an alliance with religion. In one sense, of course, it was recognized that all victories came from the gods and therefore it was only prudent to include them in any memorial concept. This memorial aspect is readily apparent in the case of the Parthenon and indeed all the buildings of the Athenian acropolis can be interpreted as a memorial thank offering for the defeat of the Persians. It has been suggested that the frieze of the Parthenon itself is a monument to the dead of Marathon, since 192 figures have been identified as representing those who fell in the battle.[21] The Greeks in Sicily commemorated their great victory over the Carthaginians at the Battle of Himera in 480 BC by constructing a magnificent series of temples at Agrigento and at Syracuse. Similarly the acropolis of Pergamon is essentially a vast war memorial, consisting of temples and altars and thereby playing an active part in the daily life of the state. In Rome the Emperor Augustus built a new forum overtly as a memorial, with a temple of Mars as its centrepiece. In the colonnades around the temple were placed statues of the military heroes of Rome, both real and legendary, with details of their conquests recorded in inscriptions. In the temple itself were preserved the imperial standards which had been lost to the Parthians by Crassus in 53 BC and recovered by Augustus in 20 BC, while Ovid recorded that on entering the forum the first thing the visitor saw was an array of weapons captured by Roman soldiers in all parts of the empire. Also on show was the four-horse chariot awarded to Augustus by the Senate in 2 BC, to mark the completion of the forum, which had been built with money raised from the spoils of conquest.[22]

Apart from an often overt memorial purpose in their foundation, ancient temples were places where captured arms and booty were deposited. In this way temples which were not themselves founded in commemoration of victories could take on a specifically memorial aspect. Weapons kept in temples could be both numerous and valuable, as the record of the Assyrian King Sargon's expedition in 714 BC against Urartu (today in eastern Turkey) reveals. There is a great deal of information about this particular campaign, since it is depicted in graphic detail on the bronze gates from Balawat and recorded on a long cuneiform inscription in the Louvre.[23] From this we learn that a staggering 333,500 items were looted from the temple in the city of Musasir, including 25,212 bronze shields, 1,514 bronze javelins, 305,412 swords and 33 silver chariots.

The idea of a temple either as a memorial foundation or, through the deposit of booty, as a memorial by association was passed on to the Christian world. A particularly interesting example is provided by the story told by Geoffrey of Monmouth in his *History of the Kings of Britain*, written in the 12th century. He relates how the legendary King Aurelius decided to build a national memorial to the memory of the men who had died in a massacre at Salisbury. However, having collected artists and craftsmen from across the land, no one could suggest an appropriate form for the monument. The answer was provided by the wizard Merlin, who transported the Giant's Ring from Mount Killaraus in Ireland, to form the monument which we know today as Stonehenge. This story is especially interesting, since it suggests that in the 12th century there was still a strong tradition that associated large round monuments with memorial structures, even if they were no longer being built.

Churches and monasteries came to be seen as memorials, and some were indeed founded by kings as thank-offerings for success in battle. The great church foundations of Constantine must be seen at least in part as monuments to the victory of Christianity and a similar element is present in the churches built in the wake of Christian conquests. One of the most famous examples preserves the memory of its foundation in its name — Battle Abbey. This was built by William the Conqueror on the site of his victory at Hastings in 1066, in fulfilment of a vow made before the battle. The high altar was sited on the spot where King Harold was slain, making the church a very conspicuous thank-offering for victory. Today almost all trace of the Norman building has disappeared, but excavations have revealed the plan and indicate that the abbey was built in a fashion which reflected its importance as a national shrine.[24]

A similar and still standing example is the church of San Juan de los Reyes in Toledo (51), the ancient capital of Spain. This was also a monastic foundation, created by the Catholic monarchs Ferdinand and Isabella to mark their victory over the King of Portugal at the Battle of Toro. The church is a large and elaborate Gothic structure, lavishly decorated as befitted a royal foundation which was also intended to serve as a mausoleum for the two monarchs. In this it continued the ancient tradition of mausolea-memorials, first encountered at Adamklissi, although in the case of Ferdinand and Isabella they were finally buried in Granada, leaving the church in Toledo as an empty tomb. It does, however, have one further memorial aspect, for the exterior is hung with the chains of prisoners, traditionally those of Christian slaves who were freed from Moorish captivity by the battles of the Catholic monarchs. This too was an ancient practice, and Herodotus records that still in his day (in the 5th century BC) one could see hanging around the temple of Athene in Tegea the chains of the Lacedaemonians who had been defeated in battle.[25] The Moorish connections at San Juan de los Reyes also serve to remind us that the establishment of religious foundations in fulfilment of a vow before battle is not a solely Christian custom. It is recorded that the early Ottoman Sultan Beyazit built the Great Mosque(50) in his capital city of Bursa with twenty domes — a prudent modification of his original vow to build twenty mosques if he was victorious in battle at Nicopolis in 1396. The mosque itself survives as one of the early glories of Ottoman architecture.

Spoils of war were also presented to the gods in ancient times. In the British Museum is a bronze helmet which was dedicated to Zeus at Olympia by Hiero, tyrant of Syracuse, from the arms captured from the Etruscans during a battle in the Bay of Naples in 474 BC. It is inscribed with the words "Hiero son of Deinomenes and the Syracusans (dedicated) to Zeus Etruscan (spoils) from Cumae".[26] One of the most impressive examples of this idea must have been the great monument erected after the sea battle at Actium in 31 BC, when Octavian defeated the fleet of Anthony and Cleopatra and secured for himself control of the whole Roman world. The battle took place near the modern town of Preveza in northern Greece, and the city of Nicopolis was founded as a thank offering; its centrepiece was a great monument, adorned with captured bronze rams from the enemy galleys. These were set in a long line into a stone terrace and recent excavations have shown that they were huge pieces of metal, up to two tons in weight. This series of gleaming bronze rams must have made a memorable trophy, not unlike the lines of captured cannon that one sees in many western arsenals.[27] Thank offerings in the form of captured weapons were sometimes given to churches, as they were to temples in antiquity. Joan of Arc revealed, in her examination of 17 March, 1431, that after she had been wounded near Paris in September, 1429, she made an offering to St. Denis of a complete suit of white armour and a sword, which she had won before Paris. Similarly in 1328, after the Battle of Cassel, Philip VI presented arms and armour to Notre Dame in Paris and perhaps also to Chartres. There is a suit of armour preserved in the cathedral at Chartres, which is traditionally said to be the gift of Philip the Fair after the Battle of Mons-en-Pévèle in 1304.[28] There is a large series of armours in the Franciscan church of Santa Maria delle Grazie near Mantua, which were said to have come from the battlefield of Marignano, fought in 1515, although they probably include other sorts of *ex-voto* offerings.[29] However, probably the most extraordinary case of a piece of armour as a gift to a church is the late Roman gilded helmet and face-mask used in the image of St Faith at Conques.[30]

An *ex-voto* gift as a thank offering for victory might also be specially made for the purpose. Some were spectacular luxury objects, none more so than the golden shrine which Charles the Bold presented to the Cathedral of Liège in 1471.[31] The circumstances in which the gift was made were unusally bloody; in 1467 and 1468 Charles had attacked and defeated the independent Prince Bishopric of Liège, which stood in the way of his political ambitions. The second of these attacks culminated in a savage massacre of the population and the wholesale destruction of all but the religious buildings in the town. It was nevertheless a victory for Charles and the gift of the reliquary was a memorial thank-offering. It is one of the most sumptuous pieces of medieval goldsmiths' work to have survived, representing Duke Charles, dressed in full armour, kneeling and offering the reliquary itself (containing a finger of St Lambert of Liège). Standing behind the Duke is the figure of his patron saint, George. The account books reveal that the whole reliquary cost the staggering sum of 1200 *livres,* which makes it somewhat ironic that Charles was to lose all his personal fortune and treasures to the Swiss at the Battle of Granson in 1476.

There is a distinctive group of medieval memorials, found mostly in France and known as *lanternes des morts.* These were normally free-standing towers or columns with a lantern at the top and they were commonly cited in cemeteries to provide a perpetual memorial to all those buried there. A fine 12th century example can be seen at Fenioux (Charente-Maritime), formed of a composite pillar of eleven columns, large enough to contain an internal stair which leads to the lantern gallery. Such monuments were once quite common, though many have now disappeared, and they are recalled in a number of 20th century memorials, such as that at Beaconsfield which has a perpetual flame for the dead.

Buildings remain the most impressive form of memorial offering, and one of the most ambitious of these was the monastery of El Escorial in Spain (52), founded by King Philip II in fulfilment of a vow made before the Battle of St Quentin in 1557, at which he defeated the forces of Henry II of France. The motive and the action may be compared with that of William the Conqueror at Hastings, but in the Escorial the Spanish monarch created a building of unprecendented grandeur and founded a new school of architecture.[32] The Battle of St Quentin was fought on the Feast of St. Lawrence, and consequently the new monastery was planned in the form of a gridiron, to recall the instrument of the Saint's martyrdom. The actual buildings are severe in style and vast in conception, resulting in a monument in which the spirit of imperial Rome is translated into that of Counter-Reformation Catholicism. Once again, as was intended at Toledo, the monument is also the mausoleum, for it contains the famous marble vaults which were to receive successive generations of the Spanish royal family. In addition to the great church and monastery, the architect, Juan de Herrera, constructed the royal palace and the library as part of a single monumental complex. The palace apartments were of great splendour and included the enormous battle fresco in the long gallery that was discussed in Chapter 2.

One of the most extraordinary memorial projects was the result of a competition organised by the Berlin Academy in 1796 to design a monument to Frederick the Great of Prussia. A young architect named Friedrich Gilly designed an extensive and extravagant monumental complex, at the centre of which was a Greek temple raised on a huge crypt, to contain Frederick's sarcophagus. This was surrounded by no less than five tall obelisks, and the monument was approached through a great triumphal arch. Thus all the most important elements of memorial design were brought together in a single scheme, but it is perhaps not surprising that it remained on the drawing board.[33] Nonetheless, Gilly's plans were influential, especially on the architects Karl Friedrich Schinkel and Leo von Klenze, the main exponents of the Neo-Classical style in Germany during the first half of the 19th century.

Leo von Klenze was responsible for the most remarkable memorial building actually constructed in the 19th century, the Walhalla near Regensburg (53). This was also the result of a competition, organised by Ludwig of Bavaria in 1814 after Napoleon's defeat in the Battle of Leipzig. It was intended as a temple in memory of great German heroes and German victories and was completed in 1842. Von Klenze adapted the idea of building a huge Greek temple, modelled on the Parthenon, which Gilly had planned for his unbuilt monument to Frederick the Great. This is sited dramatically on the banks of the Danube and raised on a high podium. The pediments of the temple are decorated with sculpted scenes of victory, one a Germanic defeat of the Romans in 9 AD, the other representing the freedom of the German states after the Battle of the Nations at Leipzig in 1813. The interior forms a great hall, with a frieze depicting German victories through the ages and with busts of heroic Germans, while a seated figure of Ludwig in Roman dress dominates the space. Here undoubtedly is the supreme example of a national memorial in Neo-Classical style, which draws together numerous strands of antique tradition.[34] However, Klenze was to build another almost equally remarkable memorial, the Hall of Fame in Munich, designed along the lines of a Greek stoa to hold the busts of eighty prominent Bavarians. The resulting structure, erected 1843-54, immediately calls to mind the Great Altar of Pergamon, which had not in fact been discovered at the time the Hall of Fame was built!

Napoleon was not to be left out of the vogue for Neo-Classical memorial buildings and planned a Temple of Glory. This was finally consecrated in 1842, the year of the completion of the Walhalla, as the Church of the Madeleine.[35] The models here were Roman rather than Greek, with the Maison Carrée in Nîmes and Hadrian's temple of Venus and Rome (in Rome) providing the inspiration for the architect, Pierre Vignon. Although Napoleon's fall caused the purpose of the building to be changed, it remains a splendid statement of the imperial spirit.

A late German example of the type is the enormous memorial to the Battle of the Nations at Leipzig. This combination of battlefield monument, mound and memorial hall was designed by B. Schmitz and built between 1898 and 1913; its opening marked the centenary of the battle in which the European tide turned definitively against Napoleon. An unattractive mixture of classical and modern styles, the monument still dominates the Leipzig skyline and seems to have provided a source of inspiration for many of the giant memorials built in eastern Europe later in the century.

Grandiose buildings such as these became part of the 20th century memorial repertoire, but there were other types of foundation which were equally influential. Religious structures such as temples and churches could be seen to be 'useful', but from an early period there was also a feeling that a memorial could have a still more practical value. The idea of making a foundation which could help the poor, and especially those who had suffered as the result of war, has always appealed to Christian soldiers. Indeed, one of the duties of the Christian knight was defence of the poor, and this lay behind the foundation of the military orders in Jerusalem at the time of the Crusades. The Templars and the Hospitallers were pledged to protect pilgrims on their way to the shrines and to care for the sick, and as their orders spread throughout Europe they founded a series of buildings devoted to charitable works.[36] Other medieval charitable foundations, especially hospitals, were built and endowed by kings and princes, as expressions both of their secular power and their Christian virtue. Many were associated with chantries, which were religious foundations established as places of perpetual prayer for the soul of the founder. The finest surviving example of a medieval hospital is probably the Hotel Dieu in Beaune, established by Nicholas Rolin, Chancellor of the Duchy of Burgundy, in 1443.

The idea of building a hospital specifically for old soldiers emerged in Britain in the 16th century and a licence was granted in 1598 to erect a hospital in Buckingham for thirty-six maimed unmarried soldiers. However, the main example was Charles II's Royal Hospital in Chelsea and the king himself laid the foundation stone in 1682 of this place 'for the reliefe of Indigent officers'. The architect was Sir Christopher Wren, whose imposing buildings still serve their original purpose.[37] The memorial aspect of the Hospital was stressed by the inclusion of a figure of the founder in Roman costume which was placed in the central hall. In this hall were laid the flags captured in various campaigns, and Wellington, the hero of Waterloo, lay in state here.

Chelsea Hospital was to provide a model for other memorial found-

66

ations. Another similar establishment was the Royal Naval Hospital in Greenwich, founded by Queen Mary at the end of the 17th century. In the same way Louis XIV founded the Hotel des Invalides in Paris in 1670 which could house up to 6,000 men. It acquired a specific memorial role in 1840 when the body of Napoleon was translated from St Helena and reburied beneath the great dome of the Invalides church. This custom of founding hospitals as memorials was to be revived in the present century, which has devised a number of other practical and useful memorial forms.

A final word should be said about cenotaphs, since they constitute one of the commonest forms of 20th century memorial although they are relatively uncommon in antiquity. In ancient Egypt the Pharaohs normally had at least two tombs prepared, one of which was destined to remain empty and form a cenotaph. The Greeks attached the greatest importance to the proper burial of the dead, to the extent that if no body was available a fictitious burial ceremony was held and a cenotaph erected over an empty grave.[38] Inevitably, it was often the bodies of soldiers who fell in foreign wars that could not be recovered for burial, and so the concept of the cenotaph became particularly, but not exclusively, associated with military memorials. Examples have also been given in this chapter of medieval cenotaphs, ranging from the Sutton Hoo ship burial, where the reason for the lack of a body is unknown, to the church of San Juan de los Reyes in Toledo, which became a cenotaph when the Catholic Monarchs were buried in Granada instead. In the 20th century, and especially after the building of the Cenotaph in London, the word has come to be synonymous with any war memorial that was not itself an actual sepulchre.

Perhaps the most surprising thing is how long-lived the more traditional types of memorial structure have proved to be and how many of those constructed in the wake of the two World Wars drew upon traditions which go back to antiquity. At the same time it was undoubtedly this traditionalism both of form and iconography that gave the modern memorial movement its strength. Using a tried and tested vocabulary of memorial forms artists of the 20th century have been able to provide war memorials with an unprecedented range of symbolism and meaning. The more we understand and appreciate this background, the better placed we are to judge their achievements. Many of the leading architects and sculptors involved were people with a profound knowledge of past traditions and among the memorials they created are some of the most sophisticated re-workings of historic and symbolic elements ever achieved.

NOTES

1 Grinsell, L, *Barrow, Pyramid, and Tomb*, London, 1975. There have been many designs for pyramid tombs and cemeteries in more recent times, especially by the French architect Etienne-Louis Boullée (1728-1799). See Curl, J, *A Celebration of Death*, London, 1980

2 Curl, *op.cit.*

3 Herodotus, Book VI, 117

4 Garland, R, *The Greek Way of Death*, Ithaca, 1985

5 See Clayton, P, & Price, M, (eds), *The Seven Wonders of the Ancient World*, London, 1988. St George's Church, Bloomsbury, by Hawksmoor (1731) was one of the earliest attempts to build a replica of the mausoleum

6 Toynbee, J, *Death and Burial in the Roman World*, London, 1971 and Curl, *op.cit.*

7 On this and other Commagene monuments see Yorukoglu, O, & Soyer, K, *The Land of Commagene*, Istanbul, n.d. (1986)

8 Daniel, G, & Bohn, P, *Ancient Places: The Prehistoric and Celtic Sites of Britain*, London, 1987

9 Jones, G, *A History of the Vikings*, Oxford, 1968, p.39. The names of the three kings are recorded in the sagas as Aun, Egill and Athils.

10 The ship burial has now been fully published in a series of British Museum monographs

11 The mound is 148 feet high and marks the spot where the Prince of Orange was wounded

12 MacKendrick, P, *Roman France*, London, 1971, pp 86-89

13 Radulescu, A, *The Triumphal Monument Tropaeum Trajani at Adamklissi*, published by the Museum of National History and Archaeology, Constanta, n.d.

14 MacKendrick, *op.cit.*, pp 99-101

15 There is an extensive literature on the subject, but see Seidel, L, *Songs of Glory: the Romanesque facades of Aquitaine*, Chicago, 1981

16 Krautheimer, R, 'The Carolingian revival of early Christian architecture,' *Art Bulletin*, 24, 1942, pp 1-38

17 Lasko, P, *Ars Sacra 800-1200*, London, 1972, p 21

18 For the Capua and Naples arches see Hersey, G, *The Aragonese Arch at Naples, 1443-1475*, New Haven, 1973

19 Pillement, G, *Unknown Yugoslavia*, London, 1969, pp 90-1

20 On the subject of modern revivals of the triumphal arch idea see Westfehling, U, *Triumphbogn im 19 und 20 Jahrhundert*, Munich, 1977 and on the Arc de Triomphe in particular Gaehtgens, T, *Napoleon's Arc de Triomphe*, Gottingen, 1974

21 Boardman, J, 'The Parthenon Frieze — Another View,' in *Festschrift für Frank Brommer*, Mainz, 1977, pp 39ff

22 See Walker, S, and Burnett, A, *The Image of Augustus*, London, 1981 (British Museum exhibition catalogue)

23 See Piotrovsky, B, *Urartu*, Geneva, 1969. The Balawat gates are in the British Museum.

24 Clapham, A, *English Romanesque Architecture after the Conquest*, Oxford, 1934, pp 28-9

25 Book I, 66

26 Finley, M, *A History of Ancient Sicily to the Arab Conquest*, London, 1968, p 195

27 *Archaeology*, Vol. 41, No 5, pp 28-35 and report in *The Times*, 27 December 1988

28 Blair, C, *European Armour*, London, 1958, pp 63-4

29 Mann, J, 'The Sanctuary of the Madonna delle Grazie, with notes on the evolution of Italian armour during the fifteenth century,' *Archaeologia*, Vol LXXX, pp117-142 and Vol LXXXVII, pp 311-351

30 Taralon, J, 'La nouvelle presentation du tresor de Conques," *Les Monuments historiques de la France*, I, 1955, no 3

31 See *The Gold Reliquary of Charles the Bold* (Victoria and Albert Museum exhibition catalogue), London, 1980, and Lightbown, R, 'Ex-votos in gold and silver: a forgotten art,' *The Burlington Magazine*, June, 1979

32 *Palacios y Museos del Patrimonio Nacional*. Madrid, 1970, pp 152-226

33 Watkin, D, & Mellinghoff, T, *German architecture and the classical ideal, 1740-1840*, London, 1987, pp 66-69

34 Watkin & Mellinghoff, *op.cit.*, pp 157-162

35 MacKendrick, *op.cit.*, pp 234-7

36 Woodhouse, F, *The Military Religious Orders*, London, 1879

37 L'Estrange, *The Village of Palaces or Chronicles of Chelsea*, London, 1880, II, pp 1-38

38 Garland, *Greek Death*, p 102

CHAPTER 5

THE MEMORIAL MAKERS

'You don't make a tombstone for the sake of giving pleasure but in order to put up a record of names and dates. If incidentally it does please you, so much the better — nay, more, it will be in some sort a proof that the work has been done properly.'

Eric Gill, *Autobiography*, 1940

At the end of the First World War there was a widespread movement to create suitable memorials to the fallen. As we have seen, there had been many forms of memorial to war in the past and the recent South African War had itself resulted in extensive memorial construction.[1] Yet never before had there been a war which so deeply affected every community. There was hardly a town or village in Europe that had not lost some of its sons in the conflict. Clearly there was a demand for national memorials and for memorials on the battlefields, but equally every local community felt the need to have its own monument to its dead. There were other distinct categories of memorial required, notably by schools and universities, which had lost many of their pupils in the fighting. Business and industrial firms also erected memorials to their employees, and specialized bodies such as the police and the nursing services added to the list. There was also the problem of what form a memorial should take and from the outset there were many who favoured practical forms of remembrance, such as homes for orphans, hospitals, or libraries. However, the great majority of communities and institutions opted for memorials in the form of monuments, even if they also created other, more practical memorials at the same time. It was almost as if an outward and visible recognition of the price and sacrifice of war provided a form of expiation.

On nearly all these memorials the style is undoubtedly conservative, contrasting with what art historians would regard as the mainstream of modern art. Most First World War memorials were produced in the 1920s, at a time when the main artistic current was flowing increasingly towards abstract and constructivist forms. There are very few war memorials which follow such trends and fewer still that do so successfully. The adherence to a version of the classical tradition undoubtedly reflects the official patronage which sponsored the building of the memorials, for such patronage is normally conservative in its choice of styles. Moreover, it was clearly felt that time-honoured ancient formulae were more appropriate to record the sacrifices of the war than transitory products of artistic fashion. Yet although the inherent traditionalism of official patronage is apparent, there is no reason why this should have been a bar to artistic excellence. The view that tradition is the enemy of artistic expression is a legacy of the Romantic movement (as the plot of Wagner's *Die Meistersinger* reminds us) but as a received opinion it has become as much of a cliché as the view which it criticises. The best of the 20th century memorial artists, men such as Lutyens, Blomfield, Goscombe John, Ledward and Jagger, were able to develop within the classical tradition a style that was distinctively their own. There is still a curious prejudice amongst critics against memorial architecture and sculpture, and an entirely erroneous view that it is all bad. Of course quite a lot is of poor quality and in an artistic enterprise on the scale of the memorial construction in the 1920s this was bound to be the case. Equally, a surprisingly large amount of the work produced is of very good quality, and a small proportion can be considered inspired. The proportion of good to bad is, I suspect, no smaller than for other forms of artistic expression across the ages, and equally the best work can stand comparison with that of any other time or form.

Today, in an era when figurative art has made a determined comeback, most people would accept that the official solution to the problem posed by war memorial design was the right one. It would have seemed inappropriate for memorial art to be experimental and equally inappropriate for it to be abstract, in the sense in which this term is normally applied to works of art. In fact, of course, many of the forms used are abstract, but they are universally recognized abstractions (such as the obelisk). The one thing a memorial has to do is to convey some generally recognized meaning about what is being memorialized. If it fails to do so, fails to communicate directly, it rapidly loses all reason for existence. The ancient and classical traditions of symbolism remained widely understood, and indeed had entered popular consciousness through centuries of repetition. At the same time we can recognize that it was the misfortune of the memorial artists to work in a period when the styles and forms they adopted were becoming increasingly unfashionable.

With hindsight it is possible to see and appreciate more clearly the achievements of the memorial makers, which resulted from a deep and conscious study of the artistic traditions of the past. The results were, for the most part, much more than poor pastiches of earlier styles; rather, they are part of a long-lived and living artistic tradition. Nonetheless, as has been observed, critical judgment of the memorials is still clouded and many art historians cling to the belief that artistic achievement only has validity if it constitutes stylistic advance. As recently as 1981 in the catalogue of the important exhibition at the Whitechapel Gallery, *British Sculpture in the Twentieth Century,* it was stated that 'the great demand for such memorials, predominantly in a traditional format, led British sculptors to opt for an unadventurous, conventional style, which set back the cause of modern sculpture in this century for over a decade.'[2] One may question whether such a developmental interpretation of the history of art is entirely justified and in this case it ignores both the underlying cause and intent of the memorial movement. It will be argued here that we should attempt to judge the memorials on their own terms since this is the only way in which it becomes possible to appreciate the measure of their success.

In the following chapters these memorials are surveyed according to their form, but we must begin with some consideration of the different categories and the method of their design and construction. This was a topic that occupied people's attention even while the war was still in progress. In 1915 Lawrence Weaver published a book entitled *Memorials and Monuments, Old and New: Two Hundred Subjects chosen from Seven Countries,* which was an unashamed attempt to influence the form of any future memorials, since Weaver believed (by no means entirely justly) that the standard of memorials to the Boer War required improvement. Immediately after hostilities ceased, the question of memorials came to the fore, with further publications and with exhibitions of memorial designs at the Victoria and Albert Museum and the Royal Academy in 1919 and 1920. The Museum also published a pamphlet, *Inscriptions suggested for war memorials* (V & A publication No. 133, 1919), in an attempt to make sure that appropriate wording might be chosen for all memorials. There was a lively correspondence in *The Times* and questions were asked in Parliament. Not surprisingly, many people expected the lead to be taken at the national level and the pattern established here was partly to determine the course followed by the other sectors. However, there was never any question of central direction for the programme of memorial construction and local memorials were for the most part the result of genuine community enterprise. The precise processes whereby a particular memorial was planned, designed, erected, and financed have been little studied, or at least little published, but the work that has been done, such as the investigation of the unusual street memorials in the Abbey parish of St. Albans or the detailed study of war memorials in the town of Rye, indicates the value of such local research.[3]

In fact the national memorials, including the main battlefield memorials, emerged from what was, at least initially, a somewhat confused and unstructured group of organizations. Before the war had ended Lord Beaverbrook had established the British War Memorials Committee, modelled on the existing Canadian War Memorials Fund.[4] However, despite its name, the primary purpose of the Committee was the commissioning of paintings as a record of the war, for display in a permanent memorial gallery in London. They were not concerned with public commemorative monuments and indeed were rather opposed to the use of sculpture at all. More will be said of their work later, but it was appropriate that they soon changed their name to the Pictorial Propaganda Committee. Of much greater significance for the development of memorials proper was the Imperial War Graves Commission, although they had not intended to play a leading role in this aspect of commemoration.

The War Graves Commission was also established while the war was still in progress and was the successor to the Graves Registration Commission, set up by a remarkable man named Fabian Ware to record and if possible to care for the graves of the fallen.[5] After the war the prime concern of the Commission was to establish proper cemeteries, but it was soon realized that the many who had died but who had no known grave presented a serious difficulty and an appropriate means of commemorating them would have to be found. At the same time there was a growing desire to erect national battlefield memorials, to commemorate some of the most significant events in the war, and this led to the setting up of a Battle Exploits Memorial Committee in 1918 and, in 1919, the National Battlefield Memorials Committee. At the prompting of Winston Churchill, the British government agreed to fund the main memorials, but it then became apparent that if such an operation were to be distinct from the activities of the War Graves Commission there was a probability that both effort and expense would be duplicated. Consequently the Memorials Committee settled for an advisory role and the War Graves Commission took on the practical task of organizing the construction of the memorials themselves.

This was not really a job that Fabian Ware relished, since he saw the primary task of the Commission as the construction and maintenance of cemeteries, but he was helped and advised in this additional role by Sir Frederick Kenyon, Director of the British Museum. It was on Kenyon's advice that the first three Principal Architects were appointed in March, 1918; Edwin Lutyens, Herbert Baker and Reginald Blomfield. All three were well-known and well-established figures, although a fourth Principal Architect, appointed in 1920, was the younger and less well-known Charles Holden. Lutyens and Blomfield had already been involved in work for the Commission, designing the basic memorial forms which would be repeated in cemeteries worldwide. Lutyens believed that these should be entirely non-denominational and designed the Great War Stone for this purpose (54). He came to the idea after his visit to the Western Front in July, 1917, although his initial reaction to the carnage was that no monument could do justice to the scale of the tragedy. He then proposed an eternal form such as a ball of bronze, but by early August he had come up with the idea for an altar-like stone. He described to his wife, Lady Emily, a meeting with Randall Davidson, Archbishop of Canterbury, in the Athenaeum: "So I went upstairs and there was Cantuar and some fellow Bishop. I said I want to speak to you Sir. He said All right, wait a mo. So I waited a mo and up he came and I told him of my big stone idea as against the cross — the permanency, the nondenominationalism etc. He was very kind and said he was greatly and favourably impressed but would think it over.' The cross was Herbert Baker's idea and Lutyens' dislike of the proposal was shared by his wife: 'Baker must be dotty!' A five-pointed cross for each of the colonies. Too silly. And India left out which will cause bitter hurt and what about the Jews and agnostics who hate crosses?'[6] The first design for the Stone was as part of a temporary War Shrine in Hyde Park in August, 1918. Its final form was a rectangular monolithic block, 12 feet long and cut with the greatest precision to ensure that all lines and surfaces were very slightly curved, using the principle of entasis he had learned from studies of the Parthenon. The Stone was raised on three steps and carved with the inscription 'Their Name Liveth For Evermore' from *Ecclesiasticus,* chosen by Rudyard Kipling.

Baker's idea for a cross was taken up by Blomfield, whose contribution was both Christian and martial, the Cross of Sacrifice. This consisted of a tall, long-shafted cross with a bronze sword applied to it (54). Blomfield described his intention as follows: 'What I wanted to do in designing this Cross was to make it as abstract and impersonal as I could, to free it from any association with any particular style and, above all, to keep clear of any of the sentimentalities of the Gothic . . . The bronze sword is there to identify it with war'.[7] He added that he never expected the sword to be

73

passed; the overt association of cross and sword is, as we have seen, of medieval origin and some criticized the design as being too strongly symbolic of Christian victory. Despite this, over 1,000 of the crosses were to be set up in cemeteries across the world and the design was also used for memorials at home, the first instance being at Old Buckenham in Norfolk. It was also adapted for use in many hundreds of other memorials, often without Blomfield's sanction and sometimes to his distress. At Aylesbury he noted 'the local man has done his best, but he has simply murdered my Cross.' There are certainly many poor, ill-proportioned imitations of the Cross, although occasionally the variations are unexpected — thus at Greenock on the Clyde the cenotaph bears a Celtic cross on which is superimposed a bronze claymore! Blomfield's original design remains unmistakable.

Between them Lutyens, Blomfield, Baker and Holden, with a handful of other senior architects, were responsible for the major battlefield memorials to the fallen erected on behalf of the Imperial War Graves Commission. Of the associate architects the most important were Sir Robert Lorimer, J. R. Truelove, W. H. Cowlishaw and H. Charlton Bradshaw, while among the sculptors employed were Sir William Reid Dick, Charles Sargeant Jagger, Gilbert Ledward, Henry Poole and Alfred Turner. The very considerable results this group of artists achieved will be discussed later, but the scale of these undertakings meant on the whole that they were to be completed rather later than the mass of memorials at home and were consequently of limited influence. Lutyens was, however, responsible for the design of one memorial that proved to be more influential than any other, the Cenotaph in London (54).[8] This was to become the British national memorial, but, ironically perhaps in view of its subsequent influence, it started life as a temporary structure. A monument was required for the Peace Celebrations to be held in London in July, 1919, and Lloyd George asked Lutyens to design it. The first sketches, dashed off in a few hours, produced a basic form that was to remain little changed and the temporary structure, built of wood and plaster, was unveiled on 19 July. This was much admired and was consequently replaced by the permanent stone structure in 1920, which was unveiled on the second anniversary of the Armistice. This version also drew upon Lutyens' studies of Greek architecture, especially the Parthenon (although he did not actually visit Athens until 1932), and used the principle of entasis, whereby all the lines and surfaces are slightly curved. In the case of the Cenotaph, the vertical lines are arcs of circles that would intersect 1,000 feet above the monument, while the horizontals are curves of circles whose centre would be 900 feet below the ground. The accurate reproduction in stone of these design specifications required masonry skill of the highest quality. Lutyens also wanted to render the flags on the monument in stone, but this was changed to allow for real flags to be used. However, he did design stone flags for some of his other monuments, notably on the pavilions in the cemetery at Etaples (194), on the arch memorial at Leicester (193) and on the Lancashire Fusiliers (66) obelisk at Bury, and these reveal how effective the device could be.

In terms of its form, the Cenotaph consists of a tomb chest set on top of a tall stepped pylon, for which there are many classical prototypes, including the tower tombs at Xanthos in Lycia (4) and Roman examples such as the Secundinii tomb at Igel near Trier. Equally, elements in Lutyens' design can be derived from Renaissance tombs and mausolea which revived these classical ideas. What distinguishes the monument is its stark severity and lack of decoration, which concentrates attention on the overall form; many who pass the Cenotaph daily are probably unaware that it represents a tomb on a pedestal, but see it simply as an abstract design — and such a reaction would no doubt have pleased its author. Lutyens' monument was to spawn many copies and variations (some by Lutyens himself) but none surpassed, or indeed equalled, the original.

Apart from the national and battlefield memorials, the famous and established architects designed some of the major civic monuments to the war — Lutyens at (amongst others) Manchester, Norwich and Southend, Blomfield at Leeds, Luton and Torquay. Holden constructed memorial buildings, such as the Deal and Walmer memorial hospital and a memorial gateway for Clifton College. Other well-known figures contributed too, and we shall come across their work, but perhaps the most striking aspect of the vast number of local memorials is the diversity of their design and construction. There was no agreed national pattern or standard, with Blomfield's Cross and Lutyens' Cenotaph providing the nearest equivalent. There was no clear conception of who should design a memorial; the War Graves Commission, working on a large scale, had gone for architects but many local communities decided it was a job for a sculptor. Most commonly, perhaps, a partnership of architect and sculptor was formed. In these cases the overall design might be provided by the community or county architect, the sculpture executed by the best artist that could be afforded. This could mean a well-known figure of the older generation from London or Manchester, or might be a talented amateur, perhaps the village school teacher. In at least one instance, at Pant in Glamorgan, the memorial was designed by the Curator of the local museum,[9] while others are known to have been both designed and executed entirely by local masons. There is more than one instance of memorial design leading to acrimonious controversy and the erection of rival monuments by the competing factions. Durisdeer in Dumfriesshire and Hartwell in Northamptonshire provide examples of this.[10]

Whatever the case, the money for the construction of a local memorial was normally raised by public subscription. Up and down the land, committees were established to raise funds and to supervise the design and construction. There was generally little difficulty in finding the money, although the sums involved varied considerably. The architectural precinct designed by Messrs Gibson and Gordon for Portsmouth cost £15,808 (176), but that was expensive and included a cenotaph and large sculptures by Charles Sargeant Jagger. Most community memorials cost a good deal less, usually coming out at between £1-2,000 and with many costing less than £1,000. Often architects or sculptors would donate their services, as Lutyens did in designing an obelisk memorial for the Lancashire Fusiliers, his father's old regiment, in Bury, but it was unreasonable to suppose that the more popular memorial artists could always forego their fees. In many cases, however, there was a balance left in the memorial fund and this was typically used to provide scholarships, help orphans, or improve nursing care.

The range of artists and designers can be illustrated from two monuments which share the rather unusual composition of three soldiers standing on top of a raised round base. The first of these is the 37th Division Memorial at Monchy-le-Preux (56), near Arras, which was designed by Lady Feodora Gleichen, the sister of the first Commander of the Division, Lord Edward Gleichen.[11] She was one of a small band of aristocratic Victorian lady sculptors, but despite her breeding and royal blood she was no amateur.[12] Born in 1861, she trained at the Slade under Alphonse Legros and was a competent artist in the best 19th century academic tradition. The three figures on the Monchy memorial stand at ease, back to back in a triangular formation, and are modelled in a naturalistic fashion, each soldier distinct in pose and character. The basic design of this memorial, which was unveiled in October, 1921, shortly before the artist's death, was followed, no doubt unconsciously, by Eric Kennington, in a well-known memorial to the 24th Division in Battersea Park (57), unveiled in October, 1924. Kennington had served with the Division and the memorial was a gift from the artist, although it was found to be rather too modern for some tastes. The trio of figures here are presented with a totemic simplicity, at the expense of realism and accuracy of detail, although the face of one of the figures was modelled on the artist's friend Robert Graves. Lady Feodora's more traditional naturalistic soldiers were more in line with the general expectation of memorial sculpture, and it is worth quoting the views of her brother, Lord Edward Gleichen, on Kennington's memorial: 'That limited group of people who admire 'futuristic' art will doubtless highly approve of this monument. It represents in stone three tin-hatted figures — a sergeant, corporal, and lance-corporal — crunched together and looking straight to their front, while a serpent disports itself among their legs — which, by the way, are held together with stone billets. The fore-end of one man's rifle has had to be cut away in order to get it under his hat; and there are no folds in their clothes anywhere.'[13] Today, of course, Kennington is seen as a major figure in the history of British 20th century art, while Feodora Gleichen is unknown to all but the most specialized students of sculpture — yet it can well be argued that she produced the more successful of the two monuments, both as a representative of the memorial concept and as a piece of public sculpture.

Many of the best of the memorial sculptors were of Feodora Gleichen's generation and included several of the most well established and respected artists of the day. Several were part of the movement known as The New Sculpture, a term coined by Edmund Gosse in 1894 to describe what he saw as a new realism and naturalism in British sculpture. In fact, the impetus for this new style came from France; Gleichen's tutor Alphonse Legros had invited his fellow-countryman Jules Dalou to Britain when he was forced out of France by the Commune in 1871. Dalou became first Professor of Modelling at the Royal College, South Kensington, where he was to be succeeded by another Frenchman, Edouard Lanteri. Thus the whole generation of British and British colonial sculptors were trained by a series of French teachers and nearly all espoused the naturalism of The New Sculpture.

A number of artists had come together in 1904 to form the Royal Society of British Sculptors, devoted to raising the standard and standing of British sculpture.[14] The leading figure was Sir William Hamo Thornycroft (1850-1925), whose father, Thomas Thornycroft, was also a distinguished sculptor and creator of the well-known Boadicea by Westminster Bridge.[15] Sir William was responsible for a number of the best known pieces of Victorian public sculpture, such as the figure of Oliver Cromwell outside Westminster Hall. He had produced many commemorative statues, including military figures such as General Gordon on London's Victoria Embankment, and had already designed war memorials, notably the Boer War memorials in Durban and Manchester. After the First World War and at the end of his career he worked only occasionally, but did contribute to the memorial at Luton (108), where he designed a bronze figure of Courage holding a palm in one hand and a small figure of Victory in the other, surmounting a pedestal designed by Blomfield.

Almost as famous as Thornycroft, but ten years younger, was Sir William Goscombe John (1860-1953),[16] Son of a Cardiff stone-mason, he rose to national fame with his figures of eminent Victorians in Cardiff and London. He was particularly active as a war memorial sculptor after both the Boer and First World Wars, specializing in dramatic compositions. Several of these memorials are, naturally enough, in his homeland of Wales, but his masterpieces were in Newcastle (186) and Port Sunlight (178), where he provided two of the finest sculptural ensembles on any British monuments.[17] On the basis of these two works alone he deserves to be recognized as one of the major British sculptors of this century, but it was perhaps his misfortune to be born too early. Despite his very long life (he died aged 93) and his prolific 20th century output, he tends to be thought of, if he is thought of at all, as a Victorian figure. The memorials will be discussed in the following Chapters and it is clear that a proper reassessment of his very considerable achievements is overdue.

Another prolific memorial maker was Sir George Frampton, who was born in the same year (1860) as John and had much experience of public sculpture.[18] His most famous pieces are in London, including Peter Pan in Kensington Gardens, and his best known memorial, that to Nurse Edith Cavell (98) erected in St Martin's Place in 1920. This severe work was criticised as being too modern in style and was somewhat unusual for Frampton, whose normal memorial mode, established after the Boer War at Bury (154) and at Radley school, was more heroic. He was a leader of the Arts and Crafts movement, as well as a member of The New Sculpture, and like a number of his contemporaries he developed a considerable skill as a metalworker.

Two other near contemporaries may be mentioned here. Albert Toft (1862-1949), came from a family of Staffordshire potters and was first an apprentice at the Wedgwood factory,[19] He then studied sculpture at the Royal College of Art and gained a reputation as a sculptor of portrait busts and naked ladies. However, he took on several important Boer War memorials, including those at Birmingham, Cardiff and Ipswich and carried on this activity after the First World War. The Royal Fusiliers Memorial in London's Holborn (167) is one of his best known works and this bronze figure of a soldier was reused in France, on the 41st Division memorial at Flers (168). He also made the four bronze figures which adorn

78

the exterior of the Memorial Hall in Birmingham (203), representing the three armed services (including perhaps the only sculptural representation of a rotary aero engine) and a female figure of Victory or Peace.

Finally there is John Tweed (1869-1933), a Scotsman who had studied in London and Paris and worked with both Thornycroft and Rodin.[20] He was responsible for several important public commissions, such as Lord Kitchener on Horse Guards Parade (138), and he also produced work for Boer War memorials. He made a number of First World War memorial figures, including those on the Rifle Brigade memorial in London (151).[21]

At the end of the First World War all these artists represented the sculptural establishment, with a proven record of success and a style that had become entirely acceptable in public monuments. There are many others in the same category, such as Adrian Jones (1845-1938), who lived to the same great age as Goscombe John, and who served for 23 years as a veterinary officer in the army. Another was John Cassidy, born in Ireland in 1860 but who studied and worked in Manchester, and who was responsible for a number of memorials in northern England. William Birnie Rhind (1853-1933) came from a famous Scottish family of artists, for both his father and his brother were successful sculptors. Working from Edinburgh, he more or less cornered the memorial market in Scotland, together with Alexander Carrick (1882-1966) and Kellock Brown (1856-1934) in Glasgow. Another significant figure was the Canadian sculptor R. Tait MacKenzie (1867-1938) who worked extensively on memorials in Canada, the United States and Britain.

Thus, memorial sculpture after the First World War was in large part a continuation of the Victorian tradition of public sculpture, carried out by artists who survived from an earlier era. The reasons for this are not simply the conservative nature of state and communal patronage, although this was paramount, but also the dearth of younger sculptors after the war. Few had been trained during the conflict and many more potential students had been killed or wounded. Probably the most admired younger figure who worked in the modern style was the Croatian artist Ivan Mestrovic (1883-1962), who came to live in London as an exile during the war and who had an enormously successful exhibition at the Victoria and Albert Museum. He was much favoured by the members of the British War Memorials Committee, but he returned to his homeland after the Armistice and was not involved in the design of memorials. The most distinguished British member of this younger group was to be Jacob Epstein (1880-1959), but his first major public commission, eighteen figures for the British Medical Association Building in 1908, caused a public outcry.[22]

They were thought to be both ugly and obscene and this ruled Epstein out as a memorial artist. He had redeemed his reputation somewhat in 1917 with a bust of a British Tommy called *The Tin Hat*, but Sir George Frampton opposed his appointment as an official war artist and Epstein's only real war memorial was to be that to Trade Unionists killed in both World Wars and erected in the courtyard of TUC Headquarters in 1958.[23] This is a powerful work, carved from a monolithic block and representing a man carrying a corpse. However, its massive stylization, acceptable in the 1950s, would have been rejected in a memorial of the 1920s. We have already seen that the modest modernity of Eric Kennington's memorial in Battersea Park caused some complaint and Epstein would have certainly offended public taste.

It is all the more surprising, therefore, that three sculptors from this younger group were found to be acceptable as memorial artists, and indeed between them produced some of the finest of all memorial works. First to be noticed was Gilbert Ledward (1888-1960), the son of a sculptor and winner of the first British School of Rome scholarship in 1913.[24] The British War Memorials Committee selected him as one of the sculptors to produce work for the proposed Hall of Remembrance, which, apart from pictures, was to contain a huge narrative sculptural frieze. Ledward was commissioned to do the section from the invasion of Belgium to the Battle of the Marne, to be 40 feet long and 7½feet high (179). Only some models and sections of this were completed before the Hall of Remembrance project was abandoned in 1918. However, he adorned the impressive obelisk memorial for Harrogate with characteristic reliefs (68), and contributed the notable figures to the Guards Memorial in St James's Park (77). He also made a group representing Britannia protecting Humanity to go in the shrine of the Memorial Hall in Stockport, and contributed to the memorials at Blackpool and Abgergavenny (149). In the former case he designed the bronze panels at the base of the obelisk, representing the outbreak and the end of the War and for the latter made a fine and somewhat unusual bronze figure of a weary Tommy resting on his rifle. He continued to produce public sculpture until after the Second World War, including the Venus fountain in Sloane Square in London, dating from 1953.

A second important sculptor of this generation was Charles Sargeant Jagger (1885-1934).[25] He was a fellow student with Ledward, and runner-up to him in the Prix de Rome in 1913. He won the prize the next year but did not take it up, joining the Artists' Rifles instead. He fought at Gallipoli and on the Western Front, was twice wounded and awarded the Military Cross. Like Ledward, he was singled out by the British War

Memorials Committee to produce work for the Hall of Remembrance project and made a large relief of the First Battle of Ypres (180). Then, already interested in making memorials, he was recommended by Sir George Frampton as a suitable designer to Hoylake and West Kirby in Lancashire. The resulting memorial was a turning point in Jagger's career, although the basic form, an obelisk, is entirely traditional. At the base are two figures in bronze, a female dressed in the semblance of a religious habit and holding a chain, representing Humanity breaking the chains of war, and a soldier, rifle in hand ready for action (172). This is the first of a series of distinctive British Tommies which Jagger included on his memorials; they are realistic figures, sculpted with the greatest care and attention to detail, yet at the same time they have an abstract and universal quality. Massive, forceful, suggesting violent action even when at rest, they are amongst the most memorable sculptures made in the decade after the First World War. They also contrast markedly with the memorials Jagger designed for Bedford and Brimington, where Victory is shown as a mythical armour-clad figure, triumphing over the evil dragon of war. However, there seems no real foundation for the suggestion that Jagger made these figures under protest, and indeed their style may be related to the work he was to produce for Imperial Chemical House in 1928.[26]

Jagger worked on a number of memorials abroad, notably the National Memorial in Brussels and the Tank Memorial at Louverval in France, but his masterpiece was undoubtedly the Royal Artillery Memorial at Hyde Park in London (187). Here the architect, Lionel Pearson, created a huge stepped plinth as a base for a massive stone howitzer and Jagger contributed a series of relief panels and large bronze figures. The sculptural quality of the work is exceptional and makes the Artillery Memorial one of the outstanding examples of 20th century British art — it is perhaps the only war memorial to have been recognized as intrinsically important in its own right. Equally powerful is Jagger's figure of a soldier reading a letter on the Great Western Railway Memorial at Paddington Station. In his later works he moved on to other subjects and his untimely death in 1934 deprived the world of an artist of exceptional talent. His finest work is probably to be found on the memorials and he remains the only major artist to have made his reputation in this way.

Eric Gill (1882-1940) was a versatile and talented artist who worked in a variety of media, including sculpture.[27] His real interest was in the development of line, whether in drawing, engraving, or in relief sculpture, and his war memorials are characterized by their linear style. He was trained both as an architect and as a stone mason and from early in his career had a particular interest in lettering. He was also converted to Roman Catholicism in 1914 and his religious beliefs were to be of profound influence on his art. His place is in the history of the Arts and Crafts movement, as it developed in the 20th century, but he contributed a number of noteworthy memorials, including that at Leeds University, which consists of a large relief panel, now in the Arts Building, depicting Christ driving out the money changers, who all appear in modern dress. The choice of subject, which is unique in terms of a memorial, was explained by Gill as the only occasion on which Christ is recorded as using physical violence and, perhaps not surprisingly, the Leeds panel became the subject of acrimonious debate.[28] More traditional but equally interesting are his crosses at Trumpington near Cambridge (127), South Harting, near Petersfield, Bisham, near Marlowe, and Bryantspuddle in Dorset and the obelisk at Chirk in Clwyd (69).

Ledward, Jagger and Gill would have been recognized as important artists at any time and in any sphere. There were other artists of this same younger generation who worked on memorials — men such as Walter Marsden, who made the sculpture for the St. Anne's (184) and Bolton (99) memorials, or Gilbert Bayes, who made the charming memorial fountain for Todmorden in Yorkshire, as well as famous equestrian figures of War and Peace for the National Gallery in Sydney, Australia. The fact remains that they were the exceptions and the great majority of memorial sculptors were either long-established senior figures or little-known artists, even including a fair number of amateurs. This in no way diminishes their achievement and the following Chapters are intended to demonstrate that, taken as a whole, the British memorials to the First World War form an impressive group of monuments, revealing a deep knowledge of the memorial traditions of the past.

The story is similar in other European countries and, although one can define national characteristics, the overall pattern of production is the same. Thus in France we find that the memorials reflect the French academic tradition, with a continuing use of allegory and allusion, but with comparatively little work of outstanding quality. Italy was more unusual in adopting a modernist approach to many of its memorials, especially in terms of architecture, but the results seldom have the authority of their more conservative counterparts.

By comparison, relatively few memorials were constructed in the aftermath of the Second World War, and for the most part the names of the fallen were added to the exisiting memorials. There were of course many exceptions, such as Great Yarmouth, where a Second World War memorial was constructed alongside that from the First War, but the new enclosure was stylistically a continuation of the existing monument. Some of the existing national memorials, notably the naval memorials by Lorimer and Lutyens, were also extended to include the Second War, with Sir Edward Maufe as architect and Sir Charles Wheeler (65) as sculptor. A great number of Second World War memorials were erected on the battlefields, and some specific services were commemorated at home, notably the Royal Air Force at Runnymede (215). However, so far as sculptors were concerned, the 1940s and '50s were a period of almost complete abstraction and their work did not conform to the public perception of a memorial style. There were a few brave attempts to adapt or revive a figurative style, such as Sir Charles Wheeler's groups for the Royal Naval memorials, or Epstein's TUC memorial, but for the most part abstraction won the day. The dilemma was well illustrated by the controversy that surrounded the competition in 1953 to produce a monument to an Unknown Political Prisoner.[29] This was won by Reg Butler, whose abstract linear steel construction was destined to be sited close to the border with East Berlin. The outrage felt by the public, and shared by many critics, was symptomatic of the inability of British sculptors to satisfy the memorial requirement. The result is that the Second World War memorials are for the most part uncomfortable and unconvincing creations in a non-current figural style, seldom executed by artists of the first rank. Perhaps the nearest thing to a truly modern memorial is the new cathedral at Coventry. It is not, of course, a memorial in the strict sense, but it preserves the ruins of the old church as a narthex, adjoining Basil Spence's new building, consecrated in 1962. Today this has a somewhat dated and faded feeling, yet many of the works of art associated with Coventry Cathedral, especially Epstein's sculptures and Sutherland's tapestry, are outstanding works of their time.

In Spain there are a number of large memorials constructed after the Civil War (89), but the main area of memorial construction since 1945 has been the Soviet Union and its eastern European satellites. The study of Soviet memorials is a massive task which has yet to be seriously undertaken, for there are many of them, often of great size. However, their forms are predominantly traditional and their iconography derives from essentially the same sources as those in the west. The quality of Soviet memorial sculpture has been much criticized and a lot of it does seem to represent the least imaginative type of state-sponsored production. However, it is likely that the monuments vary in achievement, much as British First World War memorials do. It is possible that in the future some of this

Russian sculpture will also come to be seen as a late flowering of a long-established tradition.

More recent conflicts have produced their own memorials. Korea, Vietnam, and the Falklands all have their monuments, along with contemporary and continuing conflicts. Such memorials can vary from the traditional but extremely effective Vietnam Wall in Washington, D.C. (58), made of polished black granite, reflecting the viewers' own image and incised with the names of the fallen,[30] to modern symbolic sculptures, such as the works of Michael Sandle. It is somewhat ironic that one of the longest and most savage of recent wars, between Iran and Iraq, has produced the vastly expensive Martyrs Memorial in Baghdad, clad in shining marble and dwarfing the surrounding buildings. It may be contrasted with the novel but grisly Martyrs Fountain in Tehran, in which the water flows blood red. Different though these are, they seem little more than obligatory gestures to the memorial tradition, not to spring from a genuine response to the tragedy of war. It is this that distinguishes the First World War memorials, for they were designed and built out of authentic feelings of pride and sorrow. In examining the various forms they took it is important to remember that they were envisaged as "living" memorials, to recall for current and future generations the sacrifice of war. A reminder of this is the fact that, not so long ago, when gentlemen normally wore hats they always raised them when passing the Cenotaph in London. Although the custom has died out, perhaps we should try to revive the spirit which gave rise to it.

NOTES

1 The Boer War memorials were fully published by Gildea, J, *For Remembrance and in Honour of those who lost their lives in the South African War, 1899-1902*, London, 1911.

2 Exhibition Catalogue, edited by Nairn, S, and Serota, N. The quotation comes from p19, an essay on the patronage and support of sculptors by Dennis Farr.

3 Goodman, A, *The Street Memorials of St Albans Abbey Parish* (St Albans and Hertfordshire Architectural and Archaeological Society), St Albans, 1987 and Ewart, P and L, *Monuments to Memory, The Story of Rye's War Memorials*, Hawkhurst, 1988.

4 The Minute Books of the Committee are preserved in the Imperial War Museum. See also Harries, M and S, *The War Artists*, London, 1983.

5 See Longworth, P, *The Undending Vigil: A History of the Commonwealth War Graves Commission*, London, 1968, and Edwin Gibson, T, and Kingsley Ward, G, *Courage Remembered*, London, 1989.

6 See Percy, C, and Ridley, J, *The Letters of Edwin Lutyens*, London, 1985, p345ff.

7 See Blomfield's autobiography, *Memoirs of an Architect*, London, 1932. There is also a recent study of his life and work, Fellows, R, *Sir Reginald Blomfield, An Edwardian Architect*, London, 1985.

8 For Lutyens generally see the exhibition catalogue, *Lutyens: the work of the English architect Sir Edwin Lutyens*, London, 1981, and the bibliography cited there.

9 He was C.H.C. Holder, Curator of the Merthyr Museum.

84

10 These cases are discussed in Boorman, D, *At the Going Down of the Sun,* York, 1988, pp70-71.

11 For Lady Feodora Gleichen and her contemporaries see Read, B, *Victorian Sculpture,* London, 1982. The Monchy-le-Preux figures were re-used for the memorial to other ranks at the Royal Military College, Sandhurst, unveiled in 1927. Lord Edward Gleichen subsequently wrote an excellent book on the public monuments of the capital, *London's Open Air Statuary,* London, 1928.

12 The most royal of all such sculptors was HRH The Princess Louise, Duchess of Argyll, and daughter of Queen Victoria. She designed the Boer War memorial to Colonial Troops in St Paul's Cathedral.

13 Lord Edward Gleichen's comments are to be found in his book on London Statuary cited above (note 11) p 171. The identification of one of the figures as a portrait of Robert Graves was made by Dennis Farr, *British Sculpture in the Twentieth Century,* p.19.

14 See *Modern British Sculpture,* published by the Society in 1923 and listing the names and addresses of the members at that date.

15 For the Thornycrofts see Read, *Victorian Sculpture.*

16 Pearson, F, *Goscombe John at the National Museum of Wales,* Cardiff, 1979.

17 See below, pp 114, 120 and plates 178, 186.

18 Read, *op.cit.*

19 Read, *op.cit,* Spielmann, M, *British Sculpture and Sculptors of Today,* London, 1901, and Read, B, and Skipwith, P, *Sculpture in Britain* *Between the Wars,* London (Fine Arts Society), 1986, pp 140-1.

20 John Tweed, *Sculptor, A Memoir,* London 1936.

21 For London's memorials see Gleichen, *op.cit,* and also Byron A, *London Statues,* London, 1981.

22 For Epstein see Silber, E, *The Sculpture of Epstein,* London, 1986.

23 See Harries, *The War Artists,* p 127.

24 For Ledward see the catalogue of the exhibition held at the Fine Arts Society, *Gilbert Ledward, 1888-1960, Drawings for Sculpture,* London, 1988.

25 See the catalogue of the exhibition held at the Imperial War Museum, Compton, A, (ed) *Charles Sargeant Jagger: War and Peace Sculpture,* London, 1985.

26 Compton, *op.cit.* The suggestion occurs in the essay by Glaves-Smith, J, "Realism and Propaganda in the work of Charles Sargeant Jagger and their relationship to artistic tradition," pp68-9.

27 See Read, B, and Skipwith, P, *Sculpture in Britain between the Wars* (Fine Arts Society), London, 1986, pp 76-83 and bibliography cited there, especially Speaight, R, *The Life of Eric Gill,* London, 1966.

28 Speaight, *op. cit,* pp 126-134 and Shewring, W, (ed) *The Letters of Eric Gill,* London, 1947.

29 *British Sculpture in the Twentieth Century,* p 136.

30 See Ezell, E, *Reflections on the Wall: The Vietnam Veterans Memorial,* Harrisburg, 1987.

CHAPTER 6

THE SYMBOLS REVIVED

'The national conscience is stirred to its depths, the hearts of the
people will be filled with pride and gratitude, and it is to be
hoped that the memorials will be worthy of the men and of the
occasion.'

Lawrence Weaver, *Memorials and Monuments*, 1915

W hen it came to designing monuments to the fallen of the Great
War artists turned first to those traditions of memorial art which
had been established and recognized over the centuries. In particular,
they revived the accepted symbolic forms and figures which had attained
a universal meaning. At the same time many aimed to reinterpret these
symbols, to combine one with another, and generally to impart a specific,
even consciously intellectual tone to the established vocabulary of forms.
Some were, inevitably, more successful than others but it is hard not to
be impressed by the sheer variety of solutions adopted. While many memorials are similar, very few are actually duplicates and the range of invention displayed is extraordinary. This fact alone makes the memorial movement well worthy of study, for there can be no better example of how
to achieve visual variations on a limited number of themes.

All the various symbolic forms have been widely used in 20th century
memorials. Sometimes this is in a direct and straightforward manner, but
equally one of the characteristics of many memorials in this century has
been the combination of a number of existing symbols. Both approaches
can be illustrated through the use of obelisks. In the 18th and 19th centuries obelisks continued to be among the most frequently used type of
memorial and the transportation of Cleopatra's Needles had added to the
popularity of the form. A number of Boer War memorials were obelisks,
a splendid example being that on Plymouth Hoe (**59**), where the 41-foot
pink granite pillar is decorated with Egyptian motifs. At the base is a
bronze plaque, sculpted by M. Emil Fuchs, illustrating the apotheosis of
Queen Victoria's grandson, Prince Christian Victor of Schleswig-Holstein,
who was killed in action; on the side panels are two scenes of battle by

Onslow Whiting. Obelisks were used as memorials on the battlefields, notably at Spion Kop, and in several other British cities, including Cheltenham, Nottingham and Middlesbrough. Elsewhere, as at Coombe Hill in Buckinghamshire, an obelisk was erected on the highest point in the county to commemorate the Men of Bucks and to be visible for many miles around.[1]

In a similar fashion, plain obelisks were extensively used after the First World War. At Leighton Buzzard (Bedfordshire) this involved raising a monolithic pillar 23 feet high and weighing 22 tons (60), which was, according to *The Quarry*, the largest single block of granite ever quarried in the British Isles.[2] Certainly, so far as I am aware, there are no other instances of a monolith of this size used as a memorial; the surface of the stone is left rough and a simple cross incised on the face. The use of high places also continued, with an obelisk-shaped cairn memorial set up at 1,700 feet on Rylstone Fell in Yorkshire. On the Western Front and on the Gallipoli peninsula obelisks were especially popular as battlefield memorials; at the notorious point known as Clapham Junction, the scene of fierce fighting in the successive battles of Ypres, are plain obelisks set on either side of the road, one to the 18th Division, the other to the Gloucestershire Regiment. New Zealand erected national battlefield memorials on Messines Ridge, at Delville Wood, and Passchendaele in the form of a large obelisk designed by S. K. Seager, and the 62nd West Yorkshire Division at Havrincourt (61), is a plain but elegant obelisk. The Australian memorial at Lone Pine, Gallipoli (62), is a squat obelisk with plain crosses on each face. Sometimes additional interest could be added, as on the Tank Corps memorial at Pozières, where the plain obelisk has four bronze model tanks at its base, recalling the fact that it was here on 15 September, 1916, that tanks first went into action.

The British memorial at Cape Helles, Gallipoli, is a 100-ft obelisk, designed by John Burnett as a landmark for shipping. Naval forces also favoured obelisk memorials because they made good landmarks. The large obelisk commemorating the Dover Patrol at St Margaret's Bay, is matched across the Channel by a second similar memorial at Cap Blanc Nez (63). The Imperial War Graves Commission took on the task of setting up memorials to the missing of the Royal Navy and invited Sir Robert Lorimer, architect of the Scottish National Memorial, to produce a design.[3] He created a variation on the plain obelisk form, a tapering granite pylon, stepped towards the top like the obelisks of ancient Mesopotamia. At the apex four ships' prows and female figures representing the winds support a large copper sphere, symbolizing the world. The base consists of a square plinth, with lions at the corners, and the monuments are set within spacious semicircular enclosed precincts, each slightly different in design and decorated with sculptures by Henry Poole. The memorial was erected at Chatham (64), and Plymouth and Portsmouth, the three manning ports, all were completed in 1924. They were extended after the Second World War, to the designs (65) of the architect Sir Edward Maufe, with sculpture by Sir Charles Wheeler. The architectural origins of the central form are particularly clear at Portsmouth, where three small 19th century obelisk memorials adjacent to the monument commemorate the Crimean War and the officers and men of two ships who died in epidemics of yellow fever. Similarly at Plymouth the naval memorial is seen alongside the Boer War obelisk for Prince Christian Victor.

Obelisk memorials were erected in several British cities, with notable examples at Blackpool, Southport and Scarborough — again, the value of obelisks as landmarks made them especially popular in seaside towns. Some of the well-known memorial architects also used the form, particularly Lutyens who seems to have been especially attracted to it. He designed slender obelisks for the Lancashire Fusiliers at Bury (66) and for the municipality at Southend-on-Sea, although the latter has subtle echoes of the Cenotaph in it. In York he combined an obelisk with a walled enclosure for the North Eastern Railway Company Memorial, while at Manchester (102) and Derby he built a version of his Cenotaph and flanked it by two obelisks. Blomfield used a plain obelisk for the memorial at Hampstead (67), and Gilbert Ledward carved the reliefs for the obelisks memorial at Harrogate (68), a monument which matches the grandeur of the surrounding civic buildings. At its base are large low-relief panels, one showing a bugler in front of artillery pieces, the other representing Victory, bearing a sword and wreath; only closer inspection reveals that she is standing on a ground made up of the helmeted heads of dead soldiers. Jagger used a round-topped obelisk at Hoylake and West Kirby, and Eric Gill produced a rather stumpy version for Chirk (69), bearing the sculpted relief of a soldier.

There were several variations on the plain form. One was to merge the obelisk and cross. Great Yarmouth provides a good example of this, for the memorial consists of a granite obelisk with a cross of polished granite on each face, and with bronze swords (derived from Blomfield's Cross of Sacrifice) applied to the crosses (70). The monument was designed by F. R. B. Haward, a local architect.[4] Similar combinations of obelisk and cross were to become quite popular and are found in a number of smaller local memorials. Wallington in Surrey provides a sophisticated example in which the crosses emerge gradually from the face of the truncated obelisk (72), while on a grander scale the same idea is seen on the Euston memorial (71). A Scottish version at Greenock uses a Celtic cross, while a striking combination of the two forms is seen on the Coventry memorial, where a plain cross is set at the centre of an elaborately stepped obelisk.

Another variation is the obelisk that develops into a figure at the top, normally a bust of a soldier. A simple but rather bizarre and uncomfortable version of this idea is seen on the memorial at Ripon, with a bronze bust of a soldier, sculpted by F. J. Wilcoxson, set on top of a granite obelisk (73). The form was most successfully exploited in a number of Western Front memorials; at St Julien, on the site known as Vancouver Corner, the Canadian memorial is a 35-foot truncated obelisk, with the point replaced by the head and shoulders of a mourning soldier, his rifle reversed and merging into the pillar (74).[5] The monument was designed by Frederick Chapman Clemesha, an architect who was wounded while serving with the Canadian Corps in France, and it marks an area where some 2,000 Canadians were killed. It was here also, on 22 April, 1915, that the first German gas attack took place.

The St Julien memorial may be compared with a similar French memorial at Argonne, which has the added refinment of a cross below the bust of the soldier. However, the complete development of Clemesha's design was the well-known Canadian memorial at Vimy Ridge (75). This marks the site of a famous and successful engagement on Easter Monday, 1917, but more importantly it is also the general memorial to the 60,000 Canadians who died in the war. It was designed by a Toronto architect, Walter S. Allward, and consists of two tall obelisk-shaped pillars from which emerge a series of symbolic figures including Peace, Justice, Truth and Knowledge. The pillars are mounted on a massive base, also containing sculpted figures, notably Canada mourning her dead. It is one of the most original and striking of the battlefield memorials, especially when viewed from a distance, but closer inspection reveals the disappointing quality of the figure sculpture. The monument took eleven years to construct, being unveiled by King Edward VIII on 26 July, 1936.[6]

The combination of obelisk and figures was used elsewhere in a more conservative fashion. An interesting example is Goscombe John's memorial to Marine Engineers at the Pier Head in Liverpool (76), not least because it was designed and erected in 1916, while the war was still in progress. It also differs from John's later, highly realistic memorials, comprising an unusual banded obelisk surmounted by four stylized Victories, and with equally stylized reliefs of two officers and two men at the base.

Mourning figures at the base of an obelisk are fairly common, and may be well illustrated by the London and North-Western Railway Company memorial outside Euston Station (71). This monument, designed by R. Wynn Owen, consists of a tall obelisk set on a base. Crosses and wreaths are added to each face of the pillar at the top while at the bottom stand four bronze mourning figures, their rifles reversed, representing the different branches of the armed services. The female figure at the front of Jagger's Hoylake and West Kirby obelisk is apparently mourning the folly of war, represented by the first of his distinctive and typical Tommies at the back (172).[7] Finally, the Guards' memorial in St James' Park (77), designed by H. C. Bradshaw, is in the form of a short, squat obelisk — almost a pointed cenotaph — and has five notable bronze figures by Gilbert Ledward, cast from captured German guns, representing the Grenadier, Scots, Welsh, Irish and Coldstream Guards.[8]

A distinctive group of miniature obelisks comprises the small Demarcation Stones (78) which were erected on the Western Front. A total of 119 of these were set up to mark the limits of the German advance in 1918, so forming a link with the ancient boundary stones from Egypt and Mesopotamia (such as the Narmer palette discussed in Chapter 1) which marked the agreed frontiers established after a battle. The Stones were designed by Paul Moreau Vauthier as little obelisks, crowned with a wreath and either a British or French pattern tin helmet. The sides of the Stones have items of soldiers equipment, such as gas mask and water bottle, carved in relief, and the inscription 'Here the Invader was brought to a standstill'. It is unfortunate that many of these interesting little monuments, whose ancestry can be traced back some five thousand years, have been destroyed and they are now quite rarely found.

Obelisks are therefore a key feature of 20th century memorials, continuing a tradition that goes back at least 4,000 years. Indeed, although we associate obelisks with the Egyptians, more were created between 1920-30 than at any other time in history. They continue to be made, for the Katyn memorial, erected in Gunnersbury Cemetery in 1976, is an obelisk of black Nubian granite, raised in memory of the thousands of Polish prisoners massacred at Katyn near Smolensk in 1940. This is a sombre monument to a great atrocity, so let us leave obelisks with one that, today, at least, seems less momentous. At Meriden Green, near Birmingham, a plain obelisk forms the cyclists' memorial (79). It was erected with subscriptions from cyclists and cycling clubs, following a public meeting convened in October, 1919, by the editor of *Cycling* magazine in response to a suggestion by Mr F. T. Birdlake. In the effort to raise funds for the monument the Prince of Wales even sent his own bicycle for auction. The inscription reads *To the lasting memory of those* CYCLISTS *who died in the* GREAT WAR 1914-1918[9] and those who died in the Second World War have now also been included. The base of the memorial is regularly adorned with wreaths, consisting of bicycle wheels decorated with flowers.

Columns have also been used in 20th century memorials. Indeed, in the lands of the ancient Roman Empire antique columns were sometimes re-erected; at Arsuf in Palestine the memorial to the 52nd Lowland Division was a column taken from the Roman ruins and set up at the spot where the 155th Brigade crossed the River Auja on the night of 20/21 December, 1917.[10] Similarly at Chambrecy in France an antique Roman column brought from Italy is placed in the Italian cemetery. Modern columns were also used as battlefield memorials, notably in the American cemetery of Meuse-Argonne on the Butte de Montfaucon, which was captured by American troops on 27 September, 1918. The tall column is here surmounted by a copy of the Statue of Liberty. A column flanked by lions forms the central feature of the striking memorial to Indian troops at Neuve Chapelle, which was designed by Sir Herbert Baker (**80**). However, single columns were less common than obelisks on the battlefields, although they can be found, for example, as the memorial to the 1st Battalion Loyal North Lancashire Regiment at Troyon (Aisne). This scarcity may be taken to reflect the ancient tradition that the obelisk was somehow the more sacred form. One unusual example is the Martyrs' Column in Damascus, on the spot where a number of Syrian patriots were executed by Turkish troops in 1916; the slender column is surmounted by a miniature mosque (**81**).

In Britain columns are again comparatively unusual as memorials in the 20th century, but several fine examples exist. Perhaps the best is the Elveden Column in Suffolk (**82**), erected on the Earl of Iveagh's estate. It was placed at the spot where the parishes of Elveden, Eriswell and Icklingham meet, to commemorate the forty-eight men of all three who fell in the war. The memorial consists of a Corinthian column built of Weldon stone, surmounted by a vase of Portland stone, the whole having a total height of 127 feet. It was designed by Clyde Young, a London architect, took two years to build, and was unveiled by Field-Marshal Sir Henry Wilson on 21 November, 1921. Today the column is a familiar landmark for motorists on the road from London to Norwich.

Simple columns are rarely found, although the memorial at Nairn in Scotland is a plain fluted column and capital. More common is the column as a support for an emblem or a figure. The Bermondsey and Rotherhithe memorial is an 18-foot granite column surmounted by a ball and flame, symbolizing the world and life. At Hungerford the memorial consists of a column surmounted by an orb and cross (83), while a rather weird memorial at Wittersham in Kent, designed by Sir George Frampton, consists of an octagonal column on which is perched a stone cushion bearing a crowned orb (84). Frampton had provided another version of this for the Kentish village of Knowlton, where the column also incorporates four small figures at the top, representing the Services. Erected in 1915, the monument was a prize offered by *The Weekly Dispatch* in their bravest village competition. Knowlton won, because twelve out of a total population of thirty-nine had enlisted. At Lynford in Norfolk the column is surmounted by Christ on the cross (85), while another somewhat unusual memorial is at Felixstowe in Suffolk, where an elegant Corinthian column on the seafront is capped by a dove of peace which looks, appropriately enough, rather like a seagull (86).

The idea of placing a bust on top of a column might seem less uncomfortable than placing it on an obelisk and this can be found in the memorial to Lord Allenby at Beersheba. However, columns are most frequently found as supports for complete figures; in the past it had been mainly heroes who received columns, but in the 20th century they have been largely reserved for figures of Victory. A particularly good example of this is the Boer War memorial at Newcastle (87), designed by the local artist T. Eyre Machlin. A tall tapering hexagonal column, half-way to being an obelisk, is surmounted by a huge bronze Victory bearing a wreath and a sword. At the base of the column is a second bronze female figure, carrying a standard and a palm of sacrifice and representing Northumbria. Notable First World War examples of the same idea can be found at Aberystwyth and at Uxbridge, where the sculpture is by Adrian Jones, while other figures to receive columns include saints, such as St George at Hove. Another oddity is a naval memorial on the Pier Head, Liverpool, consisting of a stone column which sprouts two ship's prows in bronze at half its height and is surmounted by a naked male figure bearing a shield and a wreath. It is the work of Bertram Pegram and dates from 1920. As a final variation on the columnar theme we should note the Sheffield memorial, designed by C. D. Carus Wilson and with sculpture by George Alexander, which consists of a slender steel mast, 90 feet high, surmounted by a golden crown of victory (88). At the bottom an elaborate bronze base bears four mourning soldiers and the badges of the various regiments.

It has already been observed that the commonest of all 20th century memorial forms is the cross. Apart from Blomfield's enduringly popular Cross of Sacrifice, every form of traditional cross was revived and widely used, especially for small local memorials. They were also set up on battlefields and incorporated in national memorials. The combination of cross and obelisk has been mentioned, and such combinations were widely developed. Plain crosses were made in all sizes, but the largest must surely be that which dominates the Spanish national memorial at Valle de los Caidos, north of Madrid (89)[11]. This was built by and for General Franco after the Spanish Civil War, which makes it a somewhat controversial national shrine. It also has the grandiose bombasity typical of dictatorial architecture and, like the monuments of imperial Rome, it is very impressive. The main part of the memorial will be mentioned later, but the cross which surmounts it is almost 500 feet high and sited in some of the most dramatic countryside in central Spain. At the base are figures of the Evangelists, each 60 feet tall, with the Cardinal Virtues above.

The Valle de los Caidos is, like most national memorials, an exceptional monument. However, its type of plain, long-shafted cross is the most common memorial form. Perhaps rather surprisingly, the crucified Christ is not most commonly depicted, because the intended symbolism was general rather than specific and because the tradition of free-standing cross monuments excluded a *corpus*. There are, of course, very many exceptions, exemplified by the battlefield memorial to the men of Hull, designed by Major C. D. Allderidge, at Oppy Wood on the Somme (90), which has a large Crucifixion as the centrepiece of an altar-like monument. Occasionally also wayside crucifixes turn out to be memorials, as at Withern in Lincolnshire, and in towns there are crucifixion memorials in churchyards; a good example of the type is the shrine outside the apse of All Saints Church in Bryanston Place, London (91). An interesting iconography is found on the memorial at Cromer in Norfolk, where the crucified Christ is placed at the top of the a long-shafted cross, with St George killing the dragon at the bottom and figures of a solider, sailor, airman and nurse on the base.

Almost as common as the plain form is the Celtic cross, derived from the many existing examples and decorated with elaborate interlace patterns. This is despite the fact that, in Blomfield's view, 'the Celtic cross is the last word in commonplace and uncouth design' (92).[12] They were naturally popular in the former Celtic kingdoms and as battlefield memorials to Scottish and Irish regiments, such as the Seaforth Highlanders' Cross at Fampoux (93), set alone on a hillside, or the memorial to the Munster Regiments in the grounds of the Cathedral at Ypres. The group of ancient crosses with relief carving on their shafts, such as Ruthwell, also inspired a number of memorials. At Eamont Bridge in Cumbria the idea was taken up by the Scottish sculptor Grant Stephenson, whose cross design included bronze portraits on the shaft of the two men killed from the village (out of four who went) in the Boer War. At Ardrossan in Ayrshire is a Celtic cross memorial with a series of Scottish heroes depicted on the shaft, from Saint Columba to David Livingstone. A variation on the Celtic form is found at Canterbury, where the thick, square shaft is decorated with interlace scrolls and includes four niches at the top, one containing a figure of St George in armour with a soldier, sailor and airman in the other three (94) (this may be compared with the iconography of the Cromer cross, mentioned above). A cross of vaguely medieval form and distinctive quality was provided by Eric Gill as the memorial for Trumpington outside Cambridge. Set on an arcaded base, this has four relief panels at the bottom of the shaft, including St George dressed as a contemporary soldier killing the dragon, while another soldier carries his rifle in a way that echoes Christ carrying his cross. The remaining panels show the Virgin and Child and one of the rare memorial instances of St Michael (127).[13] In this context too we should remember the genuine Breton cross that was transported, along with a dolmen, to form the memorial to the French 87th and 45th Divisions at the Carrefour de la Rose, near Ypres.

The victorious nature of the cross was emphasized by the figures placed beneath it. While those who flank obelisks tend to be in mourning for their comrades, with rifles reversed and heads bowed, figures next to crosses are normally alert, on guard, or ready for action. Newbury Trent designed crosses for Redbridge (95) and Tredegar with a bronze figure of a soldier presenting arms on the base. At the Royal Academy Exhibition of War Memorials held in 1919, L. S. Merrifield showed his design for a Celtic cross in front of which stood a soldier at the ready and with bayonet fixed; a version of this design was erected at Burnham in Buckinghamshire. Representatives of the various services stand alert and ready for duty at the base of the cross at Builth Wells (96) and at East Brent in Somerset, while action itself was depicted on the Lever Brothers memorial at Port Sunlight (178), the work of that most dramatic of memorial sculptors, Goscombe John.[14] This, certainly one of the finest memorials in the country, is described in more detail in the next chapter.

One of the basic Christian meanings of the cross is hope born of suffering and this is the theme of a number of cross memorials. At Derby the monument by Arthur Walker has a grieving mother standing in front of a cross, mourning a dead son but carrying a second infant child in her arms

to denote the future (97). Similarly, if more obliquely, Sir George Frampton intended a sense of hope in his rather ugly monument to Edith Cavell
in London. On this the striking marble figure of the nurse herself stands
before a massive plinth, which develops into a form of cross, itself surmounted by a half-figure of a woman and child who represent Humanity
protecting the Small States (98). Another memorial to emphasize the hope
of the cross is the private monument to Charles and Elizabeth Vyner in
Fountains Hall, Yorkshire, dating from the Second World War, which is
described in the next chapter. Once again, there are many exceptions to
the generally heroic or optimistic nature of most cross memorials. Bolton
may stand as an example, for here the cross is set within an arch that is
flanked by bronze figures by Walter Marsden representing Grief and
War (99).

Memorials were also built as copies or variations on the medieval series
of Eleanor crosses. There is a Boer War example at York, and from the
First World War at Wigan, designed by Sir Giles Gilbert Scott, while at
Hereford a similar memorial is by L. W. Barnard. The form was apparently appropriate, since the original crosses had been erected as memorials to the queen, marking the resting place of her coffin on its journey
to London. However, this association with a particular historical person
made the type less successful in a general memorial context and its use as
a war memorial form was limited. Nonetheless, one example, the memorial to the 5th Yorkshire Regiment at Sledmere, is among the most interesting. This consists of a tall Eleanor Cross of careful and accurate mediaeval
form (100), erected by Sir Tatton Sykes in 1899, the octagonal base of
which was subsequently decorated with an elaborate series of monumental brasses (101). These are directly based upon mediaeval examples, but
they represent contemporary soldiers. In some cases, as in the figure of
Captain Edward Bagshawe, we have a direct copy of a particular brass (in
this case that of Sir Robert Septvans at Chartham in Kent) supplied with
a portrait head of the soldier commemorated; in others the figure is shown
in modern dress but in mediaeval pose. These must be among the last
monumental brasses to have been made, and they help to make Sledmere
among the most fascinating of memorial sites. The Cross stands alongside
the equally unusual Wagoners memorial, which is discussed in the next
chapter.

Some further words should be added about cenotaphs, which have
become a characteristic memorial symbol in the 20th century. Although
tower tombs go back to antiquity,[15] the cenotaph form was developed
by Lutyens for his London monument. Such was the impact and popularity

of this that the type was adapted for memorials across the country. Luty-ens built more than one, including the Southampton city memorial, which was designed at much the same time as the London Cenotaph. Set on a large rectangular pier, the structure is stepped up to a tomb chest, on which a recumbent soldier may be seen. A Great War Stone, that Lutyens had designed for the Imperial War Graves Commission, is set before the monument. The whole effect is highly classical and Lutyens developed this theme in his Manchester Memorial (102). This is a complex grouping, involving several strands of the memorial tradition, with a central ceno-taph which repeats the Southampton motif of an effigy of a soldier lying on the tomb chest that crowns the monument. At the front is a Great War Stone, and on either side are typically elegant obelisks. This use of twinned obelisks, the altar-like stone, and the tower tomb suggests that Lutyens was making overt reference to the most ancient memorial traditions. A similar combination of twinned obelisks and the Great War Stone was adapted by Lutyens for Northampton, while he used his Ceno-taph form in several of the major battlefield memorials, notably Vis-en-Artois and Etaples.

Such was the influence of the London Cenotaph that even Sir Reginald Blomfield, in most respects Lutyens' chief rival and critic, drew upon it for his design of the RAF Memorial (103) on London's Embankment, although Sir William Reid Dick's golden eagle, which surmounts the monument, tends to disguise its architectural affinities.[16] In other cities Lutyens' orig-inal concept was taken to its limits, as in Sir Giles Gilbert Scott's monu-ment for Preston (104), where the cenotaph is some 70 feet tall, with the symbolic tomb at its top, and with a relief figure of Victory bearing wreaths at the base, the work of Henry Pegram. Large cities such as Glasgow and Bristol tended to erect plain but imposing memorials based on the Lon-don Cenotaph; in Belfast the cenotaph is set within a tall curved colon-nade, while a solid curved wall, adorned with plaques bearing names com-memorated, is found in Middlesbrough. At Bude in Cornwall a form of cenotaph was designed by Walter Marsden, with a stone oil-lamp at the top to symbolize eternal life; the interest of this is that Lutyens had first intended the London monument to be surmounted by an urn 'to spout a pillar of flame by night and, I hope, smoke by day.'[17] Elsewhere, ceno-taphs range from the simple and plain, as at Carshalton in Surrey, to the elaborate and complex, as at Campbeltown in Argyll, where the monu-ment is a hybrid of obelisk, cross and cenotaph.

Cenotaphs were seldom accompanied by figures, although it is clearly by design rather than accident that the Hull example was erected in close

96

proximity to the Boer War memorial, in the form of a dramatic sculpture of a soldier defending his wounded comrade. An interesting and effective combination is at Croydon (105), where the monument, designed by James Burford, consists of a cenotaph flanked by bronze figures (by P. R. Montford) of a soldier dressing his own wounded arm, and a distraught mother and child, holding what appears to be a letter. We must presume that the news of her husband's perhaps fatal wounds has just reached her. Another effective combination is seen at Bradford, where a soldier and sailor flank the cenotaph. They hold their rifles at the ready, but the bayonets which were fixed to them were removed in the 1960s as being too aggressive — with the consequent unbalancing of the bronze figures.

Symbolic figures are as common as symbolic forms and exist in a profusion of variety. Among female personifications the most common is certainly Victory, but before considering her we may note some of her sisters.[18] We have seen that the pagan Victory was transformed into a Christian angel with little change in outward form and a variety of angels adorn the memorials to modern war. Sometimes they are unspecific winged beings, such as might decorate tombstones or altar frontals. At Poplar in east London is a pathetic memorial to eighteen children killed in their school by a German bomb on 13 June, 1917, consisting of a conventional angel standing on a pillar (106). This is by A. R. Adams of Poplar, who was clearly the local purveyor of tomb monuments and the result fails to match the tragedy. Elsewhere, angels have greater character and it is often impossible to distinguish between the specifically Christian and the general characterization of emotion. Grief as a female, especially as a mourning mother, is found frequently and is often accompanied by a young child, symbolizing hope for the future. This form has already been noted at Derby and Croydon. Among many other examples is that at Halkirk in Scotland, designed by the architects Alexander Ross and Son of Inverness and depicting a mother and child in Highland dress; the inscription contains the words *'Gentle Peace returning, wi' mony a sweet babe fatherless and mony a widow mourning.'* Peace herself is also common, as on the Boer War memorial to the Royal Artillery on the Mall in London, where she is depicted (by W. R. Colton) as a winged figure controlling the Spirit of War, in the form of a large horse.

In this context we should at least take note of the monument at Volgograd in the Soviet Union, especially as we have recorded the largest cross, for here is surely the largest female figure. This is the enormous concrete sculpture by Evgeni Vuchetich representing The Motherland, which dominates the vast memorial complex for the Battle of Stalingrad. Set on a hilltop, the memorial commemorates the many who died in the great siege and battle and is approached from the river frontage by a series of memorial stairways flanked by subsidiary shrines to Fallen Heroes. One cannot but be overawed by the size of the whole construction, although the female figure is derived rather too obviously from Delacroix's famous image of *Liberty Guiding the People*.[19] There are also forerunners of this idea in John Flaxman's design for a 200-ft figure of Britannia at Greenwich as a memorial to British naval victories over the French (see above, Chapter 1) and in the Statue of Liberty. However, the representation of the Motherland is not common on British memorials, although an exception appears to be the female figure on the Blackburn memorial, supporting a wounded soldier. [20]

The theme of youth and war is also common and is the subject of another of Goscombe John's memorials. For Llandaff in the suburbs of Cardiff he designed a memorial with a classically robed female at its centre, the personification of the town, raising her hand in blessing of two boys, one still in short trousers but both carrying rifles (107). These represent the sons of Llandaff going off to war — a topic which John was to treat again, more dramatically, at Newcastle. A less successful version of the idea is K. Scott's figure of a boy in the grounds of Oundle School, with the inscription on the plinth *'Here Am I: Send Me!'*

Other unusual personifications include John Angel's figure for Bridgwater, which represents Civilization as a seated female, holding a globe in one hand and with the book of knowledge on her lap. More traditional was Britannia, seen on Goscombe John's Boer War memorial to the King's Liverpool Regiment, on Walter Gilbert's First World War memorials to the men of Crewe and of Troon, and above the memorial entrance arch of Waterloo Station. She also occurs as a free-standing sculpture by Gilbert Ledward in the apse of the Memorial Hall in Stockport. The virtues of Truth and Justice are also represented as females, on London's Submarine memorial and Charles Sargeant Jagger made Humanity female on the Hoylake and West Kirby memorial. On occasion there is an unnamed female spirit, probably Duty or Patriotism, as on John Cassidy's memorial at Clayton-le-Moors in Lancashire, where the female figure is both protecting and encouraging a soldier. On the Luton memorial the female figure, shown holding a miniature Victory in her left hand, is identified as Courage (108); it is a late work by Sir William Thornycroft.

Probably the most surprising female personification to appear on a memorial is *La Delivrance* by Emile Guillaume in Finchley (110), which commemorates the allied defeat of the German armies at the Battle of the

Marne in September, 1914. It is, therefore, a traditional victory monument and the figure of a naked girl, arms raised aloft and pointing a sword to the sky, is intended to be triumphant. The result has been aptly described as the only statue in London to be sexy.[21]

Victory is a recurring image, although she seldom appeared on battlefields, where the price of her achievement remained all too clear. An exception is provided by the two monuments to the 34th Division, on the Mont Noir (111) and at La Boiselle, which have a surprisingly French-looking Victory by Robert Emerson. However, she dominated local and town memorials, where civic and national pride could mingle and the emphatic statement 'We won!' seemed neither equivocal nor inappropriate. Traditionally a winged female figure, normally bearing a wreath and a sword, Victory surmounts many a municipal monument. The influence of Sir Thomas Brock's Victoria Memorial outside Buckingham Palace seems to have been a key factor in establishing the type, and a good Boer War example is Bertram Mackennal's memorial to the Islingtonians at Highbury Corner in London (112). The version by L. F. Roslyn for Wetherby in Yorkshire (113) may be taken as typical of many First World War monuments. The subject was so popular that sculptors sometimes reused their figures; at Leeds (109) the memorial was originally capped by a bronze Victory poised on a globe (since removed to the Crematorium), while at the base of the obelisk-shaped plinth are figures of Peace and St George, all by H. C. Fehr. He reused the same figures, slightly re-worked, for the memorial at Colchester (114), with a plinth of different design, and the Victory was used again at Eastbourne. Another case of reuse is the striking figure of Victory sheathing her sword designed by George Wade in 1904 as the Boer War memorial in Norwich (115) and reused on the memorial in Maritzburg, South Africa, in 1911. By sharing elements, and sometimes complete memorials, design costs could be kept down but there was in fact less duplication of figures than is sometimes thought. The majority of sculptors, including the best known, had at least one Victory to their credit. Thus we can admire Adrian Jones' version on a column at Uxbridge, Newbury Trent's at East Barnet Valley, Birnie Rhind's at Plymouth and so on. At Keswick an unusual relief, in the form of a Roman tombstone, bears a Victory by Derwent Wood, while a clear allusion to the original location of the Winged Victory of Samothrace was provided by Alexander Proudfoot for Greenock (117). Here Victory stands in the prow of a Viking ship, emerging from the base of a truncated obelisk, as she was originally placed in the prow of a Greek ship on Samothrace.[22]

An elaborate Victory monument was designed by John Angel for Exeter which was much admired at the time, the Victory having been exhibited in the courtyard of Burlington House during the Summer Exhibition of 1922 (119). At the top of a tall plinth stands the female figure, in bronze, her right arm raised and clasping a spray of laurel leaves, with a long sword held point down in her left hand. She tramples on a dragon which, like St George, she has slain and represents the enemy. At the base of the plinth are four seated bronze figures, personifying those whose efforts have gained victory: a soldier in a greatcoat, a sailor labouring at sea, a woman sewing, and a prisoner of war, naked and manacled but defiant. Another interesting example is the South Eastern Railway memorial in Dover Marine Station (120), which consists of a large bronze group with Victory holding a torch, while shielding a soldier and a sailor with her wings. A bugler stands rather incongruously at the back of the monument and, according to the sculptor, W. C. H. King, he has just sounded the notes of the Last Post over the fallen.[23]

Among male representations the most common in England is St George. The reasons for using the Patron Saint are obvious, but were nonetheless stated by the Duke of York when he unveiled the memorial at the Leys School in Cambridge, which has a central St George figure: 'It will stand for all time, a pivot of the school's history and tradition and the inspiration of those ideals of chivalry, self-sacrifice, and patriotism which are essential to the highest conduct and character.'[24] St George almost invariably appears in armour and is normally standing in victory on the dragon. He is sometimes shown on horseback in the act of killing the beast, as on a relief for a cross terminal designed by Newbury Trent,[25] or on Charles Hartwell's memorial to the men of Marylebone (122), near Lord's cricket ground, that has all the vigour of a Renaissance condottiere. A particularly good example is the Cavalry Memorial in Hyde Park (121), by Adrian Jones, with interesting scenes of First World War cavalry on the plinth. The two types can be compared in Newcastle, where there is a second cast of Charles Hartwell's Marylebone figure on horseback in Eldon Square, while John Reid's version outside the church of St Thomas the Martyr shows a standing figure, sheathing his sword after decapitating the monster (123). Sir George Frampton made a number of striking St Georges, begin ning with the Boer War memorial for Radley School and, after the First World War, the Maidstone Memorial (124) and the Pearl Assurance Company Memorial (125) in the courtyard of their grand headquarters building in London's Holborn. Alfred Drury's figure for Denstone College in Staffordshire is a noble knight in the tradition of Donatello, while Lutyens memorial for Wellington College (in the chapel) includes a white figure

100

of St George on top of a black marble column. Eric Gill's version on the Trumpington memorial, with St George as a modern soldier, seems an isolated interpretation.

In the British Isles St Michael is rare, although he does appear on the base of the Trumpington Cross (127). He also appears as a bronze figure by Allan Wyon, set within a small circular temple structure, at Shrewsbury and can be seen on the Royal Marines memorial on Plymouth Hoe, by W. G. Storr-Barber (129). Here the Saint is placed on a pedestal and in the act of killing a dragon, with a mourning soldier and a sailor below and he occurs again on the memorial outside the church dedicated to him in Cornhill in London (128). Richard Goulden's sculpture depicts the Saint protecting a group of children on one side, while wild animals are seen fighting on the other. A second cast of this sculpture forms the 1st Division memorial at the Le Groise crossroads, near Le Cateau. Goulden seems to have had a liking for using popular Saints that were nonetheless unusual in the memorial context and he designed the bronze St Christopher carrying a child that forms the Bank of England Memorial.

Figures of Christ, other than on the cross, are rare but one may be found in Limehouse churchyard. This represents the risen Christ, hand raised in blessing, and is the work of R. A. Walker (130); it may be compared with the unsigned figure of Christ bearing the crown of thorns which stands outside a deserted church in Walworth (131).

Other male figures and personifications cover a wide variety of themes. The South African memorial at Delville Wood, designed by Sir Herbert Baker, includes a triumphal arch surmounted by a sculptured group in bronze. This, by Albert Turner, shows two men leading a warhorse into battle and represents Physical Energy and the two (white) races of South Africa, inspired, according to Sir Herbert Baker, by Macaulay's poem of the Battle of Lake Regillus, telling how the Great Twin Brethren appeared in the sky to fight in the ranks of Rome. Certainly the sculpture appears to be based on antique figures of Castor and Pollux.[26] At Skipton in Yorkshire John Cassidy placed Victory on an obelisk with a naked male figure of Humanity breaking the sword of war at the bottom (132). For the Machine Gun Corps Memorial in London (133) Derwent Wood made a large naked figure of David, carrying a great sword and flanked somewhat incongruously by Vickers machine guns. However, the inscription, from the Book of Samuel, makes the point: *Saul has slain his thousands, and David his ten thousands.*

Naked allegorical figures were another speciality of Richard Goulden, seen at Dover, Reigate and at Crompton. The Reigate Monument (134) shows an adult struggling through what appear to be massive brambles, with a child in one hand and a flaming cross in the other. An explanatory inscription states that *The bronze represents the triumphal struggle of mankind against the difficulties that beset him in the path of life. Shielding and bearing onward the child, the figure holds aloft the symbol of self-sacrifice to light the way. The flaming cross is used to indicate the suffering endured by men in the war. Flames consume the flesh: the spirit is unconquerable.* At Crompton (near Oldham) the male figure is clearing the path to the future of the wild beasts which beset it, while the children of the next generation look on (an iconography already noted on his St Michael figures).

Unusual in a different way is the Paisley Memorial (135), designed by the Scottish architect Sir Robert Lorimer as a tall square pillar, surmounted by a sculptural group in bronze by Mrs Meredith Williams. This shows First World War Tommies trudging through mud and surrounding a mounted mediaeval knight, whose shield and pennant bear St Andrew's Cross. He presumably represents the spirit of Scottish patriotism.

One symbolic figure that seldom occurs is Death. This is probably because the traditional skeletal personification of Death as a grim and horrific spectre was found to be ill-suited to memorials that were intended to honour courage and sacrifice and to rejoice in victory. Death is seen as a noble act of self-sacrifice, not another inevitable victory for the reaper. One suggested example in Britain is Harold Brownsword's memorial for Allerton near Bradford, where a wounded soldier is supported by a cowled female figure, but this identification seems uncertain.[27] Artists were less reticent on the continent and it comes as a salutary shock to meet the memorial to the French 69th Division at the aptly named Mort Homme on the Verdun battlefield. Here a large figure of Death carries a broken spear and surmounts the proud inscription *Ils n'ont pas passé.* The sculptor was Froment Meurice. A still more dramatic, indeed bizarre version occurs on the Portuguese Corps Memorial (136) in the little village of La Couture, near Béthune, where a skeletal Death, armed with his sickle, is receiving a falling soldier into his arms, while Victory, with drawn sword, looks on helplessly from above. The whole monument is constructed on a podium in the form of a ruined church. The sculptor was F. Lopes and there can be few more unexpected village memorials in existence.

NOTES

(1) For all Boer War memorials see Gildea, J, *For Remembrance and In Honour of those who lost their lives in the South African War*, London, 1911.

(2) Information from *The Quarry*. January, 1921, quoted in files of IWM Department of Photographs, War Memorials Collection.

(3) See Longworth, P, *The Unending Vigil: A History of the Commonwealth War Graves Commission 1917-1967*, London, 1967.

(4) The Yarmouth memorial is interesting in other ways also; it is one of the few town memorials to which a separate Second World War memorial was added, in the form of an adjacent walled enclosure. The original memorial also suffered from bomb damage in the Second World War and these scars were left unrepaired as a further form of memorial (cf. Cleopatra's Needle, see Ch. 1, p 4).

(5) Nicholson, G, *We Will Remember ... Overseas Memorials to Canada's War Dead*, Ottawa, 1973, pp 16-17.

(6) Nicholson, *op. cit.* pp 32-33.

(7) See Compton, A, (ed) *Charles Sargeant Jagger: War and Peace Sculpture*, London, 1985 p 16 ff.

(8) For the Guards Memorial see Skipwith, P, 'Gilbert Ledward R.A. and the Guards' Division Memorial', *Apollo*, January, 1988, pp 22-26.

(9) Information based on notes in files of IWM Department of Photographs, War Memorials Collection.

(10) Site of the Roman city of Apollonia-Sozusa. Similar memorials were erected to the 156th and 157th Brigades.

(11) *Monument National de Santa Cruz del Valle de los Caidos* Madrid, 1974.

(12) The use of Celtic crosses as the basis for memorials was specifically advocated by Ludovic MacLellan Mann in a pamphlet entitled *War Memorials and the Barochan Cross, Renfrewshire*, Edinburgh, 1919. Blomfield's opinion is given in *Memoirs of an Architect*, London, 1932, p 176.

(13) The iconography of the Trumpington Cross was discussed by Gill in his letters to the local committee. He added that 'I hope the committee will be willing to trust me as a sculptor and will not ask for naturalism in a thing which obviously calls for symbolism.' See Shewring, W, (ed) *The Letters of Eric Gill*, London, 1947.

(14) On Port Sunlight see Curl, J, 'Victorian Garden Village: Port Sunlight, Merseyside', *Country Life* 16 December, 1976, pp 1822-4, although this does not discuss the memorial.

(15) See Chapter 1 above and Toynbee, J, *Death and Burial in the Roman World*, London, 1971.

(16) Perhaps this is why Lord Edward Gleichen described it as 'not very original' only five years after it was erected; see *London's Open-Air Statuary*, London, 1928, p 102.

(17) See the exhibition catalogue, *Lutyens*, London, 1981, no 289-2.

(18) It should be noted that allegorical figures are often left unidentified and are interpreted at will by the viewer.

(19) For the Stalingrad memorial see Warner, M, *Monuments and Maidens; The Allegory of the Female Form*, London, 1985. Delacroix's picture is in the Louvre.

(20) Boorman, D, *At the Going Down of the Sun*, York, 1988, p 137.

(21) See Byron, A, *London Statues*, London, 1981, p 304.

(22) On the Winged Victory of Samothrace, see Chapter 1, p 12.

(23) See the report of the unveiling of this memorial in *The Railway Gazette*, 3 November, 1922, pp 555-557. I am indebted to R. J. A. Tinker for drawing my attention to this entry, which gives the name of the sculptor; the piece appears to be unsigned.

(24) Quotation from notes in files of IWM Department of Photographs, War Memorials Collection.

(25) At Beckenham.

(26) The iconography of the Delville Wood memorial is explained by Baker in his autobiography, *Architecture and Personalities*, London, 1944, p 90 and in a special issue of *The African World*, 16 October, 1926.

(27) Boorman, *op. cit.*, p 98.

CHAPTER 7

EVERYMAN AS HERO

It's Tommy this, an' Tommy that, an' "Chuck him out, the brute!"
But it's "Saviour of 'is country" when the guns begin to shoot.
Rudyard Kipling, Tommy.

In previous chapters the narrative tradition and the depiction of heroes have been treated as separate strands of development, and this was indeed the case up to the 19th century. From that point on there was a gradual transformation of the heroic idea, which had been concerned only with great leaders, to embrace ordinary soldiers; such soldiers were the people whose stories were told in war narratives and consequently the distinction between the two strands of pictorial development began to blur. The result was the emergence of the heroic narrative, which was to prove one of the standbys of memorial design. This chapter considers how the depiction of heroes on the one hand survived and at the same time developed a narrative aspect.

Heroes of the past were normally commanders. In antiquity this meant the king or emperor and in practice hero portrayal was largely limited to the ruling classes until the 19th century. Then the depiction of the ordinary soldier as hero began to rival the more traditional forms. It did not, however, replace the custom of commemorating commanders with public monuments and Victorian Britain was almost profligate in this respect. Soldiers and sailors far less distinguished than Wellington or Nelson were frequently accorded imposing memorials in stone and bronze and our major cities abound in statues of military men whose names are all but forgotten. With the advent of the 20th century many fewer such traditional memorials have been erected, but they have not died out completely. At the same time the role of the ordinary and anonymous soldier as hero has grown in importance, especially through his widespread appearances on war memorials. Yet most of the forms of heroic portrayal have remained fairly traditional, whatever type or class of hero is involved.

There is one area where the leader as hero has not only survived but flourished, although its investigation lies beyond the bounds of the present study. Extreme political regimes of both right and left have made extensive use of leadership cults in the 20th century, and so developed the appropriate iconography. The Fascist rulers consciously used art for political propaganda and as a means of propagating their own preferred images. Both Hitler and Mussolini developed an imperial iconography, akin to the *Pax Romana* tradition, in which they were portrayed as all-powerful, victorious, yet beneficient.[1] Mussolini, and also Franco, liked to see themselves as heroes in action, on horseback and (rather incongruously) wielding a sword.[2] In communist countries the images of the revolutionary leaders and their successors have been equally prominent, playing an almost iconic role. In many cases these figures are of immense size, marking a direct revival of the ancient tradition of showing the ruler on a larger scale than his subjects. This emphasis on size is, as has been noted, a feature of war memorials in totalitarian regimes and both instances reflect a fundamental belief that power may be equated with physical size.

Fascist and communist hero cults form a direct link with the ancient tradition of hero portrayal and it is of interest that a comparable survival occurs in some less extreme political systems. In Turkey, for example, every town and village has its central statue of Ataturk, who is venerated as the creator of the modern Turkish nation.[3] For the most part, however, there are few such symbols in western countries; in Britain the nearest approach to a modern figure of this sort is probably Winston Churchill, but he has at present only three statues in London and few elsewhere.

If multiple images of the hero ruler, so typical of the Roman empire, have not found a place in contemporary democratic states, there have also been changes in the presentation of famous soldiers as heroes. Most notable is the decline and demise of the equestrian figure. This, of course, reflects actual practice, since commanders no longer go to war, or even perform many ceremonial duties, on horseback. The last equestrian statue in London is Alfred Hardiman's figure of Earl Haig, erected in Whitehall in 1934 (137).[4] Two other First World War commanders were given equestrian memorials in London; Maréchal Foch in Grosvenor Gardens and Lord Roberts (who died in the first few months of the war) on Horse Guards Parade,[5] but the majority of 20th century military leaders deemed worthy of commemoration stand on their own two feet. Moreover, since the fashion for tall pedestals (let alone columns) had also declined, sculptors have had to experiment with a number of other devices in the attempt to allow their subjects to dominate their surroundings.

A few examples, again from London, will suffice. Proving that traditional solutions are the best, John Tweed gave his statue of Kitchener (138) considerable presence by placing it in a simple architectural context and by giving the figure an air of calm authority. Unfortunately its position, on one side of Horse Guards Parade, means that few people bother to go and look at it, but it succeeds better than many more recent figures. Compare, for example, the figure of Churchill by Ivor Roberts-Jones in Parliament Square, which draws attention solely on account of its bulk. Nearby, Epstein's sculpture of Field-Marshal Smuts is distinguished by the oddity of its pose (neatly described by David Piper as seeming "to skate on very thin ice and to be unsuitably dressed for the occasion").[6] Along Whitehall, Oscar Nemon made Field-Marshal Montgomery fourteen feet high, to make up for the lack of a proper plinth, but he still fails to dominate the Ministry of Defence behind him. Nemon had tried another solution for Lord Portal (139), nearby on the Embankment, giving him a rough triangular slate base, but the result is somewhat awkward and no more successful than William Macmillan's traditional figure of Lord Trenchard alongside, complete with orthodox if small plinth. Both figures compare unfavourably with William Thornycroft's adjacent statue of General Gordon,(140) made for Trafalgar Square in 1882, but subsequently moved to the Embankment.[7] One of the recent additions to these ranks is Franta Belsky's 1983 figure of Lord Mountbatten, adjoining Horse Guards Parade, where the statue is placed on a small plinth at the top of some low steps, which succeed in separating the figure from its surroundings and marks it out for attention. However, it is difficult to avoid the conclusion that the traditional forms of commemorating heroic commanders, tried and tested since antiquity, have still to be improved upon.

In fact some of the more successful images of 20th century leaders are in two rather than three dimensions and there are two examples of the type painted after the First World War which make an interesting comparison. These were commissioned immediately after the conflict to commemorate (or perhaps to create) the commanding heroes involved. The military commanders were painted by John Singer Sargent, whose enormous canvas entitled *Some General Officers of the Great War* (141), dates from 1922.[8] It is a rather uninspiring work, the soldiers in question being arranged in a more or less straight line, looking more like the guests at a school reunion than the fearless conquerors of the Hun. Sargent was of course a somewhat unlikely war artist, whose unexpected masterpiece was *Gassed*. Despite his background in society portraiture, the creation of hero images was evidently not his metier and *Some General Officers* is chiefly of interest in comparison with another of these commemorative pictures, James Guthrie's group of politicians.

Guthrie, a Scottish artist, was perhaps a more surprising choice than Sargent, but he produced one of the most memorable of group hero portraits (142). The scene appears to be set in a sort of memorial hall which is dominated by a huge Winged Victory; the symbolism is perhaps over-obvious but is nonetheless dramatically effective. In the foreground, grouped round a table, some standing, some sitting, are the politicians. The grouping and the posing of the figures immediately recalls the series of 17th century Dutch portraits of Town Guards painted by artists such as Frans Hals and it is known that Guthrie made a special visit to Holland in order to study these works. He also went to Spain to see the great works of Velasquez and his picture reveals the direct influence of *Las Meninas,* notably in the handling of light and space. This combination of victory symbolism, calculated groupings, and dramatic lighting gives the picture considerable impact. By strange prophecy, the central figure of the group, the compositional lynch-pin and illuminated by a shaft of light, is Winston Churchill, whose true heroic role was yet to be played.

The contrasting story of the sculptural monuments to London's heroic commanders can be repeated in the capitals and major cities of other western countries. The images are comparatively few and seldom have the presence of their classical or their 19th century predecessors. The real continuation of the tradition of hero portrayal is to be found on the war memorials and in the anonymous soldiers they present. These derive from the late Victorian concept of the noble soldier, fighting for Queen and Country, who had figured so prominently in the battle paintings of Lady Butler and others.[9] However, in painting the heroic soldier was normally depicted as part of a unit — a Square or a "Thin Red Line" — and our attention is directed to the group rather than the individual. Considerations of size, space, and no doubt expense meant that the memorials had to concentrate more on the individual and so revived the old forms of hero presentation.

This revival began with the Boer War memorials and continued with those of the First World War. The three traditional types of heroic image were all employed: the hero in action, the hero in triumph, and the dying hero. Once again the only significant omission was the hero on horseback, since the horse was even less appropriate for the ordinary infantryman than for his commander. There were rare exceptions, such as the Paisley Memorial (135). where the central figure is a mounted mediaeval knight surrounded by 20th century Tommies; the association between these differing images was obviously intended to stress that the chivalrous qualities of the former were also characteristic of the latter. In addition

107

equestrian figures do regularly occur in the form of St George, while a delightful and different memorial is Cecil Brown's monument to the Imperial Camel Corps in London's Victoria Embankment Gardens (143). This naturally depicts a trooper mounted on a camel.

Equally surprising is the fact that the horse itself is treated as the hero on a number of occasions. The military use of horses remained very widespread up to the end of the First World War and as beasts of burden many thousands saw action and were killed.[10] In the South African city of Port Elizabeth there is a memorial in the form of a drinking trough surmounted by full-size bronze sculptures of a horse with his rider, a trooper, kneeling to offer the animal a drink of water. The inscription records that it was erected by public subscription *In recognition of the services of the Gallant Animals which perished in the Anglo-Boer War*. At Chipilly-sur-Somme the First World War memorial to the 58th London Division (144) shows an artilleryman caressing his wounded horse, the work of the French sculptor Gauquié, while at Le Cateau the memorial to the 66th Division is in the form of a horse drinking trough. This may be compared with the memorial at Lake on the Isle of Wight which incorporates a drinking trough in memory of the horses and dogs that took part in the war. A further memorial to horses is in St Jude's church, Hampstead, where a bronze statuette of a horse surmounts a plaque dedicated to the 375,000 horses killed in the war.

The most common form of soldier-hero found on memorials is related to the traditional imagery of the emperor in triumph, exemplified by the *Pax Romana* figures of Augustus. A young soldier is seen in a pose of calm confidence, standing At Ease, and gazing into the future. Hundreds of examples exist on memorials up and down the country and the sculptor John Cassidy described his figure at Heaton Moor, Greater Manchester (145) as *'typical of the majority of the soldiers who comprised the armies of Great Britain during the War. Called from the uneventful civil pursuits by the voice of duty, he carries with him the refinement of his ordinary life, whilst the knowledge of the horrors of war enhances his valour.'*[11] There are many excellent versions of the subject to be found, but a classic statement of it occurs in Alfred Drury's figures on the Men of London Memorial (146) outside the Royal Exchange. Other fine versions include John Tweed's figure for the King's Royal Rifle Corps memorial in Winchester and Goscombe John's memorial for Lampeter. There are equally good examples by lesser known sculptors — P. G. Bentham at Trowbridge, A. G. Walker at Sevenoaks (147) or C. W. Coombes at Kendal, while in Scotland memorable images of Scottish soldiers were made by Birnie Rhind and

Kellock Brown (148). One of the most impressive statements of the idea is found on the Guards' Memorial in London (77), where Gilbert Ledward presents us with five apparently identical figures, one for each regiment, but which on closer observation are seen to be all different. They stand against the squat obelisk of the monument itself, designed by H. C. Bradshaw, looking defiantly across to Whitehall in a composition that can stand comparison with the public sculptor of antiquity.[12]

A particular variation of the type using a seated figure was evolved by the Canadian sculptor Dr R. Tait Mackenzie of Philadelphia. His Scottish-American Memorial (152) in West Prince's Street Gardens, Edinburgh, entitled *The Call, 1914*, shows a young kilted soldier, rifle across his knees, gazing in anticipation towards Castle Rock: behind him a frieze depicts men joining up and setting off for war. Mackenzie made similar figures for some of his Canadian memorials, notably *The Volunteer* on the Rosamond War Memorial, Almonte.[13] This was his home town and he based the figure on a particular volunteer, Alexander Rosamond, who nonetheless stands for all those who died. He also produced a striking variation on the normal form for his victory memorial to the Men of Cambridgeshire (in Cambridge) (153). Entitled *The Homecoming*, this shows a young soldier striding forward with confidence, with the rifle at his shoulder garlanded with victory wreaths. Set on a plinth designed by architect George Hubbard, this is a memorial of unbounded optimism and an unashamed celebration of victory.

Another common version of the theme, which is also essentially a celebration of triumph, shows the soldier waving his cap in the air with a victory hurrah. An early but standard version of the type is found on Sir George Frampton's Boer War Memorial to the Lancashire Fusiliers in Bury (154) and the theme is repeated in many First World War memorials. Examples include the Twickenham Memorial (155) by Mortimer Brown, with good panels showing the Navy, RAF, and, more unusually, Womens' Services on the pedestal, the Merthyr Vale and Aberfan memorials by George Thomas, the Stafford memorial by Whitehead and Sons, and the Truro memorial.

Quite different, but also deserving to come under the heading of anonymous heroes, are the numerous mourning figures found on 20th century memorials. In origin such mourners were symbolic figures (their development is discussed in Chapter 1) and of course they retain their symbolic significance, but, with the evolution of the ordinary soldier as hero, his comrades who mourn his death are themselves by definition equally heroic. Certainly the mourning soldier, head bowed and holding his rifle

reversed with its muzzle resting on the left boot, is one of the most characteristic and moving memorial images. It was tragically apposite that the
memorial at Enniskillen, Co Fermanagh, was of this type, for when an IRA
bomb exploded there on Remembrance Sunday, 1987, killing eleven
people, pictures of the monument were seen and remembered around the
world.[14] In fact the type was very common, good examples being Albert
Toft's Boer War soldier in Ipswich (156) and the same artist's First War
Memorial in Streatham (157), Benjamin Lloyd's figure for Llandrindod
Wells, and a Scottish soldier at Glenfinnan by the firm of Scott and Rae.
Multiple mourners also occur, such as the four who surround the base of
the steel mast memorial in Sheffield (88) and those around the obelisk at
Euston Station (71).[15]

The idea and tradition of heroism could be stressed by directly linking
past and present. This is something which we have already come across
in, for example, the images of Napoleon in Roman dress. In modern memorials the link with the past is normally established by pairing a contemporary soldier with his ancestors from the same regiment. Thus Goscombe John on his Boer War monument to the King's Liverpool Regiment showed a soldier of the late 17th century and one of the early 20th
century flanking a figure of Britannia. He adapted the same idea after the
First World War on the Royal Welsh Fusiliers Memorial at Wrexham (159)
depicting two figures, a present-day soldier standing before his 18th century predecessor, who carries a flag and looks on with benign approval.
A similar theme inspired John Tweed, whose Rifle Brigade Memorial in
Grosvenor Gardens, London (151), consists of three figures, the central one
a rifleman of the First World War, flanked by an officer and a soldier of
the beginning of the 19th century. At Royston in Hertfordshire the bronze
soldier stands before a sculptured white marble panel of his military fore-
bears, going back to an archer from Agincourt (160).[16] Their ghostly appearance provides a nice and intentional contrast with the bronze central figure. Another version of the same idea is provided by the monumental
brasses on the Yorkshire Regiment's Memorial at Sledmere (100/101); these
include direct copies of medieval examples but with modern faces as well
as entirely modern figures in medieval pose. The link with the past could
hardly be made in a more obvious fashion.[17]

Another role for the hero is protecting the weak or helpless members
of the civilian population. At Warlingham (161) in Surrey J. E. Taylerson's
sculpture *Succouring the Defenceless* shows a soldier standing with rifle
at the ready, protecting a recumbent woman and child. There is a similar
depiction on W. Aumonier's memorial at Alfreton in Derbyshire, where a

soldier protects a young child, a theme which is repeated on many other monuments.

A rare development, in all senses, is the transformation of the ordinary soldier into a specifically named hero, but this can occur when an individual is singled out for a particular act of bravery, notably through the award of the Victoria Cross. The exceptional status this gives to its holder is well illustrated by the case of Sub-Lieutenant Warneford, who was awarded a VC for bringing down a Zeppelin in June, 1915. Very shortly afterwards he was killed in a flying accident and his body returned to England for burial in Brompton Cemetery. His tomb became a shrine, visited by some 50,000 people on the day of his funeral, and his monument (erected by readers of the *Daily Express*) bears a portrait of the young aviator and a relief depicting his deed. One other early flyer, Captain Albert Ball, who was awarded the Victoria Cross posthumously, received the ultimate public accolade of heroism in the form of a statue in his home town of Nottingham (162).[18] This is the work of sculptor Henry Poole and shows Ball in full flying kit, protected by a female spirit who probably represents Immortality, and with relief panels depicting some of his flying exploits on the plinth. Such public commemoration of a holder of the Victoria Cross is extremely unusual, but a precedent existed in the (then) well-known sculpture by Charles Bell Birch, dating from 1880, showing Lieutenant Walter R. Pollock Hamilton VC in action during the Second Afghan War.[19] There is also a memorial to the French air ace Georges Guynemer at Poelkappelle in Belgium. He was killed on 11 September, 1917, and his monument depicts a flying stork, the emblem of his squadron, at the top of a pillar.

The most notable heroine to be specifically commemorated was Nurse Edith Cavell, with monuments in London by Frampton and in Norwich by Henry Pegram (163). The former is massive and unsatisfactory, the latter consists of a bronze bust on top of a stone pillar bearing a relief of a soldier holding up a laurel wreath. Particular individuals were also sometimes commemorated in private memorials commissioned by the family. Francis Mond, who was killed when his aircraft was shot down in May, 1918, was memorialized in a fine statuette of St George by Frampton; Edward Horner, who died of wounds received at the Battle of Cambrai, was commemorated by an equestrian sculpture by Alfred Munnings in Mells church, Somerset. One of the most striking and poignant of such private memorials is that to Elizabeth and Charles Vyner in Fountains Hall in Yorkshire. This, somewhat unusually, is a Second World War memorial to a sister and brother, respectively in the WRNS and the RNVR, who were killed aged 18 and 19. Their memorial, designed by Lord Mottistone and Paul Paget, shows the two young people standing either side of a stone cross which is set within a stained glass window. The sculpture, by Cecil Thomas, is dignified and effective and the memorial gains much from its position above the entrance staircase to the house. It is evidence that even after 1945 the traditional memorial vocabulary could be used effectively.

The dying hero had emerged as a common type in the 18th century and was revived on a number of memorials. Several Boer War memorials show soldiers protecting fallen comrades while in other cases the body of a warrior is taken aloft by angels.[20] A dramatic First World War version of this subject was created by the splendidly named Coeur de Lion MacCarthy, one of Canada's leading memorial sculptors, for the Canadian Pacific Railway. This shows the Angel of Victory raising the body of a fallen soldier to heaven. It was erected in Montreal, Winnipeg, and Vancouver, to the memory of the 1,115 employees of the company who died.[21]

Stalybridge, near Manchester, has an ambitious memorial on the eponymous bridge, by Ferdinand Blundstone, showing a dying soldier and a dying sailor falling into the arms of winged female figures, one of whom holds a lamp of eternal light before the dimming eyes of the hero (164). Blundstone also depicted a dying soldier, supported by two very similar female figures, on the memorial for the Prudential Assurance Company in High Holborn, London (165). This type of treatment is more common on the continent and is illustrated by the memorial to the French dead at Ypres (166), which shows the body of a soldier supported by two female figures, while a winged Victory looms up behind, bearing sword and wreath. A more traditional British version of the dying soldier image was made by Birnie Rhind for Fettes School. This represents an officer who has been struck down while fighting, but with his final gesture raises his hand to signal his men to (as the memorial is entitled) Carry On. It is significant that this reappearance of the Dying Commander theme should be on a school memorial, reflecting the presumption that all ex-public school boys would automatically be officers.[22]

This is an appropriate point to turn to the depiction of heroes in action. Clearly, only a limited amount of action can be shown in a single figure, but the memorial artists developed the idea to the full. Typically we see an alert soldier, moving forward and ready for action, as on the Royal Fusiliers Memorial in Holborn, London (167), where Albert Toft's figure is advancing while at the same time glancing back, as if anticipating the order to attack. He has fixed his bayonet, indicating the approach of action, and

112

this is a common iconographic device to show that the soldier is about to engage the enemy. The same figure was used for the 41st Division Memorial at Flers on the Somme (168). Another good London example is Philip Lindsay Clark's memorial in Southwark, which shows a soldier advancing through the mud, rifle slung at his back, but with his eyes firmly fixed on the enemy ahead (169). Like many others, this memorial bears bronze relief panels on the sides of the plinth depicting air and sea combat, to provide a balance to the infantryman above, and here and elsewhere these panels contain much interesting and informative detail.

Similarly alert soldiers, ready for action, occur widely with many variations of pose. Thus at Bridgnorth the figure by Adrian Jones is pointing ahead to the enemy lines (170), while at Dingwall in Scotland, J. Stevenson's is standing his ground, rifle and bayonet ready to repel an attack. Often these soldiers are powerful and impressive pieces of sculpture; S. N. Babb's figure on the Tonbridge Wells memorial (171) stands comparison with several more famous works of 20th century sculpture and many other striking images could be singled out. An unusual and powerful variation is the weary but defiant soldier on Walter Marsden's memorial at St Anne's-on-Sea (179). A seemingly rather bloodthirsty variation on the theme is found on the Canadian memorial at Three Rivers (Quebec), where the soldier holds his rifle aloft, stabbing down on an unseen enemy below. This figure is the work of Coeur de Lion MacCarthy, but a similar pose was originally envisaged by Gilbert Ledward for one of the figures on the Guards Memorial in London, as a preparatory drawing shows.[23]

The impression of action is given added credence if more than a single figure is involved. A number of Boer War memorials present the scene of a soldier protecting his fallen comrade, as on the Marines Memorial in London (174), by Adrian Jones, or William Thornycroft's memorial in Manchester. Here we see the oft-repeated theme of the wounded soldier gallantly offering his last cartridge to his comrade, presented as a distillation of the type of corporate heroism so frequently seen in Victorian battle paintings.[24] The Boer War memorial in Birmingham, by Albert Toft, developed the action theme by showing soldiers straining to push a field gun over rough terrain, while the female figure of Peace surveyed the scene above. The Boer War Memorial to the King's Own Scottish Borderers is on a pier of North Bridge in Edinburgh (175) and shows a group of three soldiers, led by an officer, who are clearly fighting to the last man. It is the work of Birnie Rhind, the most prolific of Scottish memorial sculptors.

An interesting and effective version of the soldier in action is provided on the Portsmouth Municipal Memorial (176), where the entrance to a sunken precinct with a central cenotaph is guarded by two machine-gunners, powerfully sculpted by Jagger. An unusual but less accomplished memorial is that of West Hallam in Derbyshire, where the stone group depicts a machine-gun crew of two, one standing, the other kneeling with the gun. On Philip Lindsay Clark's memorial to the Cameronians in Kelvington Park in Glasgow (177) we see an attack taking place, with the central figure charging forward, passing the body of a fallen comrade and covered from the flank by a machine-gunner. The realistic portrayal of death and the tactile quality of the muddy ground make this one of the most vivid examples of memorial sculpture.

A similarly dramatic composition forms the National Memorial in Confederation Square in Ottawa. This shows a marching column of men and horses, struggling with cheerful optimism through the Flanders mud. It is one of several colonial memorials to have been commissioned from English sculptors; in this case the figures are the work of the Kentish artists Vernon Sydney and Elsie March.

The finest example of this genre is the outstanding memorial at Port Sunlight (Cheshire), designed and executed by Goscombe John in 1921, to commemorate the more than 600 who died out of the 4000 employees of Lever Brothers Company who went to the war (178). It consists of a cross mounted on an octagonal base and set within a raised circular podium. On the base, at the foot of the cross, is a large sculptural composition in bronze, while further reliefs decorate the circular podium wall. The main sculptural group, on the front of the base, shows a defiant group of soldiers, one standing, rifle at the ready, one kneeling, one lying wounded. Rather curiously, the standing figure shelters a boy, apparently a boy scout. A nurse approaches from the left to tend the wounded man. On the back of the base the sculpture is a mother with her infant children, while two slightly older children are running expectantly towards the future. This theme of youth and war, a favourite with Goscombe John, is repeated on the podium wall, where a series of bronze reliefs, presenting pairs of children bearing wreaths and garlands, alternate with panels showing the war at sea (action stations on the bridge of a warship), on land (machine gunners in a trench), in the air (anti-aircraft gunners) and the medical services (carrying the wounded). The ensemble is in no sense a continuous narrative, but the juxtaposition of action and symbolic scenes gives to the whole a dramatic coherence. In addition the quality of both the three-dimensional and the relief sculpture is remarkable and make this a public monument of unique distinction.

Such three-dimensional sculptural monuments showing heroic action

114

clearly verge on narrative, but it remains true that pictorial narrative is essentially a two-dimensional form, in sculptural terms suggesting a relief or frieze treatment. Moreover, the fact that the ordinary soldier had become the hero meant that any war narrative immediately became a form of heroic portrayal. In antiquity the technique of a continuous narrative depiction of campaigns had developed in Assyria, while the Greeks had evolved the "highlight" technique for illustrating well-known episodes from mythical stories. As a consequence of the change in the nature of the hero from commander to commoner the 20th century "highlight" technique also became non-specific. Whereas we recognize a classical scene as being, for example, Hercules killing the Hydra, its modern memorial equivalent can only be recognized as a general depiction of, for example, trench warfare.

Extended pictorial narratives are uncommon in modern art, partly because other ways of telling stories have been evolved. The development of moving picture film made it possible to provide the sort of campaign record that artists had previously produced and one of the first true documentaries is the film of *The Battle of the Somme*, made by official British cameramen and first shown to the public in London in 1916.[25] Interestingly and perhaps inevitably this has much in common with the traditional pictorial narrative, consisting of a series of short vignettes of action, linked by captions. The technique of providing a genuinely continuous narrative flow had yet to be perfected, but it was already clear that, as a form of record, film had many advantages. It showed (or purported to show[26]) real not reported action and could tell a genuinely continuous story; even the best pictorial narratives of the past had consisted of a series of "highlights" which merged into one another, giving the impression of a continuous flow. With the arrival of film, an actually continuous narrative with images existing in time rather than space, became a possibility. Thus, for patrons as well as artists, the traditional form of pictorial narrative lost much of its appeal. The surprising thing is not so much the decline of this form of traditional visual narrative in the 20th century but the extent to which it has survived.

The most ambitious narrative scheme proposed after the First World War was part of the intended decoration of the Hall of Remembrance.[27] This project was the brainchild of the British War Memorials Committee and was along the lines of similar Canadian proposals. There was to be a great memorial gallery built in some appropriate space such as Hyde Park, and filled with specially commissioned works of art. The majority of these were to be paintings but they would not form a narrative sequence. However, around the lower walls of the gallery would be a series of friezes which would depict the story of the war. The exact way in which this would be done caused considerable argument in the Committee, some members favouring realistic narrative, others arguing for symbolic presentation.[28] This is perhaps why, although many of the paintings were commissioned, only two sculptors were appointed, to carry out preliminary studies. The choice was nonetheless fortunate, for Gilbert Ledward was asked to prepare a scheme for portraying the events from the invasion of Belgium to the Battle of the Marne (179), while Charles Sergeant Jagger was to work on the First Battle of Ypres. The intention was to make friezes 40 feet long and 7.5 feet high, but Ledward made only a small plaster model of his proposals and one large-scale plaster detail; only a single large plaster panel by Jagger appears to have been completed. A short time later the Hall of Remembrance scheme was abandoned and the many completed paintings, along with the plaster fragments, were placed in the collection of the Imperial War Museum.

Jagger's panel is in very low relief, with the figures shown in profile, and directly reflects his admitted admiration for the Assyrian reliefs he knew in the British Museum.[29] It depicts the Worcesters at Gheluvelt and by concentrating in this way on a detail and by showing violent action between opposing forces he provided a vivid allegorical highlight of the whole of the Battle of Ypres (180). However, we do not know what else Jagger had in mind if the project had gone on. We do have Ledward's model of his complete frieze, together with a detailed treatment of the Violation of Belgium, which shares the low relief and profile presentation of Jagger's work, but adopts a rather more symbolic approach, with Belgium represented by a female figure.

The sculptural studies for the Hall of Remembrance were carried out in 1918-19 and although the project was abandoned the experience was later put to good use by both artists — Ledward on the Guards Memorial and Jagger on the Artillery Memorial. Before turning to these we should look at other examples of continuous or semi-continuous narratives which occur on other national memorials. The Scottish National Memorial (see Chapter 8) has a frieze on the walls of its shrine chapel, representing all the different branches of the Scottish forces which took part in the war. It is not therefore a proper narrative, but rather a long procession, reminiscent again of the armies of Assyria or Rome on the march. The sculptors were the husband and wife team of Morris and Alice Meredith Williams and their achievement is undoubtedly impressive.[30]

Other national or state memorials have also included frieze panels, such

116

as the National War Memorial of Victoria in Melbourne.[31] Here the structure itself is interesting (see Chapter 8), but the interior bears a series of relief panels by the young Australian sculptor Lyndon Dadswell, showing the various branches and activities of Australian forces during the war. They include the Navy, both ashore and afloat, the Flying Corps, the Artillery, Engineers and Tunnellers, the Medical Corps, the Cavalry and the Infantry, fighting on foot, in tanks and in the trenches. The nine panels are carved in high relief, with none of the Assyrian symmetry seen in Jagger's work, but the result is curiously stiff and lacking in vitality. Once again, this is a series of highlights, not a true narrative, but it did represent the first attempt in Australian art to portray everyday scenes of war. Rather more accomplished are the two friezes representing the Eastern and Western Fronts in the Anzac Memorial in Sydney. They are the work of Rayner Hoff, who was Dadswell's teacher and the leading sculptor in Australia during the 1920s. He completed the panels for the Anzac Memorial in the 1930s, in a low relief profile style that suggests the influence of Jagger's Artillery Memorial in London.[32] His natural style was Art Deco, seen in the central sculpture, entitled Sacrifice, of the Sydney Memorial and on the Adelaide Memorial of 1927-31.

Perhaps the most unusual, interesting, and entertaining use of an extended narrative on a memorial is to be found on the Wagoners Monument at Sledmere in Yorkshire (181). This is placed alongside the equally unusual Eleanor Cross, with its monumental brasses on the base, and make Sledmere one of the most interesting memorial sites. The Wagoners Memorial is a small round structure, with a pointed roof supported on four colonnettes. The whole form is consciously medieval and the circular drum is decorated with three rings of narrative frieze. An inscription records that the monument was designed by Sir Mark Sykes (the well-known Member of Parliament, expert on the Middle East and head of the hereditary land-owning family of Sledmere) as a memorial to the Wagoners Reserve, a corps of over 1,000 drivers which he raised from his estates. The sculptor was Carlo Magnoni, who is not otherwise recorded but who reveals an unsophisticated and amusing style which is (either intentionally or unintentionally) an excellent medieval pastiche. The top register shows the Wagoners at work in the fields; the postman arrives with a letter and the recruit duly presents himself before Sir Mark Sykes to enrol. In the second register the new soldiers say farewell to loved ones and embark for France, in carefully depicted ships, and arrive before a fortified building. The bottom register shows scenes of fighting; in one a gallant Wagoner with fixed bayonet chases a fleeing Hun, while in another we see a most unusual depiction of the supposed German atrocities, including setting fire to a church and executing an innocent civilian. There is also an inscribed doggerel verse, in five stanzas, describing the exploits of the Wagoners.[33] For all its charm and *naïveté*, this is an example of narrative which has few equals among modern memorials and the parallels are, as they were intended to be, with the narrative art of the distant past.

The best-known and perhaps most successful First World War narrative was not an official commission either, and it was painted rather than sculpted. Stanley Spencer had already produced a number of war pictures when the suggestion for a memorial chapel was made by his friends Louis and Mary Behrend.[34] Mary's brother had died in Macedonia in 1919 from an illness contracted during the war and the chapel at Burghclere in Hampshire was to be a memorial to him. Spencer had also served in Macedonia and the idea of creating a proper memorial appealed to him greatly. He also saw it as an opportunity to achieve a major work for a private patron, just as Giotto had done in the Arena Chapel in Padua. The Behrends finally decided to go ahead with the project in 1924 and the building was entrusted to an architect friend, Lionel Pearson. Spencer first intended to paint frescoes on the walls, but abandoned this in favour of specially shaped canvasses. The side walls of the chapel were arcaded and for each arch he provided rectangular panels at the bottom, which he referred to as predellas, with a second scene above following the curve of the arch. Over the four-arch arcade, on each side, was a single large scene, while the whole of the eastern wall of the chapel was devoted to the Resurrection of the Soldiers at Kalinova, a village in Macedonia where Spencer had camped. The building was finished in May, 1927.

Spencer had enlisted in the Royal Army Medical Corps and worked at Beaufort Hospital in Bristol, where war casualties were cared for. In 1916 he went to Macedonia with the RAMC and transferred to the infantry in 1917. These various aspects of his service are recorded at Burghclere chapel, with the predellas devoted to a series of scenes from life at Beaufort Hospital; the arched panels also begin with two scenes at Beaufort Hospital, the arrival of a convoy of wounded soldiers and ablutions. Next is a scene of kit inspection at Tweseldown camp, where Spencer was in transit to Greece, followed by Stand To, with men emerging from their dugouts in Macedonia. The remaining arched panels are also scenes from the front, entitled Reveille, Filling water bottles, Map-reading, and Making a Fire-belt. Similarly, the two large scenes above are of Macedonia, one showing the camp at Karasuli, the other the river-bed at Todorova. Finally, the Resurrection on the east wall is also given a Macedonian setting. It is

118

unusual to find this subject as part of a traditional memorial but there is an interesting parallel in Arthur Walker's monument in Limehouse churchyard, where a large bronze figure of the Risen Christ stands on a podium which bears a bronze relief panel showing the bodies of soldiers lying in the trenches. This dates from 1921 and it is not impossible that Spencer knew of it.

There is clearly a form of narrative sequence in the Burghclere paintings, even though they do not present a coherent or continuous story. Spencer's cycle is the supreme example of what may be termed the anonymous highlight technique. The scenes themselves are ordinary and certainly do not depict heroes in the accepted sense. Yet the result is perhaps the most memorable narrative sequence to be inspired by the First World War. The Resurrection, with its ordinary soldiers emerging from a graveyard of simple crosses, is a culmination of previous experience and completes this most moving memorial. Spencer was a controversial figure in his day and his painting still has its detractors as well as its admirers, but even those who are resistant to the artist's idiosyncratic style must admit to its powerful impact.

Burghclere chapel forms an interesting contrast with the most ambitious narrative cycle to emerge from the Second World War. This is the Overlord Embroidery (182), also the result of a private commission, which provides a pictorial record of the Normandy invasion and was intended to commemorate the sacrifice of those who served.[35] Here we have an old-fashioned formula, complete with conquering hero figures such as Eisenhower and Montgomery. The intention was to create a 20th century equivalent of the Bayeux Tapestry, but the format, which was itself ancient 900 years ago, is difficult to apply in the context of a contemporary and historically accurate narrative. The result is that the embroidery, though a marvel of workmanship, seems to have no clear purpose. No one who wishes to know the story or see the action of the battle of Normandy would use this as a source; they would rather read books and look at films and photographs. The Bayeux Tapestry, on the other hand, was at the time of its production (and even more today) a prime source of information about the Battle of Hastings. This immediacy contributed directly to its evolution as a work of art. The Overlord Embroidery has no such record purpose and the result is that it appears an anachronism, with limited artistic value. It is, perhaps, the final proof that traditional pictorial narrative is no longer a current form for artists.

While attempts to produce continuous or semi-continuous war narratives have been comparatively uncommon in the present century, single-scene action highlights have been regularly used. The idea was first extensively developed on Boer War memorials, and the panels of the Plymouth Hoe Memorial have already been mentioned. The Royal Marines Memorial in London, by Adrian Jones, also cited above, has reliefs of action in South Africa and China, and similar action scenes occur on First World War memorials, such as Lindsay Clark's in Southwark or Arthur Walker's in Sevenoaks, both of which have panels depicting naval and aerial action, to complement the infantry soldier above.[36] Walker's scene of trench warfare on the Limehouse Memorial may also be mentioned. A particularly impressive panel was created by Gilbert Ledward for the back of the Guards Memorial, showing an 18-pounder field gun in action, in the presence of a representative of each of the five Guards divisions.[37] Sometimes a rather more elaborate representation was attempted, as on the Stourbridge Memorial (183) by John Cassidy, which consists of a tall cenotaph surmounted by an unusual kneeling Victory, and with relief panels on the base. These show the activities of the armed forces, including sailors loading a gun and the infantry on the march, executed in a low relief and profile style. More ambitious is Walter Marsden's memorial for St Anne's-on-the-Sea (184), which has a suppliant female figure at the top of a squared column, with a soldier and a mother and child at the base. On the rectangular plinth is a continuous relief depicting various scenes from the life of an infantryman, from leaving home to serving in the trenches, where the wounded and dead are carried away, while a group of gas victims stagger along in Indian file.

A similar frieze-like treatment is found on the Scottish American Memorial (185) in Edinburgh by Dr R. Tait Mackenzie, as a backdrop to the seated heroic figure mentioned above. Here the relief represents *The Spirit of 1914* and shows a crowd of recruits falling in behind a pipe band and setting off confidently to war. In fact this theme of recruitment and departure for war occurs a number of times and provided the subject for one of the most spectacular of British war memorials. Once again this is by Goscombe John and is his monument in Newcastle entitled *The Response 1914* (186 a & b), erected, as the inscription states, to commemorate the raising of four Batallions of the Northumberland Fusiliers by the Newcastle and Gateshead Chamber of Commerce in 1914. The memorial was the gift of Sir George and Lady Renwick and was erected in 1923. It consists of a procession of lifesize figures, representing volunteers joining up and going off to war. At the head of the procession are drummer boys leading uniformed soldiers, with a winged Victory blowing a horn above. Behind we see the ordinary men of the district, dressed in their working

120

clothes but for the most part carrying rifles. They are saying farewell to wives and children and setting forth with what seems unbounded enthusiasm.

The monument represents the patriotic confidence with which Britain entered the war and it is remarkable that Goscombe John was able to recapture this almost a decade later and with the full experience of the war behind him. John himself was born in 1860 and his allegiance to Victorian ideals is understandable; today we can see his vision as an accurate portrayal of the spirit of 1914, which makes its function as a memorial the more poignant. It is also a magnificent statement, displaying John's virtuosity to the full and deserves to be recognized as another key work in this genre.

If, at Newcastle and on other monuments, Goscombe John presents us with a traditional view of the soldier hero, a different and, to most modern eyes, more easily acceptable image was given by Charles Sargeant Jagger.[38] Jagger is today recognized as one of the major talents in 20th century British sculpture and he and Gilbert Ledward were the only leading artists of their generation to devote themselves largely to memorials. The Battle of Ypres relief was one of Jagger's earliest war commissions and in this he demonstrated both his interest in the sculptures of ancient Assyria and a tough, uncompromising attitude to his subject matter. On his earliest memorial, for Hoylake and West Kirby (172), he established his version of the soldier-hero: a tough, battle-scarred figure who hides neither the violence of his calling nor his nature. The Great Western Railway memorial on Paddington Station gives a similar impression, despite the fact that the soldier is seen reading a letter from home, while for Portsmouth (176) Jagger carved a soldier and a sailor, both manning machine guns with solid if weary determination. The heroism remains but the glamour has departed.

All these elements came together in the Royal Artillery Memorial at Hyde Park Corner (187 a-d). This once controversial monument is now generally recognized as his masterpiece and has been considered at length elsewhere. Here it is only necessary to pick out certain of its features. Firstly, it is important to remember that the memorial was a joint project, with the overall architectural design provided by Lionel Pearson, who was later to design the Burghclere Chapel. The fact that Pearson provided the backdrop for major works of art by Spencer and Jagger suggests that his talents deserve particular recognition. It was he who designed the podium of the Artillery Memorial, giving its basic shape and providing the base for the massive stone howitzer. Around this podium Jagger placed three standing bronze figures; an officer, a driver and a shell carrier. As the design developed a fourth recumbent figure of a dead soldier was added on the north side. The long sides of the podium were also decorated with reliefs, showing heavy artillery, horse artillery, trench howitzers and signallers. These reveal a further development of the relief style which Jagger had first used for his Hall of Remembrance panel of the Battle of Ypres. The dense nature of the composition, their powerfully expressive carving and their direct link with the traditions of antiquity make these panels memorable and impressive works. They are in fact much more striking than the more abbreviated and abstract reliefs of trench warfare which Jagger made for the Tank Memorial at Louverval in 1927 — one of his last memorial commissions.

It is the bronze figures on the Artillery Memorial which make the most lasting impact on most viewers. They are extraordinarily expressive, with the figure of the driver conveying a relaxed yet sinister power, the cape suggesting some monstruous bat-like creature. The shell-carrier exudes determination and force, while the officer, a captain, has a similar calm power. The inclusion of the fourth, dead figure was a daring stroke, and such recumbent effigies were normally placed on tall pedestals, as on Lutyens' Manchester Memorial. Here the dead man lies directly on the plinth, at the same height as the viewer, and the impact of the figure is immediate and shocking.

The Royal Artillery Memorial is perhaps the finest expression of the concept of everyman as hero and provides the best example in its reliefs of heroic narrative highlights. Yet the quality of Jagger's work should not lead us to ignore the many other effective ways of handling the subject, some of which have been indicated in this chapter. The establishment of the ordinary soldier as hero, and his portrayal in a wide range of forms, remains one of the major achievements of the memorial makers.

NOTES

1. See for example Kershaw, I., *The Hitler Myth: Image and Reality in the Third Reich*, Oxford, 1987, which discusses the non-visual ways in which the Führer's image was projected. Most recently, see the excellent study by Golomstock, I., *Totalitarian Art*, London, 1990.

2. There is a famous photograph of Mussolini on a visit to Libya in March 1937, on horseback and holding aloft the 'sword of Islam' — which had been made for him in Florence! It is reproduced in Mack Smith, D., *Mussolini*, London, 1981.

3. In addition to the statues of Ataturk there is his tomb at Ankara, which is a mausoleum on a truly imperial scale.

4. This is a somewhat uninspired piece and it is unfortunate that the commission did not go to Gilbert Ledward, who was very anxious to have it.

5. Curiously, both these are second versions. Lord Roberts is by Harry Bates and is a replica of an equestrian statue set up in Calcutta; similarly the figure of Foch is a replica

of Georges Malissard's figure on Mont Cassel, the Maréchal's headquarters during the First World War.

6. Piper, D., *The Companion Guide to London*, London, 1964, p 105.

7. On all these figures see Gleichen, *op. cit.*, for those prior to 1928 and Byron, *op. cit.*, for the later additions.

8. Both pictures are in the National Portrait Gallery, London, but were discussed in a leaflet published by the Scottish National Portrait Gallery entitled *Some Statesmen of the Great War*, n.d. (?1984).

9. Further discussed by Hichberger, J., *Images of the Army*, Manchester, 1987.

10. Cooper, J., *Animals in War*, London, 1983.

11. This quotation is inscribed in the sculptor's hand on the back of a photograph of the Heaton Moor memorial in the IWM Department of Photographs, War Memorials Collection.

12. Skipwith, P., 'Gilbert Ledward RA and the Guards' Division Memorial,' *Apollo*, January, 1988, pp 22-26.

13. See Shipley, R., *To Mark Our Place: A History of Canadian War Memorials*, Toronto, 1987, and *The Municipal Review of Canada: War Memorials Souvenir Number*, Vol XXI, no 11, Montreal, n.d. (?1926), p 85. A related work is the figure by Kathleen Scott for the Huntingdon Memorial, which is known as The Thinking Soldier; see Boorman, D., *At the Going Down of the Sun*, York, 1988, pp 85-6.

14. The Enniskillen memorial is by S. C. Gassin of Regent's Street, dated 1920. I have no other record of this sculptor, but I am grateful to Marriane Maguire of the Fermanagh Divisional Library for this information.

15. Designed by R. Wynn Owen. See above p 90.

16. The Royston Memorial is unsigned and I have been unable to discover the name of the artist. I am grateful for the assistance of Mr. J. Haslam, Librarian of Royston Public Library, who explained the reason for the presence of a crow on the memorial; it is a Royston crow, symbol of the town.

17. The apotheosis of this idea is seen on the First World War memorial in Newark, New Jersey. Entitled The Wars of America, it presents 42 figures and 2 horses, all sculpted in the round, and representing American soldiery from the Revolution onwards.

18. Bowyer, C., *Albert Ball VC*, London, 1977.

19. Reid, B., *Victorian Sculpture*, London, 1982, pp 349-50.

20. As, for example, on the panel entitled 'Towards Another World' on the Plymouth Hoe memorial. See above, p 86.

21. Coeur de Lion MacCarthy was based in Montreal and specialized in heroic figures, such as the Three Rivers and the Browne County memorial at Knowlton, Quebec, which shows Victory protecting a soldier. See Shipley, *op. cit.*, and *The Municipal Review* cited in note 13.

22. For the Fettes memorial see Kernot, C., *British Public School War Memorials*, London, 1927, pp 262-3.

23. *Gilbert Ledward R.A.*, Exhibition catalogue, The Fine Arts Society, London, 1988.

24. The development of the 'last cartridge' image deserves further study. It certainly occurs in some Victorian paintings of group heroism, such as Fripp's *Battle of Isandhlwana* but I do not know its origin or first occurrence.

25. See *The Battle of the Somme: Viewing guide* (Imperial War Museum), London, 1987.

26. It is now generally accepted that a few scenes, including the famous Over the Top sequence, in *The Battle of the Somme* film were 'faked' — that is re-staged shortly after the event.

27. Harries, M. & S. *The War Artists*, London, 1983, pp 91-4.

28. The issue of sculpture was discussed at length in a letter from Robert Ross to Arnold Bennett, dated 23 April, 1918, and preserved in the files of the IWM Department of Art. Both men were members of the War Memorials Committee and the letter gives a fascinating insight into their views.

29. Jagger's admiration for Assyrian sculpture is revealed in his writings, such as *Modelling and Sculpture in the Making*, published in *The Studio's* 'How To Do It' series in 1933.

30. Weaver, L., *The Scottish National War Memorial*, London, 1927.

31. Pratt, A., & Barnes, J., *The National War Memorial of Victoria*, Melbourne, 1934, and Sturgeon, G., *The Development of Australian Sculpture, 1788-1975*, London, 1978.

32. Elliott Napier, S., (ed) *The Book of the Anzac Memorial, New South Wales*, Sydney, 1934, and Sturgeon, *op. cit.*

33. These verses, written by Sir Mark Sykes, are no longer entirely legible, but were recorded in the *Yorkshire Herald* on 5 July, 1920. The first verse, written in a curious Anglo-Saxon dialect, reads as follows:

These steanes a noble tale do tell
Of what men did when war befell
And in that fourteen harvest tide
The call for lads went far and wide
To help to save the world from wrong
To shield the weak and bind the strong.

See Boddy, G., & Wilson R., *A History of the Wolds Wagoners Special Reserve*, Beverley, 1988.

34. Carline, R, *Stanley Spencer at War,* London, 1978.
35. The Overlord Embroidery is now housed in the D Day Museum in Portsmouth.
36. Walker also designed the unusual memorial in Limehouse churchyard, which is in the form of a bronze figure of the risen Christ, and has a relief of trench fighting on the pedestal. See Gleichen, *Open Air Statuary,* p 201.
37. See the article by Skipwith cited in note 12.
38. *Charles Sargeant Jagger: War and Peace Sculpture,* 1985.

CHAPTER 8

FORM AND FUNCTION

For this will stand in our Market-place
Who'll sell, who'll buy
(Will you or I
Lie each to each with the better grace)?
While looking into every busy whore's and huckster's face
As they drive their bargains, is the Face
Of God: and some young, piteous, murdered face.
Charlotte Mew, The Cenotaph, September, 1919

Although most traditional forms of memorial survived into the 20th century and were reused in various ways, the mound or tumulus is something of an exception. Mounds of burial and triumph on the battle-field are primarily associated with ancient civilizations, although they continued to be widely used by Scandinavian peoples in the Middle Ages. The mound on the battlefield at Waterloo may be the last of its kind and was an exceptional and rather eccentric monument for its period. Yet, although no true mounds have been raised (so far as I am aware) on the battlefields of the 20th century, the tradition survives in the selection of natural mounds, ridges, and places of eminence as the sites for contemporary memorials. In a number of instances the particular action commemorated took place on or around a hill, which became thereby the natural location for a commemorative monument. Particularly striking is the obelisk memorial to the 5th Australian Division which forms the backdrop to Buttes New British Cemetery, near Ypres (**188**), for it is set on top of Hill 60, a much contested artificial mound formed from the spoil of a nearby railway cutting. At the same time the nature of the Western front terrain, which is predominantly either flat or gently undulating, made it difficult to site all memorials in prominent positions. Nonetheless, a surprising number are raised above the plain, the clearest examples being the Canadian National Memorial at Vimy Ridge (**75**), the Australian National Memorial at Villers-Bretonneux, and the memorial to the missing of the Somme at Thiepval. The memorial to the missing of Newfoundland at

Beaumont Hamel (189) is one of the few to be set on a purpose-built high point, for the bronze caribou is placed on top of an artificial rock outcrop. It is by no means entirely fanciful to suggest that this tendency to build battlefield memorials on hills can be connected in a general way with the ancient tradition of mound-building on the field of victory. Equally, some regimental memorials are set in high places, notably that to the Sherwood Foresters which consists of a 63ft-high tower set on Crich Hill in Derbyshire. The tower contains a lamp, linking it also with the medieval tradition of *lanternes des morts* and with another lamp-bearing memorial tower at Beaconsfield.

Another ancient custom which has only survived in a transmuted fashion is the erection of trophies, made up in the first instance of piles of enemy arms recovered from the vanquished and later represented symbolically by stone monuments. In the present century captured equipment tends to go on display in museums rather than adorn the memorials of the victors and there has been a conscious reaction against such overtly triumphant forms of commemoration. It is, however, worth noting that there was a clear memorial intention behind the foundation of the Imperial War Museum in London,[1] and the Australian War Memorial in Canberra was conceived as a combination of museum and memorial building. A recent extension of the concept is the commemorative museum opened as part of the South African National Memorial at Delville Wood in 1987 (190). Here the building, which encloses the Cross of Consecration that formed an integral part of the original monument, is based on the design of the Castle of Good Hope, an eighteenth century fort in Cape Town.

Clearly such museums are very different in purpose from the ancient mounds of captured arms made as a monument to victory. In antiquity such mounds had been transferred into trophies in stone, but the nearest thing to a stone trophy on a contemporary monument is the great 9.2-inch howitzer which dominates the Artillery Memorial (187), and this was an allied not an enemy weapon. In the same way the display of actual weapons and equipment on the battlefields is rare and when it does occur it is seldom in the form of a trophy. Thus the bow section of HMS *Vindictive*, which was used to block the harbour entrance at Ostend in 1918, was preserved there as a memorial. Large items are often designated as memorials when they survive, such as the submarine HMS *Alliance* which is preserved at Gosport as a memorial to all submariners, or the Spitfire, Hurricane and Lancaster aircraft preserved by the RAF as the Battle of Britain Memorial Flight. Although such memorials clearly have a triumphal element, this is found to be acceptable today in a way that the memorial display of captured equipment would not be. There is a further commemorative aspect in the preservation of sunken ships as war graves. Normally, of course, such wrecks lie deep in the ocean and are so far beyond the limits of terrestrial commemoration. In a few cases, however, ships were sunk close to the shore and their wrecks have become memorials. This is particularly the case at Pearl Harbor, where several of the vessels destroyed in the Japanese attack remain close to the surface. The USS *Arizona* sank in a mere 20 feet of water, with the loss of over 1,000 men, and her hulk has been transformed into a memorial. A structure erected over the ship allows thousands of visitors to look down into the rusting hull, which has thereby become the antithesis of the memorial formed from a captured trophy of arms.

There is one entirely traditional use of captured arms that has survived into the present century, namely the making of memorials from the metal of enemy guns. This ancient custom had been frequently revived, for example on Napoleon's Austerlitz column in the Place Vendôme in Paris[2] and in London for Richard Westmacott's Achilles statue in Hyde Park, presented to Wellington by the women of England, and for the Guards Memorial to the Crimean War in Waterloo Place (17).[3] The Guards tradition was continued when Gilbert Ledward made his five figures for the First World War Guards Memorial (77), since these were cast from the metal of captured German guns.[4]

When we turn to the architectural forms that have developed primarily or exclusively for memorial purposes, the survival of antique elements is much more apparent. Triumphal gates can be traced back at least to Babylon and probably before, while the Romans had evolved the characteristic form of triumphal arch that had survived and been revived over the centuries. It was only to be expected that the triumphal arch would play a key role in the memorials to the Great War and indeed it was to become one of the most important forms used. Between 1889-92 a Soldiers' and Sailors' Memorial Arch, designed by J. H. Duncan, was erected in New York and after the Boer War arch memorials were erected by the Royal Engineers in Chatham and by the Royal Dublin Fusiliers in Dublin.[5] These were directly inspired by Roman examples, and similar classical pastiches were constructed after the First World War, especially in Italy. An example of the type is the memorial arch at Genoa, designed by Marcello Piacentini, and decorated with a series of Roman-style friezes by Arturo Dazzi, showing the various branches of the Italian forces in action.[6] However, in the hands of some of the leading British memorial architects the triumphal arch theme was developed in new and imaginative ways that would have astonished their classical predecessors.

A number of the major battlefield memorials adapted the triumphal arch motif, including three of the most impressive structures. The South African Memorial at Delville Wood (190) was designed by Sir Herbert Baker with a tall and somewhat incongruously domed arch as its centre-piece.[7] This is surmounted by bronze sculptures by Alfred Turner, mentioned above (see p. 101). From either side of the arch runs a semi-circular wall, terminating in pavilions at either end. These are based on the Summer House built by Simon Van der Stel on the slopes of Table Mountain and contain the Roll of Honour of South African dead commemorated on the memorial. Placed on the central axis of the arch and visible from it is the Cross of Sacrifice in Delville Wood Cemetery, while on the same axis but through the arch is the Cross of Consecration, now enclosed in the museum mentioned above.

Imposing and dominant in its setting, the Delville Wood memorial is nonetheless something of a hybrid. A much more successful interpretation of the arch idea was applied by Reginald Blomfield to the Menin Gate at Ypres (191 a and b).[8] Along with the Cenotaph in London, this is the most famous of all British war memorials and it had been immediately clear that a major monument must stand at Ypres, the centre of so much destructive action. Indeed, Churchill's initial idea was to preserve the whole of the ruined town as a memorial, but not unnaturally this suggestion found little favour with the remaining inhabitants. The site of Vauban's original Menin Gate, destroyed before the war, had been crossed by almost every allied soldier who fought in the battles of Ypres and so provided the ideal site for the sort of imperial memorial that was envisaged. The form of a triumphal arch was obviously suitable in terms of location, imperial purpose and Blomfield's own predilection for Roman monuments. The idea of inscribing the names of the dead on the walls of the arch had already emerged on the Arc de Triomphe, but at Ypres both the geography of the site and the sheer number of names to be recorded dictated an elongated or stretched arch form. This concept was influenced, Blomfield recorded in his *Memoirs,* by the fortifications at Nancy, dating from the 17th century and involving a brick tunnel over a road, lit from above by oculi. The memorial is in fact a combination of arch and memorial hall, although the depth of the monument is not immediately apparent. The facades are superficially highly classical, and one could be misled into thinking that this was nothing more than Roman revival architecture. Closer inspection reveals a number of unclassical devices, notably the fact that the side openings are rectangular not arched, the capitals are Doric rather than Corinthian, and the sculpture that surmounts the structure, including the massive lion by Sir William Reid Dick, is applied in a distinctly un-Roman fashion. The subtlety of the design of the monument becomes clear to the visitor who mounts the adjoining ramparts to view the lateral sides of the Gate, for here the arch aspect is entirely hidden, and it appears to be some form of memorial pavilion.

On entering the hall-like interior one is confronted with the apparently endless columns of the names of the missing. There are in fact 54,896 of them, but even so the available space proved to be woefully short and a further 34,888 had to be inscribed on the walls of Tyne Cot cemetery. It still comes as a shock to realize that these are only the names of the missing who have no known grave.

The Menin Gate is an extraordinary and moving monument to appalling carnage. Its effect is most powerful during the daily evening ceremony when the Last Post is played. Blomfield has succeeded in giving the triumphal arch a new and sombre meaning, which accepts the imperial overtones of the form but confines its triumphalism to death. He was not dissatisfied with his achievement and wrote later: *'With me the Menin Gate is perhaps the only building I have ever designed in which I do not want anything altered, and if I am ever remembered I hope it may be by the Menin Gate'.*[9] However, the most daring and imaginative use of the arch form was Lutyens' great memorial at Thiepval(192) on the Somme.[10] The initial ideas were developed in plans for a War Graves Commission memorial at St Quentin, but this was abandoned because the French were becoming concerned about the large number of proposed memorials. Instead a single major monument was planned for Thiepval and Lutyens transferred and further developed his arch scheme for this project. The structure, of brick and stone, was erected between 1927-32.

The Thiepval Memorial is most immediately striking on account of its size and its site, neither of which can be satisfactorily captured in photographs. Closer analysis reveals it as a highly complex concept, in which the essentially flat form of the traditional triumphal arch is extended into three dimensions, with pavilions of minor arches building up towards the main central arch. The result is more than just an impressive and original variation on the arch theme, but an assertion of three-dimensional values which suggests a link with the ancient concept of a burial mound. Lutyens, who was an avid student of his architectrual heritage, was certainly aware of the significance both of triumphal arches and of burial mounds and we can be sure that the various different strands of meaning that exist in the monument were all intended. The 73,357 names carved on the walls are again only those of the missing who have no known grave; the monument is also their tomb. Its complexity of form and meaning dervive from Lutyens' own understanding of the most ancient memorial forms and it is important for those who view it today to understand some of its designer's intent.

Lutyens used the triumphal arch form elsewhere in his memorial architecture, but never with such elaborate overtones. The Leicester Memorial presents a relatively simple version of the theme, and Lutyens also opted for a plain arch form for the All India War Memorial in Delhi, designed in 1920 but not completed until 1931.[11] Dramatically sited at the eastern end of the King's Way, it makes its effect by virtue of its simplicity of form. For the famous and dignified cemetery at Etaples (194), dating from 1924, he designed pavilions which combine the arch motif with his own Cenotaph form, intended to be visible (as they still are) to travellers on the Paris-Calais railway train. The carved flags seen on these, and on the Australian Memorial at Villers-Bretonneux (195) (also by Lutyens) were of the sort originally envisaged for the London Cenotaph. The effectiveness of the device is particularly apparent at Etaples.

It is perhaps inevitable that, in the light of Lutyens' supremely imaginative use of the arch form, some of the more traditional arches created for the Great War cemeteries, such as W. H. Cowlishaw's arch at Pozières, (196) appear less innovative.[12] There are nonetheless many confident and dignified arches adorning the Western front cemeteries, which succeed precisely because the traditional meaning of the form is retained.

Arches were normally reserved for monuments of a national character and consequently they are not commonly found in other categories of memorial. Lutyens' elegant arch memorial for Leicester (193) has already been mentioned; at Nottingham the City Engineer, T. Wallis Gordon, produced a triple arch flanked by a curved colonnade. An interesting variation is provided by the main entrance arch of Waterloo station,(198) which was designed as a memorial by the staff of the station under the supervision of the architect A. W. Szlumper.[13] The sculpture by Charles Whiffen includes a large seated Britannia at the apex of the arch and with symbolic groups representing 1914 and 1918 on either side. The year 1914 comprises a central seated figure grasping a sword and a torch, while those around her mourn a figure of a dead man. The year 1918 has a central figure of Peace, holding a palm and a small figure of Victory, with a group of three giving thanks. The grimacing figures seem overemotional, but nonetheless it is a pity that this impressive memorial is regularly ignored by the thousands of commuters who pass beneath it each day.

Arches are naturally uncommon for small or local memorials, although there is an unusual example in the Scottish Rugby Union Memorial at Murrayfield. A French exception is in the little village of Proyart on the Somme where a miniature triumphal arch, roughly half normal size, forms the frame for a standard figure of a *poilu*. As a contrast, the Argyllshire village of Kilmartin has a memorial (**197**) in the form of an arch into the churchyard, on which each stone bears the name of one of those killed in the war.

Another common architectural device, much used on the great battle-field memorials but also widely adapted for local and civic monuments, was the curved wall forming a precinct, as seen on the Delville Wood monument (**190**). Such precinct walls are also an antique device for marking an area as special or sacred. The particular origins of the idea can be found in Roman tomb enclosures, such as that of the Concordii at Regio Emilia or of the Statii at Aquilea[14] and similar precincts were also used in 19th century public monuments. One of the best known examples of the form is the Victor Emmanuel monument in Rome (1885-1911).[15] The application of the scheme to war memorials can be seen on the Boer War Monument to the Royal Artillery in London which is backed by a high curved wall, and similar enclosures are common on First World War memorials. They serve to give the central feature of the monument a frame and to make it separate from the immediate surroundings, providing a sort of sanctity. A good example is the Evesham Memorial by Harold Dicks, where a curving wall rises in steps to the centre and flanks the tall podium that provides the base for Henry Poole's figure of a soldier (**150**).[16] Another striking version is Blomfield's Belgian Memorial, presented to the British nation from the grateful people of Belgium and sited on London's Embankment. Here the curved precinct gives a grandeur to the central sculpture by Victor Rousseau which it certainly otherwise lacks. At Portsmouth the tall curved rear wall forms the backdrop to a central cenotaph (**176**), while the entrance to the precinct is guarded by Jagger's sculptures of machine-gunners.[17] The theme could also be varied considerably, as at Huddersfield where Sir Charles Nicholson created a curved open colonnade as the backdrop for a memorial cross. In other cases the precinct walls are straight, forming a rectangular enclosure (Great Yarmouth), or angled to produce triangular or polygonal forms (Pant, Glamorgan). However, the most dramatic use of the precinct idea was on the national battle-field memorials and cemeteries, largely because the area enclosed was so much greater than in a local civic memorial. The naval memorials at Chatham (**64**), Portsmouth and Plymouth are set against great open precincts, formed by curving walls that terminate in pavilions. These give the central obelisks a grandeur of setting which is appropriate to their national purpose. Undoubtedly the most impressive use of this form is in the Tyne Cot cemetery (199), designed by Sir Herbert Baker and J. R. Truelove, which is both the largest and the most beautiful of the War Graves Commission cemeteries on the Western Front. A great curved wall is pierced by two doorways, leading to circular enclosures, and with all the surfaces bearing the lists of the missing whose names would not fit onto the Menin Gate. Another impressive enclosure, this time rectangular, is Lutyens' Australian Memorial at Villers-Bretonneux (195). Here the idea of the precinct wall as a frame and backdrop remains, but in some instances the walls are continued to form an actual enclosure. This was the solution adopted by Sir Herbert Baker for the Indian Memorial at Neuve Chapelle (200), dating from 1927. The intention was to give the monument a distinctly Indian feeling, and the central feature was a column flanked by lions, modelled on those which the Emperor Asoka had set up and inscribed with his edicts, to mark his royal progress through the sub-continent.[18] Similarly, one half of the enclosing wall is a trelliswork in stone, recalling the sanctuary walls of Indian temples, and resulting in one of the most individual and expressive of the national memorials. In terms of scale, the culmination of the enclosure concept was probably provided by the German memorial at Hohenstein in East Prussia, commemorating the battle of Tannenberg, where a vast octagonal court was ringed with eight square fortress towers.[19] This was destroyed during the Second World War.

In antiquity a sacred precinct often enclosed an altar, and a number of memorials consciously adopt an altar-like form. Lutyens' Great War Stone clearly makes reference to the concept of a sacrificial altar, while a specifically Christian altar is evoked by a memorial such as that to the men of Hull at Oppy Wood,(90) with its central Crucifixion. The main civic memorial in Liverpool, designed by Lionel Budden, takes the form of an altar and has a bronze relief frieze on the front, sculpted by H. Tyson Smith, showing men and women bringing wreaths to a soldier's coffin, with the headstones of a war cemetery forming the background (201).

Arches and precincts comprise architectural forms which are essentially external for they provide no real interior space. Such internal space was created most simply by building a memorial hall, which could provide a covered area for contemplation. This is an essential feature of a true memorial hall, which, like a statue or a cross, has no other purpose than to memorialise the dead; it remains a 'useless' memorial. We have seen that by stretching the arch form Blomfield had created a memorial hall within the Menin Gate, but the idea was by no means a new one. It is related to both the temples and the tomb buildings of antiquity, but such specifically memorial structures really developed in the late 18th and 19th centuries, finding their full expression in buildings such as the Walhalla in Germany (53) (above p 65). The best known British example is the Scottish National Memorial in Edinburgh Castle (202), by Sir Robert Lorimer.[20] This was the outcome of an idea first put forward in 1917 and then developed by a committee, under the chairmanship of the Duke of Atholl. The memorial was opened on 14 July, 1927, by the Prince of Wales. Lorimer chose to adopt a late medieval Scottish Baronial style to harmonize with the rest of the castle, and designed a long hall with short wings at either end and a central entrance, giving the plan the form of the letter E. An apsidal chapel opens off the hall, opposite the entrance, and contains the Shrine, in the form of a steel casket which holds the Roll of Honour. The walls of the Shrine chapel carry the sculpted friezes discussed in Chapter 7.

The Shrine chapel gives the Scottish Memorial an ecclesiastical feeling, but its lateral plan reminds us that it is not a church. It stands, defiantly in a sense, simply as a memorial and is therefore as impractical as a statue or a triumphal arch. However, by providing an internal space it does perhaps encourage contemplation and reflection on what is being memorialized. Certainly, on the windy heights of Edinburgh Castle, an entirely external memorial would have considerably less chance of causing the visitor to stop and think. The interior space also allows for non-sculptural decoration, notably some good stained glass windows by Douglas Strachan.

The difficulty about memorial halls is nonetheless apparent in Edinburgh. An external monument can have no other purpose than to commemorate or record something, whereas people seem unconsciously to expect that a building will be intended for a particular use. It might be though that a church has an equally unspecific purpose, but this is not the case since the faithful are expected to appear at more or less regular intervals to attend services. A memorial hall has no such regular usage and this is perhaps why the form did not evolve on its own in antiquity but was always connected with a building of some other, normally religious, purpose.

Despite the problems of identity and purpose posed by the non-functional memorial hall, the type has proved popular in the 20th century, especially in the United States and in Commonwealth countries. Like triumphal arches, such halls have been found to be especially suited to national or state commemorative monuments, and only rarely were they constructed as civic memorials. There are, however, some good civic examples, such as the Birmingham Hall of Memory (**203 a - e**), which consists of an octagonal structure by S. N. Cooke and W. N. Twist, suggesting Palladian style. The four external bronze figures are by Albert Toft and represent the different branches of the armed services, while the interior displays reliefs by William Bloye, depicting the departure for war, life at the front, and the return home. Another good civic example is at Stockport,(204) where the classically styled structure adopts the plan of a lateral hall, not unlike the Scottish memorial, with a central apse which contains a sculpture of Britannia by Gilbert Ledward. The difficulty of knowing what to do with such structures has been solved at Stockport by turning it into an art gallery.

The most spectacular examples of memorial halls are to be found outside the British Isles. In Australia the type was to become popular and includes the Australian War Memorial in Canberra,[21] as well as a number of State memorials. The National War Memorial was designed by architects John Crust and Emil Sodersteen as a Hall of Memory in Byzantine style, with cloisters in which the names of the dead are inscribed on the walls. Attached to the Memorial and an integral part of it is a war museum. The Victoria State Memorial in Melbourne is also of interest since it is in the shape of a great stepped pyramid, designed by a local architect Philip Hudson, on the basis of reconstructions of the Mausoleum at Halicarnassus.[22] The Anzac Memorial in Sydney is built in what can best be described as a classical Art Deco style, by C. Bruce Dellit, then only thirty years old, and with sculpture by Rayner Hoff. The decision of the competition judges in favour of their design was unprecedented, since up to then Art Deco had been associated almost exclusively with the worlds of commerce and entertainment. The building has a tall circular hall with Hoff's *Sacrifice* as its focal point, achieving a remarkable dignity of expression. Classical prototypes were favoured in the United States, the most remarkable example being the Indiana War Memorial Plaza in Indianapolis. This consists of Cenotaph Square, Obelisk Square and the Memorial Shrine, the latter influenced by both the Mausoleum of Halicarnassus and temple plans. Roman rotunda design lies behind the extraordinarily lavish memorial for the Order of Elks in Chicago.[24]

Modern, or at least non-traditional, forms in memorial architecture are uncommon after the First World War, just as sculpture in a contemporary or avant-garde style is seldom seen. The reason is the same in both cases, namely a desire to keep to established forms that have stood the test of

134

time and to avoid anything that might appear as transitory fashion. Attempts to break with convention are on the whole tentative and seldom entirely successful, although the Sydney Memorial is an exception. The grim ossuary at Douaumont, on the Verdun battlefield, is a less happy experiment.[25] Designed by a trio of architects, Azema, Edrei and Hardy, this was begun in 1923 and opened in 1932. It consists of a long, low barrel-vaulted hall, with a tall central lantern tower that derives from a combination of obelisk and cross forms. The interior of the hall is flanked by niches containing sarcophagi, and the whole edifice surmounts huge vaults which are filled with the anonymous bones of unidentified soldiers killed in the battle. As a monument to the horror of modern war it cannot fail to impress, but its style, which derives from Art Nouveau and eschews straight lines, seems curiously inappropriate and reminiscent of melting ice-cream. Something of the Douaumont style seems to reappear in the vast underground basilica built beneath the huge cross at Valle de Los Caidos (**89**) (see p 93), the Spanish National Memorial created by General Franco. Here the form is largely dictated by the nature of the enterprise, which involved tunelling into solid rock, but the result has an unfortunate resemblance to an underground railway station. This, however, is not, strictly speaking, a memorial hall since it is also a consecrated church.

Blomfield had demonstrated on the Menin Gate that a memorial hall need not be an entirely enclosed structure and others took up what might be termed the open hall plan. This is the form which Lutyens adopted for his memorial to the Merchant Navy on Tower Hill in London (**205**), where the interior space is defined by open colonnades and pierced by arches at either end. The result is broadly classical in appearance, but, perhaps because Lutyens originally designed an alternative monument of arch form to stand on the Thames Embankment, it seems somewhat insignificant in its setting.[26] The sunken precinct added by Sir Edward Maufe after the Second World War helps to give some presence but this remains one of Lutyens' less successful solutions to the memorial problem. A related but perhaps more convincing handling of a similar idea is Charles Holden's design for Buttes New British Cemetery in Belgium, dating from 1925 (**206**).[27] Here two pavilions, of starkly simple design, are linked by a colonnaded passage, giving the impression of an open hallway. A variation on the theme is the rotunda, open to the sky, which was designed by H. Charlton Bradshaw as the memorial to the missing at Ploegsteert (**207**). This, with its two guardian lions by Ledward, makes a unique and attractive Western Front monument, directly recalling Roman prototypes such as Adamklissi (**44**) (above p 56). A similar idea is seen in Sir Ninian Comper's entirely open rotunda which forms the Welsh National Memorial in Cardiff (**208 a & b**), with sculptures in the centre representing soldiers holding victory wreaths. Gilbert Ledward produced a design for these in 1924, but the commission eventually went to Bertram Pegram.[28] The design of this monument suggests that Comper may have been familiar with the story of the building of Stonehenge, as related by Geoffrey of Monmouth (see above, p. 61).

Among the most interesting memorial hall projects have been those that were never built. Mention has already been made of the Hall of Remembrance proposed by the British War Memorials Committee as a form of picture and sculpture gallery, but is seems that no architect was ever appointed to this project and no building designs are known. However, Gilbert Ledward produced a series of drawings for a memorial hall in 1918, along with detailed plans for its decoration.[29] The building was to be of classical inspiration, based on a rotunda and set in an elevated position, allowing an impressive stairway. The sculptural decoration, for which he made a number of drawings, was to be a series of reliefs in which the fourteen Stations of the Cross would be paralleled with a similar number of wartime equivalents; thus Jesus carrying his Cross was matched by a soldier marching with his rifle, while the body of Jesus in the arms of the Virgin was compared with a scene of figures mourning over a soldier's corpse. Despite the detail of the proposals and the amount of time they must have involved, it is believed that Ledward had no particular site or commission in mind.

The feeling that memorials should have a directly useful purpose is one that can be traced from classical times. Initially, such useful memorials were conceived of in purely regligious terms and first temples and then churches were constructed as or converted to memorials. Such ideas enjoyed a particular vogue after the First World War, and chapels, transepts and aisles, along with fittings such as pulpits and windows, were added to existing churches. There are also entire church buildings and a good example is St George's Memorial Church in Ypres (**209**) designed by Blomfield following a suggestion from Lord Haig. This is a small and not especially distinguished building, with an aisleless nave and a generally Late Gothic feeling. It is of interest that virtually all the fittings in the church also have a memorial intent.

The idea of constructing churches and chapels as memorials was taken up particularly by the public schools, which were quick to seize the opportunity provided by the disaster of war to enlarge or modernize existing buildings.[30] One of the most ambitious and impressive of these projects

136

was the new chapel designed by Sir Giles Gilbert Scott for Charterhouse School (210), which was consecrated in 1927. This is a large Gothic hall church, the architectural origins of which are to be found in the cathedral of Albi in southern France, but which achieves a distinct stylistic character of its own. The same architect undertook the completion of the nave of Downside Abbey as a memorial for the School, this time in the elegant High Gothic style of the Ile de France. Another fine example is the chapel of Oundle School (211), designed in an English Gothic style by Sir Reginald Blomfield.

Probably the largest single memorial church project has already been mentioned. This was General Franco's memorial to the dead of both sides in the Spanish Civil War in the Valle de los Caidos and here, no doubt in conscious imitation of Philip II's nearby foundation of the Escorial, he also established a monastery.[32] Churches that were destroyed or damaged could also be preserved as memorials, and this sometimes occurred on battlefield sites, as at Bailleul near Ypres where the ruins of the parish church of St Amand form the town memorial. There was an imaginative scheme after the Second World War to preserve bombed London churches as war memorials and a pamphlet about the idea was published, with various distinguished contributors.[31] Although the proposals did not develop in London, the idea recurs in the ambitious project for the rebuilding of Coventry Cathedral, where Sir Basil Spence retained the bomb-scarred ruins of the old building, forming a vast narthex to his new church (212).[33] In Berlin the ruined stump of the Kaiser Wilhelm memorial church is one of the city's most familiar landmarks, while in Dresden the preserved rubble of the famous Frauenkirche, where Bach played the organ, provides a poignant memorial to the devastating air raids of February, 1945.

Cloisters provided another traditional form that could be converted to memorial use, especially in schools. There are examples at Sedburgh, Cheltenham, and Lancing schools, and at Winchester, which is among the best. Here the memorial cloister was designed by Sir Herbert Baker, based upon the round arches and paired columns of Romanesque examples such as Arles. Kipling was most impressed with the result and wrote to Baker, 'I think - indeed I know that so far as my own experience goes, it is incomparably the best of all the War Memorials.'[34] A number of the battlefield memorials to the missing developed a claustral theme, without creating a complete cloister. One of the best of these is J.R. Truelove's memorial at Le Touret,(213) where the long vaulted walkways and three-sided enclosures are clearly inspired by cloister design. Lutyens achieved a similar effect at Arras, where the Royal Flying Corps Memorial (214) is set within a cloistered area adjoining the main colonnade. A genuine cloister was built for the Runnymede Memorial to the Royal Air Force, constructed after the Second World War to the design of Edward Maufe (215).

Schools were also quick to see that memorial funds provided an opportunity to improve the general facilities and many entirely practical memorials were built. Among the wide variety of schemes adopted were new buildings as memorial libraries, classrooms, assembly halls, cricket pavilions, and, at Leeds Grammar School, a swimming pool. Trent College in Derby built a house for the Headmaster as a memorial. Comparatively few schools opted for the traditional form of memorial, but crosses and statues can be found, as at Fettes (see above p 112).

The topic of school memorials provides an illustration of the more general debate as to whether or not memorials should be useful. This was a hotly contested question after the First World War and again after the Second. It was known that there was a long tradition of treating religious foundations as memorials and that this had then extended to buildings of charitable purpose, such as hospitals and alms houses. A survey carried out by Mass Observation had revealed that the majority of people felt that a memorial should have some use and be of benefit to those who came after.[35] On the other hand most of the official bodies decided against the creation of practical memorials, on the grounds that their initial purpose would be soon forgotten. This argument is sustained by experience and many people who have used or benefited from institutions established with memorial funds are unaware of the source of their benefaction. Proponents of the practical memorial idea would argue that such ignorance is unimportant and the memorial character is preserved simply through existence of the charitable institution. It might equally be argued that since most people today ignore the stone memorials which surround them, it is better to provide a form of remembrance that will be of some practical value.

It is not a question now of deciding between these two views but it is important to be aware of the debate they engendered in both government and public circles. One solution to the dilemma was to give a memorial what might be termed a passive rather than an active use. A good example of this is a clock tower, which can stand as a prominent monument but also has a practical value. A number of memorial clock towers were built, typified by that at Stockwell which takes the form of a tall cenotaph, with a classical figure of mourning carrying a reversed torch on the front and a clock on each face.(216) Similar clock memorials were constructed in a number of other places, including Golders Green,(217) Reading University, Stockbridge near Sheffield and Llangefni on Anglesey, where a splendid Gothic tower was built in memory of George Rayner, who died in the Boer War. The clock tower in Edinburgh's Haymarket is a memorial to the players of Heart of Midlothian football club who died in the Great War. Another Scottish example, at Galashiels, plays tunes on its chimes. This variation on the clock tower theme was developed at Loughborough, where a tall carillon tower was erected (218).[36] Carillons proved more popular across the Atlantic (although one was proposed for the Victoria Tower in the Houses of Parliament),[37] and examples may be found in the imposing memorial tower of the Canadian Parliament building in Ottawa and in the Virginia State Memorial in Richmond.

However, there remained a strong feeling that genuinely practical and useful buildings were needed. Much favoured in villages up and down the land were functional memorial halls, which could form a meeting place and community centre. These have indeed served a valuable purpose and it is interesting to notice that in the village of Fownhope in Herefordshire the old hall, built in 1920 and which had become unserviceable, was taken down and a replacement built in 1987, preserving the original memorial intention. Hospitals were also much favoured, in a tradition that goes back at least to the charitable foundations of the Middle Ages. Like churches, such memorials could involve either an entirely new building or an addition to existing ones. A number of new Cottage Hospitals were established, while in urban areas existing hospitals were enlarged. Sometimes quite grand buildings were designed, as at Woolwich and Darlington. A particularly attractive example was the Deal and Walmer Memorial Hospital, designed in Neo-Georgian style in 1922 by Lionel Pearson and incorporating a memorial hall at the entrance.[38] This, like many of the other memorial hospitals, is still in use, but the rapid advances in medical technology have often demanded new, purpose-built structures and some of the First World War buildings have become redundant or been destroyed.

Memorials which enhance civic amenities have proved most durable. In a number of instances the memorial involved the erection of or extension to the local museum and art gallery; at Aberdeen the memorial consists of a lion sculpted by William MacMillan set against a curving colonnaded wall, the construction of which provided an extension for the Art Gallery. Kirkaldy's memorial consisted of a park in which the museum and art gallery were set. In such projects one can see the concept of the useful memorial merging with the hall of memory and such memorials at least have the virtue of providing the visitor with some form of uplifting experience. The same can no doubt be said of the building of a memorial Opera House in San Francisco, but a cultural purpose was not always envisaged. The iron-girder bridge memorial at Carlisle and the Rowing Tank at Chiswick, designed to teach the art of rowing under cover, were obviously of an entirely practical nature. Similarly practical were the railway engines used as memorials by at least three companies, *Remembrance* by the London, Brighton and South Coast Railway, *Patriot* by the London and North Western Railway, and *Valour* by the Great Central Railway.[39]

Outdoing all other practical schemes in ambition was the proposal for an Empire War Memorial.[40] This was put forward with great seriousness in 1918, accompanied by a detailed architectural scheme by Major Charles Fawley, and envisaged the wholesale rebuilding of the City of Westminster as a memorial. Introducing the idea *The Building News* commented, 'The scope of the Great War is so vast that any memorial scheme adequate thereto, however it may challenge criticism otherwise, can hardly do so by reason of its scale'. Fawley's plans were indeed on a grand scale. The central feature was the creation of a new Empire Avenue, stretching from the Embankment to Victoria Station and forming a highway 120 feet wide. This was to be constructed to the latest standards of town planning, to include pedestrian subways, shopping precincts and electric lighting. It would also incorporate three 300-foot-diameter circuses as the sites for trophies and memorial sculptures, commemorating the part played by the various nations of the Empire. The Avenue led to a new War Memorial Bridge, replacing Lambeth Bridge and decorated with bronze statues of wartime heroes, in the manner of the Charles Bridge in Prague. A huge memorial shrine in the shape of a Maltese Cross was planned to go alongside Westminster Abbey,[41] built in a suitable Gothic style, and there would be new buildings to house London University, together with a Shakespearian theatre, a memorial picture gallery, concert hall, and Hall of Nations. A new War Museum was also planned, incorporating the Banqueting Hall in Whitehall and running from there to Parliament Square, making it the largest museum in the country. Needless to say, none of this ever happened and the newly founded Imperial War Museum was to end up in the former Bedlam lunatic asylum.[42]

After the Second World War there was a real opportunity to rebuild the bomb-scarred inner cities. London was the most obvious and immediate candidate and, as early as 1943, plans were being developed to renew the City once the war was over. A comprehensive scheme was drawn up by William Holford and Charles Holden, including a processional way from

140

the river to the south transept of St Paul's. W. H. Ansell produced a similar scheme, involving a series of memorial gardens and courtyards, but also preserving the view of the south side of the Cathedral that had been opened up by the bombing.[43] Unfortunately these and other ideas failed and the result was the piecemeal development of the area.

If such schemes of civic improvement on a large scale were doomed to fail, some other visionary ideas have been no more successful. A proposal for a United Nations University, probably to be sited on the Isle of Wight, was put forward by J. Schreiner in 1945.[44] This was not an isolated suggestion, for a similar idea was suggested in a letter to *The Times* in that year, signed by a host of literary and artistic figures, including Arnold Bax, Augustus John, Esmond Knight and Laurence Olivier. However, nothing was to come of it. A more immediately practical proposal was the creation of a fund to be used for the preservation of aspects of British countryside and this resulted in the establishment of the Land Fund in 1945. However, this excellent intention never developed much vitality and the fund was robbed by successive governments for a variety of purposes. The creation of the National Heritage Memorial Fund in 1980 as the successor to the Land Fund revived the original idea and since its inception the NHMF has been instrumental in saving or preserving a whole range of items from works of art to the nesting sites of bats.[45] Here indeed is a practical memorial which not only works but provides real benefit to society and which should, providing its funds are maintained, fulfil its purpose and memorial character into the future.

It is appropriate to close this study by reference to another 'useless' memorial; indeed, the various tombs of Unknown Soldiers which were established in a number of countries after the First World War are distinguished by the fact that they hardly constitute physical memorials at all, yet for many they provide the most moving of all tributes to the human cost of war. The idea originated in Britain, probably at the suggestion of the Reverend David Railton, who had served as a chaplain in Flanders, and who proposed to the Dean of Westminster early in 1920 that an unknown soldier should be buried in the Abbey.[46] The suggestion was adopted and it was agreed that the burial should take place on Armistice Day, 1920, when the permanent structure of Lutyens' Cenotaph was also to be dedicated. Great care was taken that the identity of the soldier should never be known, and the body was selected by Brigadier-General L. J. Wyatt, of the Imperial War Graves Commission, from four recovered from different sectors of the Front. This was done at midnight on 8-9 November and the chosen corpse was immediately sealed in a coffin and taken to London.

On the morning of 11 November the coffin was taken in procession from Victoria Station, where it had lain overnight, to the Abbey, by way of the Cenotaph, and there laid to rest in a solemn ceremony.

The very simplicity of the tomb, which consists of a black marble slab inscribed 'An Unknown British Warrior', makes it intensely effective. It is in many ways the complete antithesis of the Menin Gate or the Thiepval Memorial but serves its purpose no less powerfully. Other Unknown Warriors were also buried on the same day in other countries, in equally prominent places. In France the tomb was placed under the Arc de Triomphe and here, and elsewhere, it is accompanied by an eternal flame. The association of this simple monument with the most grandiose of triumphal arches also makes a point about the commemoration and memorialization of war. Vast size and imposing position are not of themselves a requirement for a good memorial. Ultimately, war memorials are about the deaths of individuals, whether a single unknown tomb or a seemingly endless list of names carved on a wall. Those who designed and built the thousands of memorials erected in this century faced a daunting task; today we can do more than simply respect their efforts, for we can look with an open mind and admire the extent of their success. Let us hope that no future generation of artists is ever called upon to try and match their achievement.

NOTES

1 See ffoulkes, C, Arms and the Tower, London, 1939, especially Chapter V.
2 Saint Simon, F de, La Place Vendôme, Paris, 1983.
3 See Gleichen, E, London's Open Air Statuary, London, 1928, p.19. Achilles was cast from twelve 24-pounder French guns taken at Vittoria, Salamanca, Toulouse and Waterloo. The guns at the back of the Crimean Memorial are actual Russian examples taken at Sevastopol, making this closer than most other examples to the form of an antique trophy. Nonetheless, Gleichen did not like it, commenting 'It looks best in a fog.'
4 Gleichen, op.cit., p.46.
5 See Gildea, J, For Remembrance.
6 L'Arco della Vittoria ai Genovesi caduti in guerra 1915-18, Genoa, 1931.
7 See The African World, Special Souvenir Edition, South African National War Memorial, Delville Wood, 16 October, 1926.
8 This memorial has been often published but seldom discussed. For the basic information see Longworth, P, The Unending Vigil, 1967.
9 Memoirs of an Architect, London, 1932, p.189.
10 Catalogue of the Lutyens exhibition, Arts Council, 1981.
11 See the Lutyens exhibition catalogue and bibliography cited there.
12 Stamp, G, Silent Cities, London 1977.
13 See Cherry, B, and Pevsner, N, London 2: South (The Buildings of England), London, 1983, p.362: 'the only 20th century station building in London with architectural ambitions'. Also Gleichen, op.cit., p.206.
14 Toynbee, J, Death and Burial in the Roman World, London, 1971, pp.80-1.
15 This monument was begun by Guiseppi Sacconi in 1885 and completed in 1911.
16 Henry Poole (1873-1928) was the sculptor who worked with Sir Robert Lorimer on the naval memorials at Chatham, Portsmouth and Plymouth. See Johnson, J, and Greutzner, A, The Dictionary of British Artists, 1880-1940, London, 1980.

17 See Compton, A, (ed) *Charles Sargeant Jagger*, London, 1985.

18 Longworth, *op.cit.*

19 Curl, J, *A Celebration of Death*, London, 1980, p.333.

20 *The Scottish National War Memorial. Official Guide.* Edinburgh, n.d.

21 See Stanley, P, *A Guide to the Australian War Memorials*, Sydney, 1986.

22 Pratt, A, & Barnes, J, *The National War Memorial of Victoria*, Melbourne, 1934.

23 Elliott Napier, S, *The Book of the Anzac Memorial*, Sydney, 1934.

24 Harper, F, *The Elks National Memorial* (The Grand Lodge of the Benevolent and Protective Order of Elks), Chicago, 1957.

25 For Douaumont see Curl, *op.cit.*, pp.329-30.

26 A drawing for Lutyens' original design is reproduced in The Fine Arts Society, Spring 1989 Catalogue, No. 52.

27 Karol, E, & Allibone, F, *Charles Holden, Architect 1875-1960*, London, 1988 (exhibition catalogue).

28 See the catalogue of the Gilbert Ledward exhibition, Fine Arts Society, London, 1988, No. 24.

29 Ledward Catalogue, nos. 14-21.

30 Kernot, C, *British Public School War Memorials*, London, 1927.

31 Casson, H, (ed) *Bombed Churches as War Memorials*, London, 1945.

32 *Santa Cruz del Valle de los Caidos*, Madrid, 1974 (official guide).

33 *Coventry Cathedral after the Flames*, Coventry, 1987.

34 Quoted by Herbert Baker in his autobiography, *Architecture and Personalities*, London, 1944, p.97.

35 See Whittick, A, *War Memorials*, London, 1946.

36 Bray, M, *Bells of Memory, A History of the Loughborough Carillon*, Loughborough, 1981.

37 See *The Times*, 21 April, 1920.

38 See the catalogue of the Holden exhibition cited in note 26.

39 I am most grateful to Mr R. J. A. Tinker for this information. There is a model of *Remembrance* and the name-plate of *Valour* in the National Railway Museum in York.

40 See *The Building News and Engineering Journal*, 30 October, 1918.

41 It is interesting to note that Sir Herbert Baker also drew up plans for a memorial adjacent to Westminster Abbey, in the form of a circular cloister. This scheme had perhaps more chance of success and Baker even revived the proposals during the Second World War. See *Architecture and Personalities*, pp 103-6.

42 Charles Holden also made a sketch for a new War Museum, in a very different severe style. See the Holden exhibition catalogue, p.21.

43 Whittick, *op.cit.*

44 Whittick, *op.cit.*

45 The National Heritage Memorial Fund, Annual Reports 1980 to present.

46 Carpenter, E, (ed) *A House of Kings*, London, 1966, p.370.

THE PLATES

All photographs are by the author,
unless otherwise stated.

1 The obelisks of Tuthmosis III and of Constantine Porphryogenitus in the Hippodrome of Constantinople, modern Istanbul.

2 Left: Cleopatra's Needle on the Victoria Embankment, London.
3 Right: The obelisk erected at St. George's Circus by Brass Crosby in 1771, now in the Geraldine Mary Harmsworth Park, London.

4 Left: Tomb of the Harpies, Xanthos (southern Turkey).
5 Right: Honorific column and tower tombs at Palmyra, Syria.

6 Trajan's Column, Rome (Archivi Alinari).

7 Left: Column in the Place Vendôme, Paris, erected in 1806 to commemorate the Battle of Austerlitz and based on Trajan's Column.

8 Right: Column of Constantine, marking the foundation of Constantinople
as capital of the Roman Empire on 11 May, 330, now in Istanbul.

9 Left: Colonne de la Grande Armée, Boulogne, 1804-5.
10 Right: Nelson's Column, London.

11 Left: Detail of the Victory Column in Berlin, showing the decoration of captured cannon.
12 Right: Column memorial to the old boys of Westminster School who died
in the Crimean War, by Sir Giles Gilbert Scott (1861).

13 a & b The Narmer Palette, (Egyptian Museum, Cairo).

14 Battle of the Gods and the Giants from the Great Altar of Pergamon in the Pergamon Museum, Berlin.

15 Left: The Winged Victory of Samothrace, (Louvre Museum).
16 Right: Victory on her column in Berlin, by Friedrich Drake, 1873.

17 Victory on the Guards Crimean Memorial by John Bell. The figures are
made from the metal of captured guns.

18 Cross marking the death of King John of Bohemia on the battlefield of Crécy, 1346.

19 John Hassall, *Vision of St. George in the Trenches* (Imperial War Museum).

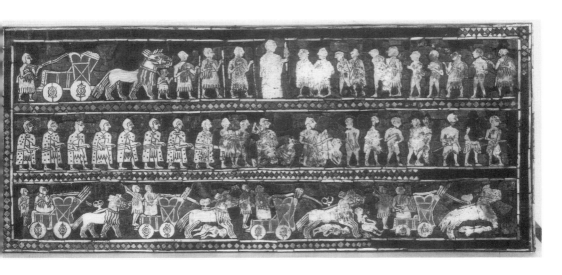

20 a & b The 'Standard' from the Royal Cemetery at Ur. (British Museum).

21 a & b Stele of the Vultures (Louvre
Museum).

22 Stele of Naramsin. (Louvre
Museum).

23 Relief from Abu Simbel showing the Battle of Qadesh.

 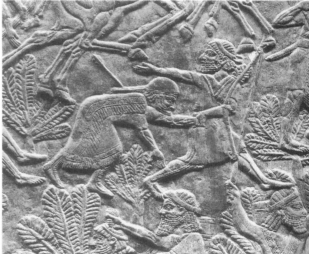

24 Left: Relief of the Siege of Lachish, from the palace at Nineveh. (British Museum).

25 Right: Relief of the battle of Ulai, from the palace at Nineveh. (British Museum).

26 The Siege of Verona, as depicted on the Arch of Constantine, Rome (Archivi Alinari).

27 The Bayeux Tapestry, coloured engraving by Charles Stothard (Society of Antiquaries of London).

28 a & b The Hall of Battles in the Escorial.

29 Column in the Place Vendôme, Paris. Detail of reliefs.
30 Head of Alexander the Great in the Archaeological Museum, Istanbul.

31 Statue of the Emperor Augustus in the Museo Vaticano. (Archivi Alinari).

32 Bronze statue of Marcus Aurelius on horseback, Rome. (Archivi Alinari).

33 Paolo Uccello, *Sir John Hawkwood*, Florence Cathedral. (Archivi Alinari).

34 Left: Donatello, *Erasmo da Narni* or *Gattamelata, Padua. (Archivi Alinari).*

35 Right: Verrocchio, *B. Colleoni,* Venice (Archivi Alinari).

36 A. Schluter, *Frederick William of Brandenburg, the Great Elector,* Charlottenburg Palace, Berlin.

37 Uccello, *The Rout of San Romano* (National Gallery, London).

38 *Dying Gaul*, National Museum, Naples (Archivi Alinari).

39 B. West, *The Death of General Wolfe*. (National Gallery of Canada).

40 J. Wollen, *The Last Stand at Gandamak* (Trustees of the Essex Regiment Association).

41 J. Wootton, *George II at Dettingen* (National Army Museum).

42 Burial mound of the Commagene queens, south-eastern Turkey.

43 Silbury Hill, Wiltshire.

44 Trophy monument, Adamklissi, Romania.

45 Left: The Arch of Titus, Rome. (Archivi Alinari).
46 Right: The façade of Amiens cathedral.

47 Left: Triumphal Arch of Emperor Charles V, Palermo.
48 Right: The Arc de Triomphe, Paris.

49 The Arc du Carrousel, Paris.

50 The Great Mosque of Sultan Beyazit, Bursa, Turkey.

51 San Juan de los Reyes, Toledo.

52 The Escorial.

53 a & b The Walhalla, Regensburg (Bildarchiv Foto Marburg).

54 The Great War Stone (Lutyens) and the Cross of Sacrifice (Blomfield) in Tyne Cot Cemetery.

55 The Cenotaph in Whitehall (Lutyens).

56 Left: The 37th Division at Monchy-le-Preux by Feodora Gleichen.
57 Right: The 24th Division in Battersea Park, London, by Eric Kennington.

58 The Vietnam Wall, Washington D.C.

59 a & b Boer War memorial, Plymouth Hoe.

60 Left: Havrincourt, 62nd West Yorkshire Division Memorial.
61 Right: Monolithic obelisk at Leighton Buzzard.

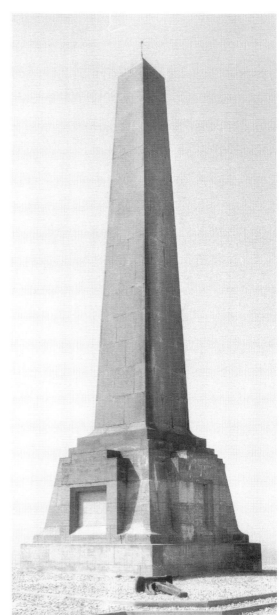

62 Left: Australian memorial at Lone Pine, Gallipoli.
63 Right: Dover Patrol memorial at Cap Blanc Nez.

64 Royal Naval memorial at Chatham.

65 Left: Royal Naval memorial at Plymouth; added Second World War sculpture by Sir Charles Wheeler.

66 Right: Lancashire Fusiliers Memorial at Bury by Lutyens.

67 Left: Hampstead Memorial by Blomfield.
68 a & b Right: Harrogate Memorial by Gilbert Ledward.

IN MEMORY OF THESE
HABITANTS AND INDWELLERS
OF THE PARISH OF CHIRK
WHO GAVE UP THEIR LIVES
FOR THE CAUSE OF THEIR COUNTRY
DURING THE WAR OF 1914-1919
THIS MONUMENT WAS ESTABLI-
SHED BY THEIR FELLOWS
OF THE PARISH
IN·RIGHTEOUSNESS·

69 Left: Chirk Memorial by Eric Gill.
70 Right: Yarmouth Memorial.

71 Euston Memorial by R. Wynne Owen.

72 Left: Wallington Memorial.
73 Right: Ripon Memorial by F. J. Wilcoxson.

74 Canadian Memorial at St. Julien by
   F. C. Clemesha.

75 a & b Canadian Memorial on Vimy Ridge by Walter Allward.

76 Marine Engineers Memorial, Pier Head, Liverpool, by Goscombe John.

77 a & b Guards' Division Memorial in St. James's Park, London, by Gilbert Ledward.

78 Left: Demarcation Stone on the Western Front.
79 Right: The Cyclists Memorial at Meriden.

80 Left: Indian Memorial at Neuve-Chapelle by Baker.
81 Right: Martyrs Memorial, Damascus.

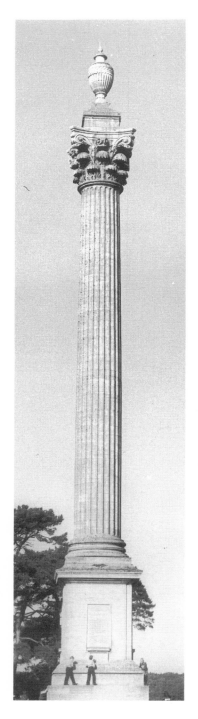

82 Left: The Elveden Column by C. Young.
83 Centre: Column Memorial at Hungerford.
84 Above Right: Wittersham Memorial by Sir George Frampton.
85 Below Right: Lynford Memorial.

86 Top: Felixstowe Memorial.
87 Left: Boer War Memorial in Newcastle by T. Eyre Macklin.
88 Right: Base of Memorial mast, Sheffield.

89 Spanish National Memorial at Valle de los Caidos.

90 Left: Memorial to the Men of Hull at Oppy Wood by C. D. Allderidge.
91 Right: Memorial at All Saints Church, Bryanston Place, London.

92 Left: Lunga, Argyllshire, to members of the MacDougall family.
93 Right: Seaforth Highlanders at Fampoux.

94 Left: Canterbury, Civic Memorial.
95 Centre: Redbridge Memorial by Newbury Trent.
96 Right: Builth Wells Memorial.

97 Left: Derby Memorial by Arthur Walker.
98 Centre: Nurse Cavell's Memorial, London, by Sir George Frampton (detail).
99 Right: Bolton Memorial, sculpture by Walter Marsden.

100 Left: Sledmere, Eleanor Cross, 1899.
101 Right: Sledmere, brasses to men of the 5th Yorkshire Regiment.

102 Manchester Memorial by Lutyens.

103 Left: R.A.F. Memorial, London, by Blomfield.
104 Right: Preston Memorial by Sir Giles Gilbert Scott, sculpture by Henry
Pegram.

105 a & b Left: Croydon Memorial, with sculpture by P. R. Montford.
106 Right: Memorial to children killed by a German bomb in Poplar in 1917,
     by A. R. Adams.

107 Llandaff Memorial by Sir William Goscombe John.

108 Left: *Courage* on the Luton Memorial, by Sir William Thornycroft.
109 Centre: *Peace* on the Leeds Memorial by Henry Fehr.
110 Right: *La Deliverance* by Emile Guillaume in Finchley.

111 Left: The 34th Division Memorial on Mont Noir by R. I. Emerson.
112 Right: Boer War Memorial to the Islingtonians by Bertram Mackennal.

113 Left: Wetherby Memorial by L. F. Roslyn.
114 Centre: Colchester Memorial by Henry Fehr.
115 Right: Boer War Memorial in Norwich by George Wade.
116 Below: Weston-super-Mare Memorial.

117 Left: Greenock Memorial by Alexander Proudfoot.
118 Right: Stourbridge Memorial by John Cassidy.

119 a-c Exeter Memorial by John Angel.

120 Left: Memorial on Dover Marine Station by W. C. H. King.
121 Right: Cavalry Memorial in Hyde Park, London, by Adrian Jones.

122 Left: Memorial to the Men of Marylebone by Charles Hartwell.
123 Right: Northumberland Fusiliers Memorial in Newcastle by John Reid.

124 Left: Maidstone Memorial by Sir George Frampton.
125 Right: Pearl Assurance Company Memorial, London, by Sir George Frampton.

126 Left: Colchester Memorial by Henry Fehr.
127 Right: Trumpington Memorial by Eric Gill.

128 Left: St. Michael's, Cornhill, London, by Richard Goulden.
129 Right: Marines' Memorial, Plymouth Hoe, by W. G. Storr-Barber.

130 Left: Limehouse Memorial by Arthur Walker.

131 Centre: Walworth Memorial.

132 Right: Humanity breaking the Sword of War, Skipton, by John Cassidy.

133 Left: Machine Gun Corps Memorial, Hyde Park Corner, by Derwent Wood.

134 Centre: Reigate Memorial by Richard Goulden.

135 Right: Paisley Memorial by Mrs. Meredith Williams.

136 Portuguese Memorial at La Couture by F. Lopes.

137 Left: Earl Haig by Alfred Hardiman.
138 Right: Lord Kitchener by John Tweed.

139 Left: Lord Portal by Oscar Nemon.
140 Right: General Gordon by Sir William Thornycroft.

141 *Some General Officers of the Great War* by J. S. Sargent
  (National Portrait Gallery).

142 *Some Politicians of the Great War* by James Guthrie
  (National Portrait Gallery).

143 Imperial Camel Corps Memorial by Cecil Brown.

144 Left: The 58th London Division Memorial at Chipilly-sur-Somme by F. Gauquie.

145 Above Right: Heaton Moor Memorial, Greater Manchester, by John Cassidy.

146 Below Right: London Memorial by Alfred Drury.

147 Left: Sevenoaks Memorial by Arthur Walker.
148 Centre: Inverary Memorial by Kellock Brown.
149 Right: Abergavenny Memorial by Gilbert Ledward.

150 Left: Evesham Memorial by Harold Dicks.
151 Centre: Rifle Brigade Memorial, London, by John Tweed.
152 Right: Scottish-American Memorial in Edinburgh by R. Tait Mackenzie.

153 Left: Cambridge City Memorial by R. Tait Mackenzie.
154 Right: Boer War Memorial at Bury by Sir George Frampton.

155 Left: Twickenham Memorial by Mortimer Brown.
156 Centre: Boer War Memorial, Ipswich, by Albert Toft.
157 Right: Streatham Memorial by Albert Toft.

158 Left: Deptford Memorial.
159 Right: Wrexham Memorial by Goscombe John.

160 Left: Royston Memorial.
161 Right: Warlingham Memorial by J. E. Taylerson.

162 Left: Albert Ball V.C. in Nottingham by Henry Poole.
163 Right: Edith Cavell in Norwich by Pegram.

164 Left: Stalybridge Memorial by Ferdinand Blundstone.
165 Right: Prudential Assurance Company Memorial, London, by Blundstone.

166 French Memorial at Ypres by A. Debeule.

167 **Left:** Royal Fusiliers Memorial, Holborn, by Albert Toft.
168 **Centre:** 41st Division Memorial, Flers, by Albert Toft.
169 **Right:** Southwark Memorial by Philip Lindsay Clark.

170 Left: Bridgnorth Memorial by Adrian Jones.
171 Right: Tonbridge Wells Memorial by S. N. Babb.

172 Left: Hoylake Memorial by C. S. Jagger.
173 Right: St. Anne's-on-the-Sea Memorial by Walter Marsden.

174 Marines Boer War Memorial, London, by Adrian Jones.

175 Boer War Memorial on North Bridge, Edinburgh, by Birnie Rhind.

176 a & b Portsmouth Civic Memorial, with sculpture by C. S. Jagger.

177 The Cameronians Memorial in Glasgow by Philip Lindsay Clark.

THESE ARE NOT DEAD
SUCH SPIRITS NEVER DIE
+   +
ON THE ADJOINING PANELS ARE INSCRIBED
THE NAMES OF THOSE
FROM THE OFFICES AND WORKS OF
LEVER BROTHERS LIMITED
AND THEIR ASSOCIATED COMPANIES OVERSEAS
AND ALSO FROM PORT SUNLIGHT
WHO LAID DOWN THEIR LIVES IN THE GREAT WAR
1914 +

ACTON A.C.
ADAMS A.M. 'LCABAR'
ALDERWOOD A,
ALLMAN I.
ALLWORK W.J.
ANSELL C.E.
ANSELL H.
ANYON J.
ASPINALL A.
ATKINSON F.J.
ATKINSON W.B.
BAILEY S.J.
BAKER C.A.
BAKER F.
BANNON R.D.
BANNON M. "M.M"
BARBER W.
BARCLAY E.
BARTLEY J.
BARTLEY G.
BARTLEY J.M.
BATHER J.R.
BAXTER J.C.

BENSON A.
BENSON G.
BERGOT
BIRCH T.W.
BLACOE H.
BLAKEWAY J.N.
BLAKEWAY J.N.
BLUNDELL G.W.
BOLTON G.W.
BOTHAM T.
BOTTCHER A.
BOWEN W.
BOWLER G.
BOYLAN J.J.
BRADD
BRANCH W.A
BRAYNE W.
BRESLIN E.
BRIGGS E.W.
BRINDLEY G.
BROCKBANK W.
BROOKE F.J.
BROOMSGROVE A.J.

178 a-c Port Sunlight Memorial by Goscombe John.

179 Battle of the Marne Memorial by Gilbert Ledward (Imperial War Museum).

180 Left: First Battle of Ypres Memorial by C. S. Jagger (Imperial War Museum).
181 Right: Sledmere, the Wagoners Memorial.

182 The Overlord Embroidery, Panel 24 showing British and Canadian Divisions (D Day Museum, Portsmouth).

183 Stourbridge Memorial by John Cassidy.

184 St. Anne's-on-the-Sea Memorial by Walter Marsden.

185 Scottish-American Memorial, Edinburgh, R. Tait Mackenzie.

186 a & b The Response by Goscombe John in Newcastle.

187 a-d The Artillery Memorial by C. S. Jagger.

188 Australian 5th Division Memorial, Buttes New British Cemetery.

189 Newfoundland Memorial, Beaumont Hamel.

190 a & b South African Memorial, Delville Wood, by Herbert Baker.

191 a & b The Menin Gate at Ypres by Blomfield.

192 The Thiepval Memorial to the Missing by Lutyens.

193 Leicester Memorial by Lutyens.

194 Etaples Cemetery by Lutyens.

195 Australian Memorial at Villers-Bretonneaux by Lutyens.

196 Pozières cemetery by W. H. Cowlishaw.

197 Kilmartin Memorial, Argyllshire.

198 a & b Waterloo Station entrance.

199 Tyne Cot Cemetery by Herbert Baker and J. R. Truelove.

200 Indian Memorial at Neuve Chapelle by Herbert Baker.

201 Liverpool Civic Memorial by Lionel Budden and H. Tyson Smith.

202 Scottish National Memorial by Lorimer (by courtesy of the Trustees of the Scottish War Memorial).

203 a-e Hall of Remembrance, Birmingham, by S. N. Cooke and W. N. Twist, the sculpture by Albert Toft.

204 Hall of Remembrance, Stockport.

205 Merchant Navy Memorial, Tower Hill, by Lutyens.

206 Buttes New British Cemetery by Charles Holden.

207 Ploegsteert Cemetery by Charles Bradshaw.

208 a & b Welsh National Memorial, Cardiff, by Sir Ninian Comper, the sculpture by Bertram Pegram.

209 The English Church, Ypres, by Blomfield.

210 Charterhouse School Chapel by Sir Giles Gilbert Scott.

211 Memorial Chapel at Oundle School, by Blomfield.

212 Kaiser Wilhelm Memorial Church, Berlin.

213 Le Touret Cemetery by J. R. True-love.

214 Faubourg d'Arras Cemetery by Lutyens.

215 Royal Airforce Memorial, Runnymede.

216 Clocktower, Stockwell.

217 Clocktower, Golders Green.

218 Carillon Memorial, Loughborough.

INDEX